The Price of Admission

Campaign Spending in the 1990 Elections

Larry Makinson

Center for Responsive Politics
Washington, D.C.

The Center for Responsive Politics was founded in January 1983 to conduct research on congressional and political trends. It has since become one of the nation's leading institutions studying the role of money in American politics. The Center issues numerous reports and publications and provides computer research for the news media and others through the National Library on Money & Politics. This, the 16th major publication of the Center, documents the realities of campaign spending in the 1990 congressional elections.

Board of Directors

Acknowledgements

This book was written and assembled by Larry Makinson, with the assistance of Ellen Miller, Joshua Goldstein, David Mendeloff, Kevin Huffman, Adam Rappaport and Carol Mallory. Special thanks goes to the helpful and knowledgeable staff of the Federal Election Commission, particularly to Kent Cooper, chief of the public records office, and Bob Biersack, head of the FEC's data processing division.

Partial funding for the project was provided by the HKH Foundation. Computer equipment used in the production of this book and analysis of the data was provided by Apple Computer.

Sources and Methodology

Campaign finance data for the 1990 elections was compiled by the Center for Responsive Politics from reports filed by the candidates with the Federal Election Commission. The records cover the period from the start of their campaigns through December 31, 1990. All numbers were current as of June 1991. Final official figures for the 1990 election will be issued by the FEC in late 1991, so some of the numbers in this book could be affected by late amendments filed by the candidates. Such amendments, however, are likely to be minor, and should affect only a small number of candidates. Historical data on elections prior to 1988 were gathered both from FEC records and from *Vital Statistics on Congress 1987-1988* by Norman Ornstein, Thomas Mann and Michael Malbin (published by *Congressional Quarterly*).

This entire book and all the data, charts and graphs in it, was produced using Apple Macintosh® computers. The maps were created with Atlas MapMaker™. Congressional district boundaries were supplied by Strategic Locations Planning of San Jose, Calif. Microsoft Word™ was used for word processing. Panorama II™ and FoxBase+/Mac™ were the database programs used to assemble the data. Charts and graphs were created using DeltaGraph™ and Canvas™. The finished pages were assembled in PageMaker™. Final proofs were produced on an Apple LaserWriter IINTX™.

Introduction

Two important counter-currents in congressional politics can be seen in the facts and figures of campaign spending in the 1990 elections. On the one hand, the gulf in fundraising between challengers and incumbents grew wider than ever before — underscoring the increasing difficulties faced by congressional challengers who find themselves frozen out of the money loop that is accessible to incumbents. At the same time, however, the average margin of victory for incumbent members of the House and Senate declined in 1990, the number of challengers who won election to the U.S. House — though still very small — more than doubled from 1988. And those challengers who did win spent considerably less, on average, than successful challengers in recent elections.

These two seemingly disparate trends illustrate what may be the most important lesson of the 1990 elections: that had it not been for the massive financial buffer that incumbents enjoyed, the turnover rate in the U.S. Congress would likely have been far higher than it actually was on election day.

In many respects, 1990 was a year that incumbents should have had plenty to worry about. Anti-Congress sentiment was high in all regions of the country — made more so by the lingering and divisive budget negotiations that highlighted an apparent inability by Congress to deal effectively with the national budget, the rising deficit, and scores of other problems currently besetting the nation. But the wide dissatisfaction — except in a relative handful of districts — did not translate into a "throw the bums out" movement that would have swept incumbents from office.

The reasons why can be found on the pages that follow. In district after district, credible opponents were unable to raise the funds it takes to compete. In more than half the congressional districts, incumbents outspent challengers by a factor of ten-to-one or more. At the Senate level, a number of potentially strong challengers simply declined to run at all. Four U.S. Senators won reelection in 1990 without even facing a major party opponent — the first time that has happened since 1852. The one Senate challenger who was successful on election day — Democrat Paul Wellstone of Minnesota — had to overcome a nearly six-to-one spending disadvantage in winning a 50.4 percent victory at the polls.

In race after race, the story was the same. Of the 422 House and Senate incumbents who sought reelection in 1990, all but 14 outspent their opponents. Nor does the situation seem likely to change in 1992. Incumbent members of the U.S. House ended the 1990 election year with an average of nearly $157,000 already in the bank, with nearly two full years of fundraising ahead.

Such facts as these begin to explain the apparent discrepancies between voters' attitudes toward Congress and the sky-high reelection rates. Many other facts about the current relationship of money and politics can be found within the pages of this book. The aim of this second edition of *The Price of Admission*, like that of the original edition two years ago, is to illustrate — through dozens of charts, graphs and maps — both the details and wider trends in the financing of our modern American elections.

Washington, D.C.
September 1991

Contents

Appendix

Index

How this book is arranged...

1. The Big Picture

The first section gives an overview of the trends uncovered both in the 1990 election and in previous elections dating back to 1974, when the Federal Election Commission first began collecting data on campaign finances. This is where to find the historical perspective on such topics as the rising cost of campaigning, the role of political action committees, and reelection rates for the House and Senate. An abundance of charts translate the raw numbers into easy-to-read graphics.

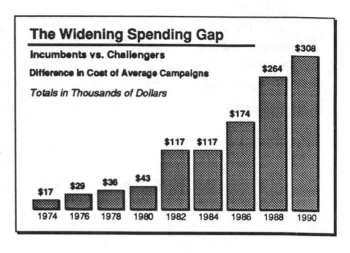

The Summary of Findings spotlights a variety of notable facts and figures distilled from the overall research. The Rising Price of Admission shows the patterns in campaign spending over the past 16 years. The Dollars and Cents of Incumbency examines the advantages that incumbents bring to their reelection campaigns. The Role of PACs shows the growing emergence of political action committees since they began to mushroom in number and influence in the 1970s. *The Big Picture begins on page 8.*

2. The Senate

This eight-page section *(beginning on page 18)* looks at the national trends in the 35 U.S. Senate races that were contested in 1990. A series of maps and charts examine the level of competition in Senate races, the costs of running and winning, the reliance of candidates on political action committees, and the year-end campaign bank balances of winning candidates. On page 19, a full-page chart shows which seats are up for election in 1992, 1994 and 1996.

3. The House of Representatives

A counterpart to the Senate section that precedes it, this 14-page digest analyzes the national trends in races for the U.S. House of Representatives. This is where to find national maps showing all 435 House districts, broken down into a number of categories, including party affiliation, type of race, closeness of the vote, amount spent by winners, proportion of funds received from PACs, and leftover cash for the next campaign. *The section begins on page 26.*

4. The Regions

These eight pages divide the nation into four regions: the Northeast, the South and border states, the Midwest and the West. Each region features two individual maps showing congressional districts within the region, and spotlighting the regional breakdown of party affiliation and campaign spending in the 1990 election. *The regional breakdowns begin with an introduction on pages 40-41.*

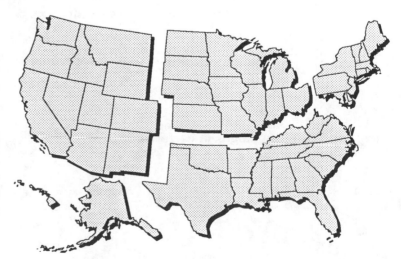

5. The States

This is the largest single section of the book, covering 96 pages with maps, charts, statistics and narrative rundowns of the congressional elections in each of the 50 states. For the most part, states appear in two-page spreads, with the maps on one page and statistics and charts on the other. Larger states have four-page spreads. States with only one or two congressional districts are grouped with others nearby. The states are arranged alphabetically. *An introductory section that explains all the charts, maps and statistics can be found on pages 50-51.*

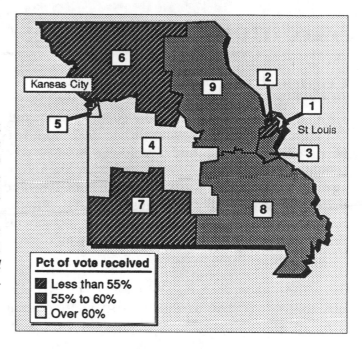

Pct of vote received

- ▓ Less than 55%
- ▒ 55% to 60%
- ☐ Over 60%

6. Member-by-Member Spending Index

This unique index provides a way to tell at a glance how each congressional winner in the 1990 elections compared with all others, through a variety of campaign measures. Using an index in which 100 equals the national average, the relative standings can be found for each member of the House of Representatives and the 35 Senators who won election in 1990. Included in the index are the members' total campaign receipts, total PAC receipts, the amount they spent, the amount their opponent spent, and the size of their campaign fund balance at the end of 1990. An index value of 100 means the member spent at exactly the national average, a value of 200 indicates double the national average, a value of 50 equals half the national average, etc. *The spending index begins on page 148.*

7. Subject and Member Index

This is the traditional index, where you can search for a subject, like PACs, or for all mentions of a particular member of Congress. Entries for incumbent members of Congress include their state and party affiliation.

Where to find ...

Summary of Findings

Competition

• Despite a surge in anti-incumbent and anti-Congress sentiment in the nation in late 1990, more than 96 percent of House and Senate incumbents who sought reelection in 1990 were successful. Their average margin of victory was narrower than in 1988 and there were considerably more close races in the House, but the towering financial advantage that incumbents brought to their campaigns helped nearly all of them weather the electoral storm.

• The number of financially one-sided races continued to rise in 1990, as did the gap in fundraising between incumbents and challengers. In more than 57 percent of House races (250 out of 435 seats), the winner outspent the loser by a factor of ten-to-one or more. The financial disparity was closer in Senate races, but even there eight of the 35 races saw one candidate outspend the other by at least ten-to-one.

• Of the 32 Senate incumbents who ran for reelection only one — Republican Rudy Boschwitz of Minnesota — was defeated. Four Senate incumbents ran unopposed by any major party challengers at all; it was the first time that many Senators won reelection without a race since 1852.

The Cost of Campaigning

• The cost of the average *winning* campaign for the U.S. House of Representatives rose to more than $407,000 in 1990, though the cost of an average House campaign — including both winners and losers — declined. House incumbents spent more than ever (an average of $413,000), but spending by challengers dropped for the third election in a row, to just $105,000. In fact, spending by challengers in 1990 was lower than the level in 1980, despite ten years of inflation and ever-rising campaign costs.

• Spending in Senate campaigns declined in 1990 — largely because there were no Senate races in either California or New York, while four Senate incumbents (in Arkansas, Mississippi, Georgia and Virginia) faced no opposition from major party challengers. Senate winners spent an average of less than $3.9 million, compared with slightly more than $4 million in 1990.

The Role of PACs

• Political action committees contributed a total of $159.3 million to federal candidates and incumbents in the 1989-90 election cycle — a hair over the $159.2 million given in 1988. Of that amount, 79.1 percent went to incumbents, an even higher proportion than in 1988. Only 10.2 percent went to challengers, and the remaining 10.7 percent went to candidates in open seat races.

• The average winning House candidate collected nearly half his or her campaign dollars from PACs in 1990. Senate winners got an average of just over one-fourth of their money from PACs.

• Democrats remained more heavily dependent on PAC dollars than Republicans. The average winning House Democrat drew more than $233,000 in PAC donations. House Republican winners averaged just over $172,000. The margin was closer among Senate winners, but there too Democrats held the edge in PAC dollars, collecting an average of slightly more than $1 million compared with the Republicans' $895,000.

• Business PACs (those representing corporations, trade and professional associations) accounted for more than two-thirds of all PAC contributions — nearly $109 million. The biggest sector within that group was the finance, insurance and real estate sector; they gave $25.2 million.

• Labor PACs gave $36.9 million in the 1990 elections. Of that amount, 92 percent went to Democrats.

• Ideological and single-issue PACs accounted for $13.9 million in contributions in 1989-90. Two-thirds of the dollars went to Democrats. Pro-Israel PACs were the leading category within the ideological sector; they gave just over $4 million.

1990 Election Statistics at a Glance

	1990 Election	1988 Election
Senate		
Average winner spent*	$3,870,621	$4,045,682
Average loser spent†	$1,674,658	$1,877,612
Most expensive campaign	$17,761,579	$14,656,367
	Jesse Helms (R-NC)	Pete Wilson (R-Calif)
Least expensive winning campaign	$533,632	$790,710
	Nancy Kassebaum (R-Kan)	Spark Matsunaga (D-Hawaii)
No. of incumbents seeking reelection	32	27
No. of incumbents reelected	31	23
Reelection rate	96.9%	85.2%
Number of close races (55% or less)	10	11
Races where winner outspent loser 10:1 or more	14	8
Average winner's vote percentage	64.7%	60.4%
Average receipts from PACs	$978,329	$1,079,774
Most receipts from PACs	$1,814,595	$2,617,311
	Tom Harkin (D-Iowa)	Lloyd Bentsen (D-Texas)
Average end-of-year campaign balance**	$465,153	$82,141
Biggest end-of-year campaign balance	$4,147,378	$855,659
	Phil Gramm (R-Texas)	Donald Riegle (D-Mich)
House of Representatives		
Average cost of winning campaign	$407,556	$390,671
Average loser spent†	$116,665	$116,763
Most expensive campaign	$1,707,539	$1,755,892
	Marguerite Chandler (R-NJ)††	Bob Dornan (R-Calif)
Least expensive winning campaign	$6,766	$8,397
	William Natcher (D-Ky)	William Natcher (D-Ky)
No. of incumbents seeking reelection	440	409
No. of incumbents reelected	422	402
Reelection rate	96.1%	98.5%
Number of close races (55% or less)	58	37
Races where winner outspent loser 10:1 or more	250	230
Average winner's vote percentage	69.2%	72.6%
Average receipts from PACs	$209,581	$197,870
Most receipts from PACs	$761,537	$558,417
	Richard Gephardt (D-Mo)	Robert Michel (R-Ill)
Average end-of-year campaign balance**	$465,153	$82,141
Biggest end-of-year campaign balance	$1,859,603	$1,251,053
	Steven Solarz (D-NY)	David Dreier (R-Calif)

* Includes incumbents' spending over their full six-year term
† Spending by second-highest vote-getter in November election. Unopposed races are counted as $0.
** Among Senators elected or reelected in 1990
†† Lost on election day

The Dollars and Cents of Incumbency

Incumbents, for any office at any level of government, have always enjoyed a natural advantage at election time. Their names are already well known, they have established a record of service for all to see, and if they have served their constituents well, the voters are likely to be reminded of it come election time. Congressional incumbents also have the benefit of regular news coverage during their term in office — coverage which often gives them credit for federal grants and projects in their districts. And they have the congressional franking privilege, enabling them to send correspondence and periodic newsletters to their constituents postage free.

Members of Congress also have the inside track on contributions from political action committees. In 1990, PACs accounted for nearly half of all the dollars received by House incumbents, and almost one-quarter of total contributions to Senators. More than 79 percent of the dollars contributed by PACs in 1990 went to incumbents.

What all this adds up to is an overwhelming advantage by incumbents over challengers, particularly in races for the House of Representatives. The vast majority of candidates opposing House incumbents, financially speaking, were never in the race. Even those who spent large amounts of money (see charts on the facing page) found tough odds against them. In the 1990 elections, more than 96 percent of the House and Senate incumbents who sought reelection were successful at the polls.

There was one bright side to the otherwise cloudy outlook for House challengers in the last election. Though the vast majority of challengers seeking to upset incumbents were vanquished at the polls, the 16 who did manage to win in 1990 did it with considerably less money than was necessary two years earlier. In 1990, the cost of beating incumbents ranged from a low of just over $178,000 (by Republican Scott Klug in Wisconsin's 2nd district) to the $883,000 campaign of Democrat Jim Moran in northern Virginia's 8th district. Two years earlier only six incumbents fell to challengers and the cost of those campaigns ranged from $316,000 to $1.3 million.

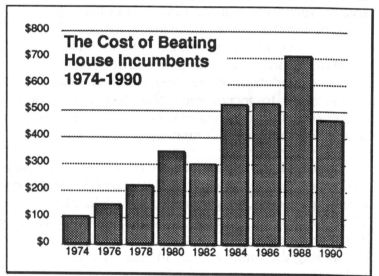

The Cost of Beating House Incumbents 1974-1990

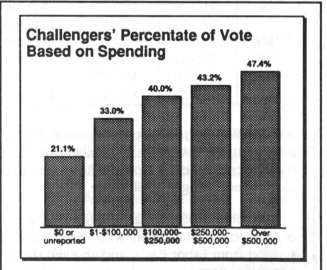

Challengers' Percentate of Vote Based on Spending

| | 21.1% | 33.0% | 40.0% | 43.2% | 47.4% |
| $0 or unreported | $1-$100,000 | $100,000-$250,000 | $250,000-$500,000 | Over $500,000 |

Even though adding extra money to a campaign was no guarantee of winning, there was a clear correlation between the amount of money spent by challengers and their share of the total votes on election day.

Year	Avg Challenger	Avg Incumbent	No.
1974	$100,435	$101,102	40
1976	$144,720	$154,774	12
1978	$217,083	$200,607	19
1980	$343,093	$286,559	31
1982	$296,273	$453,459	23
1984	$518,781	$463,070	17
1986	$523,308	$562,139	6
1988	$703,740	$876,678	7
1990	$462,546	$631,025	16

Reelection Rates through the Years

Reelection rates for incumbents in both the House and Senate were 96 percent in 1990, indicating the extreme difficulty faced by challengers trying to break into Congress. The Senate figure was the highest in 30 years, with only one incumbent out of 32 losing his seat. But in the House, the 96 percent reelection rate was actually a *drop* from the rates in the last two elections.

As the charts at right show, reelection has historically been more of a sure thing for House members than for Senators. Reelection rates for the House have rarely dipped below 90 percent in the past 30 years, while Senate rates have risen and fallen in response to national political trends.

The 1980 election, which brought Ronald Reagan to the White House, saw the defeat of nine Senate incumbents — all of them Democrats. In the same year, even though Democrats did lose 33 seats in the House, some 91 percent of House incumbents were reelected.

The last time the reelection rate for House members dropped below 80 percent was in 1948, when it was 79 percent. In every election since 1976 the rate has been 90 percent or above.

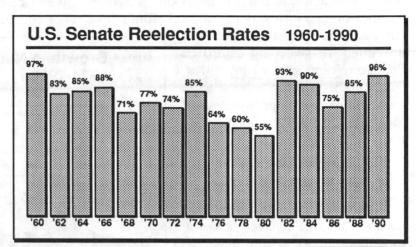

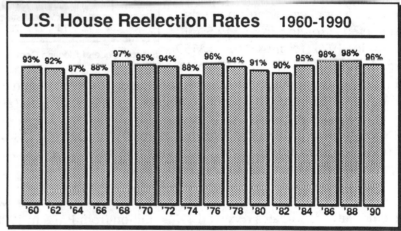

The 10 Top-Spending Challengers in House Races

Challenger	Spent	Vote Pct	Party	District	Outcome
Reid Hughes	$1,067,366	44.0%	Dem	Fla 4	Lost
John H. Carrington	$890,838	42.0%	Rep	NC 4	Lost
James P. Moran Jr.	$883,216	51.7%	Dem	Va 8	Won
Mike Kopetski	$844,797	55.0%	Dem	Ore 5	Won
Bob Williams	$817,944	46.0%	Rep	Wash 3	Lost
John A. Johnson	$781,224	47.0%	Rep	Ind 5	Lost
John A. Boehner	$732,765	61.1%	Rep	Ohio 8	Won
John Linder	$696,859	48.0%	Rep	Ga 4	Lost
Dick Waterfield	$679,117	44.0%	Rep	Texas 13	Lost
Manny Hoffman	$642,391	41.0%	Rep	Ill 4	Lost

The High Cost of Losing

While having enough money to wage a serious campaign is a clear prerequisite for winning a seat in Congress, money alone won't guarantee victory — as the chart on the left plainly shows. Of the 10 highest-spending challengers in 1990 House races, seven lost at the polls. Still, that was an improvement from 1988, when nine out of 10 lost.

The Role of PACs

Political action committees, or PACs, have been a part of the American political scene since 1943, when the first one was formed by organized labor's Congress of Industrial Organization (which later merged with the American Federation of Labor to become the AFL-CIO). A few business associations began to pick up the idea in the 1950s and '60s, but until the boom in business PACs in the early 1970s PACs were still largely an instrument of labor unions — a way of collecting funds from union members and delivering them to favored candidates (primarily Democrats). With the enactment of sweeping campaign finance reforms in the early 1970s, large numbers of corporations, trade associations, and other business and ideological groups began forming PACs and using them as a major new source for delivering campaign dollars.

The number of PACs grew from 608 in 1974 to 4,172. Over the years, total contributions from PACs to congressional candidates have skyrocketed, growing from $12.5 million in 1974 to more than $159 million in 1990. In recent years,

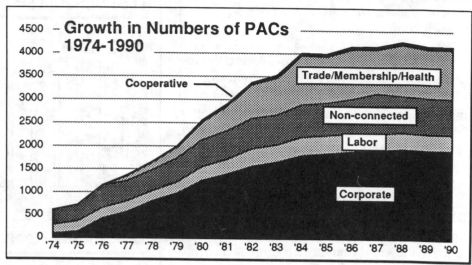

Source: Federal Election Commission

however, the number of PACs has stabilized, and even begun to decline. Total PAC dollars have also stabilized, though the amounts going to incumbents — particularly in the House — continues to rise with each new election.

In the last election, PAC dollars accounted for nearly half the revenues received by winning House candidates, and just under one-fourth of the money that went to Senate winners. More than three dollars out of every four given by PACs went to incumbents.

Democrats, particularly in the House of Representatives, were the prime recipients of the money. House Democratic candidates received $73.4 million from PACs in 1990, while House Republican candidates collected $36.9 million. Part of the reason for the lopsided Democratic advantage was that most of the money went to incumbents, and most of the incumbents are Democrats. Another reason is that labor unions, still an important segment of the PAC community, give their dollars overwhelmingly to Democratic candidates.

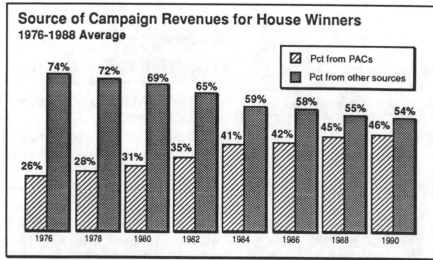

Source: Federal Election Commission
NOTE: Base data includes contributions to non-voting House Delegates

The average Democratic House winner collected $233,555 from PACs in the 1990 elections. The average Republican winner got $172,024.

Contributions to Senate candidates also favored Democrats, though by a narrower margin. Democrats drew nearly $24.9 million in PAC funds during the 1989-90 election cycle, while Republicans got $23.9 million. Among Senate winners, Democrats drew an average $1,056,761 while Republicans collected $895,283. (For incumbents, those averages include contributions received over their full six-year term preceding the 1990 election.)

Profiles of PAC Giving

Though often thought of as a monolithic source of campaign dollars, political action committees actually fall into three main groups: business, labor and ideological interests. Business PACs supply the bulk of the money, and the biggest source of funds within the business world came from the financial-insurance-real estate sector. Within that group, insurance PACs led all others, with more than $8.7 million in contributions during 1989-90. Commercial bank PACs gave nearly $6.4 million, while real estate groups gave $4.0 million. Other major contributors were physicians and other health professionals ($6.8 million), the oil and gas industry ($4.0 million),

defense aerospace PACs ($4.5 million), the telecommunications industry ($4.8 million), electric utilities ($3.5 million), and PACs representing lawyers and law firms ($4.3 million). Overall, business PACs split their dollars nearly evenly between Democrats and Republicans.

Labor PACs accounted for only a fraction of what business PACs gave, but 92 percent of their dollars went to Democrats. Public sector PACs — representing postal workers, teachers and public employee unions — were the biggest single source of labor PAC dollars, combining for nearly $10.9 million in contributions during 1989-90. PACs representing construction workers gave $6.2 million. Manufacturing unions gave nearly $5.4 million, and transportation unions gave $8.6 million.

Ideological and single-issue PACs aim their dollars at influencing issues as specific as abortion or gun control and as broad as those supporting "conservative" or "liberal" candidates. During 1989-90, pro-Israel PACs led all other ideological groups, with $4.0 million in contributions. "Leadership PACs" operated by members of Congress and other political leaders gave nearly $2.4 million. "Human Rights" PACs, representing women's groups, gay rights groups and a wide range of minority and ethnic groups, gave a combined $1.5 million. Social security and senior citizens PACs gave just over $1.0 million, while Democratic-liberal PACs gave $1.2 million. The issue of gun control drew $914,000 in PAC contributions — mostly from the National Rifle Association. Abortion groups, pro and con, gave a combined $747,000.

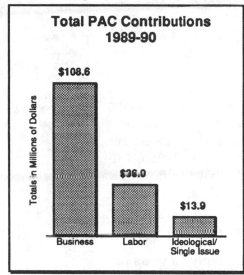

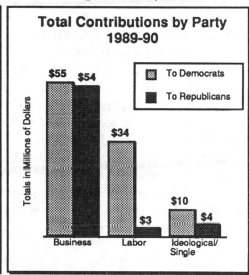

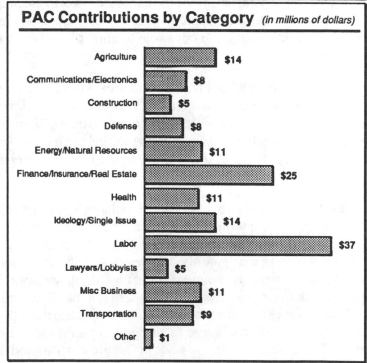

Incumbents reap by far the biggest share of the PACs' dollars. PACs with specific legislative agendas often target their money at those incumbents on committees of particular interest to their industry. Members of the House and Senate banking committees, for example, are likely to draw contributions not from one or two banking PACs, but from dozens.

Looking Ahead to 1992 . . .

Two major events could provoke an unusually large turnover in congressional seats in the 1992 elections — congressional reapportionment (following the 1990 census) and an end to the so-called "grandfather clause" that enabled senior congressmen to convert their campaign accounts to their personal use when they retired.

Reapportionment

The reapportionment of congressional districts, mandated by law following each federal census, will literally redraw the map of political boundaries in the U.S. House of Representatives. The constitution requires that congressional districts be roughly equivalent in population to all others. As population shifts occur, the boundaries must be redrawn to maintain the balance. Some states will gain new seats in Congress, others will lose them. But even in those 29 states that will send the same number of representatives to Congress after the next election, the boundaries of each congressional district will have to be adjusted to keep pace with the moving population. This means that virtually every incumbent will have to face new constituents — and possibly lose some old ones — as the boundaries are redrawn. The only states spared this process are those that have only a single at-large seat in Congress.

The process of reshaping the districts every 10 years has been a part of federal law since the earliest days of the republic. Congressional reapportionment, in fact, was the primary legal rationale for instituting the census in the first place, beginning in 1790.

The redrawing of political boundaries has always been a traumatic event, and often a contentious one, at every level of government. Hardball politics, the gerrymandering of districts — even legal challenges by those who feel slighted — have become a way of life in many parts of the country whenever political districts are adjusted.

Particularly in states where populations are rising or stagnating, the redrawing of lines on a map can also change the face of the political landscape. In fast-growing regions of the country — particularly sunbelt states like California, Florida and Texas — reapportionment brings with it new opportunities for ambitious politicians looking to break into Congress. In regions where growth has stalled— like the industrial Northeast and Midwest — it can serve to nudge long-term incumbents from office, as the number of seats in Congress is trimmed. The nation's two largest states reflect the opposite poles of these electoral patterns. New York will lose three congressional districts after 1992, while California gains seven new ones.

The chart at right lists the changes in congressional delegations that will go into effect when the next Congress convenes in January 1993.

Before & After:
Shifts in State Delegations

State	1990 Seats	1992 Seats	Change
Alabama	7	7	0
Alaska	1	1	0
Arizona	5	6	+1
Arkansas	4	4	0
California	45	52	+7
Colorado	6	6	0
Connecticut	6	6	0
Delaware	1	1	0
Florida	19	23	+4
Georgia	10	11	+1
Hawaii	2	2	0
Idaho	2	2	0
Illinois	22	20	-2
Indiana	10	10	0
Iowa	6	5	-1
Kansas	5	4	-1
Kentucky	7	6	-1
Louisiana	8	7	-1
Maine	2	2	0
Maryland	8	8	0
Massachusetts	11	10	-1
Michigan	18	16	-2
Minnesota	8	8	0
Mississippi	5	5	0
Missouri	9	9	0
Montana	2	1	-1
Nebraska	3	3	0
Nevada	2	2	0
New Hampshire	2	2	0
New Jersey	14	13	-1
New Mexico	3	3	0
New York	34	31	-3
North Carolina	11	12	+1
North Dakota	1	1	0
Ohio	21	19	-2
Oklahoma	6	6	0
Oregon	5	5	0
Pennsylvania	23	21	-2
Rhode Island	2	2	0
South Carolina	6	6	0
South Dakota	1	1	0
Tennessee	9	9	0
Texas	27	30	+3
Utah	3	3	0
Vermont	1	1	0
Virginia	10	11	+1
Washington	8	9	+1
West Virginia	4	3	-1
Wisconsin	9	9	0
Wyoming	1	1	0
Total	**435**	**435**	

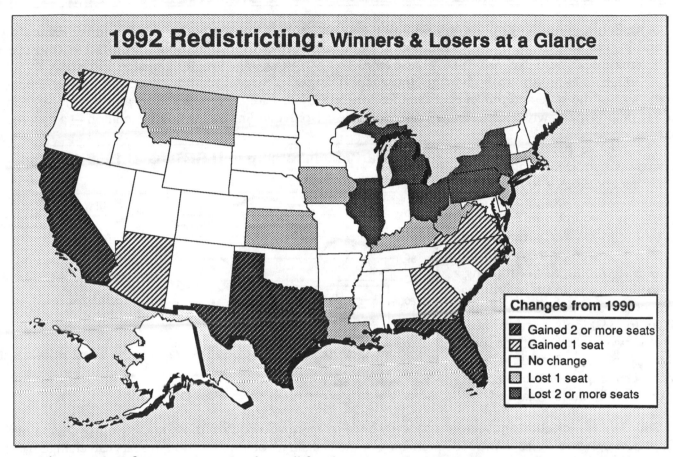

1992 Redistricting: Winners & Losers at a Glance

Changes from 1990

- Gained 2 or more seats
- Gained 1 seat
- No change
- Lost 1 seat
- Lost 2 or more seats

The patterns of reapportionment that will first be seen in the 1992 elections reflect regional shifts in population — and political power — that can be seen in the map above. The states with the biggest losses in congressional seats were those in the "Rust Belt" of the industrial Northeast and Midwest. The biggest gains were in California, Florida and Texas — Sunbelt states whose populations have swelled both with migration from other states and from the nation's biggest influx in foreign immigrants since the early 1900s.

Sunset for the Grandfather Clause

Further complicating the picture in 1992 is a one-time "golden parachute" for senior House members to retire at the end of their current terms. As part of its 1989 ethics and pay raise package, the House of Representatives voted to end the so-called "grandfather clause" that allowed senior members (those already in office on Jan. 8, 1980) to convert their leftover campaign funds to personal income when they retire. To take advantage of the old rule, those 165 representatives who are eligible must retire at the end of their current term. Any incumbent seeking reelection in 1992 will lose the right to convert their remaining campaign dollars into a personal retirement fund.

No one knows how many members will take advantage of this expiring offer, but the amount of money involved in many cases is temptingly large. A 1991 study by the Center for Public Integrity found that the average eligible member had over $245,000 in available revenues. Twenty of them had half a million dollars or more.

The "grandfather clause" does not apply to Senators. When they retire, their remaining campaign funds cannot be converted to personal use.

The Senate Today

Since Senators run only once every six years, they may enjoy some temporary relief from the immediacy of fundraising pressures faced by their colleagues in the House. But the advantage is offset by the fact that most Senate campaigns are far more expensive than House races. In 1990, the average Senate campaign cost nearly $4 million — almost ten times more than the average House race. The costs of Senate races vary widely, however, depending on the size of the state and the level of competition. In 1990, Senate contests in Texas and New Jersey topped the $12 million mark, while Jesse Helms' reelection race in North Carolina cost nearly $18 million — a new record.

The relative parity in numbers between Senate Democrats and Republicans contributes to lively competition in Senate races, as both parties seek to encourage strong candidates so they can tip (or preserve) the balance of power. On the other hand, the often numbing cost of running a competitive race acts to discourage competition and keep incumbents in office. In 1990, only one incumbent Senator was defeated at the polls, while 31 were reelected — many against challengers whose campaigns were woefully under-financed.

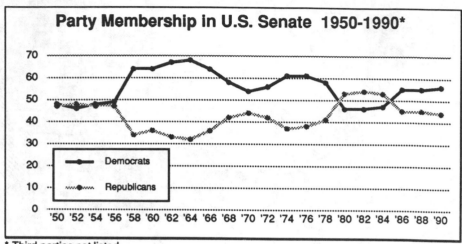

Party Membership in U.S. Senate 1950-1990*

Legend: Democrats, Republicans

* Third-parties not listed
Source: *Vital Statistics on Congress* (Congressional Quarterly)

Still, Senate reelection rates have historically been far more volatile than those in the House. During periods of political upheaval — as in the 1980 launching of the Reagan revolution — enough seats can change hands to put the other party in power. In the House of Representatives, the Democratic majority is so solid (and the power of incumbency so strong) that no single election is likely to seriously upset the status quo.

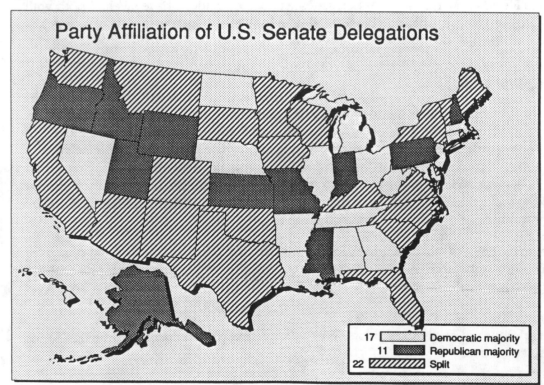

Party Affiliation of U.S. Senate Delegations

17	Democratic majority
11	Republican majority
22	Split

The map at left shows the current party makeup of the U.S. Senate. After the 1990 elections, 17 states had two Democratic Senators, 11 had two Republicans, and 22 states had one member from each party.

Americans have only been able to directly elect their Senators since a constitutional amendment was ratified in 1913. Prior to that time, the two Senators from each state were selected by the state legislatures.

Senate Seats Up for Election in 1992

State	Current Senator	Party	First Elected	State	Current Senator	Party	First Elected
Ala	Richard C. Shelby	Dem	1986	Md	Barbara Mikulski	Dem	1986
Alaska	Frank Murkowski	Rep	1980	Mo	Christopher "Kit" Bond	Rep	1986
Ariz	John McCain	Rep	1986	Nev	Harry Reid	Dem	1986
Ark	Dale Bumpers	Dem	1974	NH	Warren Rudman	Rep	1980
Calif	Alan Cranston	Dem	1968	NY	Alfonse D'Amato	Rep	1980
Calif	John Seymour	Rep	1991*	NC	Terry Sanford	Dem	1986
Colo	Timothy E. Wirth	Dem	1986	ND	Kent Conrad	Dem	1986
Conn	Christopher J. Dodd	Dem	1980	Ohio	John Glenn	Dem	1974
Fla	Bob Graham	Dem	1986	Okla	Don Nickles	Rep	1980
Ga	Wyche Folwer Jr.	Dem	1986	Ore	Bob Packwood	Rep	1968
Hawaii	Daniel K. Inouye	Dem	1962	Pa	Arlen Specter	Rep	1980
Idaho	Steven D. Symms	Rep	1980	Pa	Harris Wofford	Dem	1991††
Ill	Alan J. Dixon	Dem	1980	SC	Ernest F. Hollings	Dem	1966
Ind	Dan Coats	Rep	1990†	SD	Thomas A. Daschle	Dem	1986
Iowa	Charles E. Grassley	Rep	1980	Utah	Jake Garn	Rep	1974
Kan	Bob Dole	Rep	1968	Vt	Patrick J. Leahy	Dem	1974
Ky	Wendell Ford	Dem	1974	Wash	Brock Adams	Dem	1986
La	John Breaux	Dem	1986	Wis	Bob Kasten	Rep	1980

* Appointed in Jan. 1991 to fill Pete Wilson's unexpired term through 1992.   † First appointed in Dec. 1988.
†† Appointed in May 1991 following the death of Sen. John Heinz. An election to fill the remainder of Sen. Heinz's term was set for Nov. 1991.

Senate Seats Up for Election in 1994

State	Current Senator	Party	First Elected	State	Current Senator	Party	First Elected
Ariz	Dennis DeConcini	Dem	1976	NJ	Frank Lautenberg	Dem	1982
Conn	Joseph Lieberman	Dem	1988	NM	Jeff Bingaman	Dem	1982
Del	William V. Roth Jr.	Rep	1970	NY	Daniel Patrick Moynihan	Dem	1976
Fla	Connie Mack	Rep	1988	ND	Quentin Burdick	Dem	1960
Hawaii	Daniel K. Akaka	Dem	1990*	Ohio	Howard Metzenbaum	Dem	1976†
Ind	Richard Lugar	Rep	1976	Pa	Harris Wofford	Dem	1991††
Maine	George Mitchell	Dem	1982**	RI	John H. Chafee	Rep	1976
Md	Paul Sarbanes	Dem	1976	Tenn	Jim Sasser	Dem	1976
Mass	Edward M. Kennedy	Dem	1962	Texas	Lloyd Bentsen	Dem	1970
Mich	Donald W. Riegle Jr.	Dem	1976	Utah	Orrin G. Hatch	Rep	1976
Minn	Dave Durenberger	Rep	1978	Vt	James Jeffords	Rep	1988
Miss	Trent Lott	Rep	1988	Va	Charles Robb	Dem	1988
Mo	John C. Danforth	Rep	1976	Wash	Slade Gorton	Rep	1980†††
Mont	Conrad Burns	Rep	1988	WVa	Robert C. Byrd	Dem	1958
Neb	Bob Kerrey	Dem	1988	Wis	Herb Kohl	Dem	1988
Nev	Richard Bryan	Dem	1988	Wyo	Malcolm Wallop	Rep	1976

* First appointed in May 1990 to fill the unexpired term of the late Spark Matsunaga.   ** First appointed in 1980.
† Also served Jan-Dec 1974.   †† Appointed May 1991. See note above.   ††† Lost in 1986, elected again in 1988.

Senate Seats Up for Election in 1996

State	Current Senator	Party	First Elected	State	Current Senator	Party	First Elected
Ala	Howell Heflin	Dem	1978	Mont	Max Baucus	Dem	1978
Alaska	Ted Stevens	Rep	1970*	Neb	J. James Exon	Dem	1978
Ark	David Pryor	Dem	1978	NH	Robert C. Smith	Rep	1990
Colo	Hank Brown	Rep	1990	NJ	Bill Bradley	Dem	1978
Del	Joseph Biden Jr.	Dem	1972	NM	Pete V. Domenici	Rep	1972
Ga	Sam Nunn	Dem	1972	NC	Jesse Helms	Rep	1972
Idaho	Larry E. Craig	Rep	1990	Okla	David L. Boren	Dem	1978
Ill	Paul Simon	Dem	1984	Ore	Mark O. Hatfield	Rep	1966
Iowa	Tom Harkin	Dem	1984	RI	Claiborne Pell	Dem	1960
Kan	Nancy Kassebaum	Rep	1978	SC	Strom Thurmond	Rep	1954
Ky	Mitch McConnell	Rep	1984	SD	Larry Pressler	Rep	1978
La	J. Bennett Johnston	Dem	1972	Tenn	Albert Gore Jr.	Dem	1984
Maine	William S. Cohen	Rep	1978	Texas	Phil Gramm	Rep	1984
Mass	John Kerry	Dem	1984	Va	John Warner	Rep	1978
Mich	Carl Levin	Dem	1978	WVa	John D. Rockefeller IV	Dem	1984
Minn	Paul Wellstone	Dem	1990	Wyo	Alan K. Simpson	Rep	1978
Miss	Thad Cochran	Rep	1978				

* First appointed in 1968.

Competition in Senate Races

Whether the yardstick is fundraising, vote percentages, or reelection rates, campaigns for the U.S. Senate have long tended to be more competitive than those for the House of Representatives. Though the Democrats currently enjoy a relatively strong majority in the Senate, the balance between the parties in recent years has generally been close. From 1981 through 1986, the Republicans held the majority, though they lost it again in the 1986 elections. This relative parity between the parties in the Senate prompts both parties to try to field strong candidates in hopes of forcing party turnovers, or in the case of the Democrats, maintaining their majority.

But 1990 proved to be an unusually strong year for the status quo. Only one incumbent (Republican Rudy Boschwitz in Minnesota) was defeated, out of 32 who sought reelection. That 96.9 percent reelection rate was the highest in the Senate since 1960. Even more unusual was the fact that four incumbent Senators — Sam Nunn (D-Ga), Thad Cochran (R-Miss), David Pryor (D-Ark) and John Warner (R-Va) — didn't even face major party opponents. The last time that many Senate incumbents had such easy sailing was in 1852.

Still, on balance Senate contests remained more competitive than House races. The average Senate winner in 1990 captured 64.7 percent of the vote, while House winners averaged 69.2 percent. The spending differential between winners and losers was also closer in the Senate, with winners spending an average of 2.4 times more than losers. (In the House, winners outspent challengers by a factor of 3.5 to one.)

Of the five incumbent Senators who won reelection with over 80 percent of the vote, only David Boren faced a major-party opponent. Voters in Virginia did have an alternative to Republican John Warner — a supporter of political extremist Lyndon LaRouche who appeared on the ballot as an Independent.

Senate Candidates Winning with 80 Percent or More

Name	Party	State	Vote Pct	Race Type
Sam Nunn	Dem	Ga	100.0%	Reelected
Thad Cochran	Rep	Miss	100.0%	Reelected
David Pryor	Dem	Ark	99.8%	Reelected
David L. Boren	Dem	Okla	83.2%	Reelected
John W. Warner	Rep	Va	80.9%	Reelected

Closest Senate Races in 1990

Name	Party	State	Vote Pct	Race Type
Bill Bradley	Dem	NJ	50.4%	Reelected
Paul Wellstone	Dem	Minn	50.4%	Beat incumb
Mitch McConnell	Rep	Ky	52.2%	Reelected
Larry Pressler	Rep	SD	52.4%	Reelected
Jesse Helms	Rep	NC	52.6%	Reelected

Sen. Bill Bradley's embarrassing close call in his 1990 reelection bid may have hurt his stature as a potential presidential contender. He outspent his Republican opponent 15-to-one, but barely survived at the polls, as New Jersey voters expressed their outrage over recent state tax hikes from the Democratic governor and legislature by lashing out at the highest-profile Democrat on the November ballot.

Incumbents seeking reelection spent an average of $4.1 million in their 1990 campaigns, as opposed to an average $1.5 million for their opponents. Spending in the three open seat races was considerably lower, with winners spending under $2.3 million, versus $934,000 for the losers. But those races were in relatively small states — Idaho, Colorado and New Hampshire. The biggest gap of all was in the one race where an incumbent was defeated. In that race, Minnesota Democrat Paul Wellstone spent just $1.3 million against Sen. Rudy Boschwitz's campaign of nearly $7.9 million.

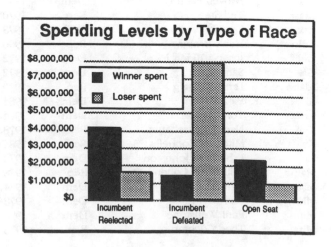

Spending Levels by Type of Race

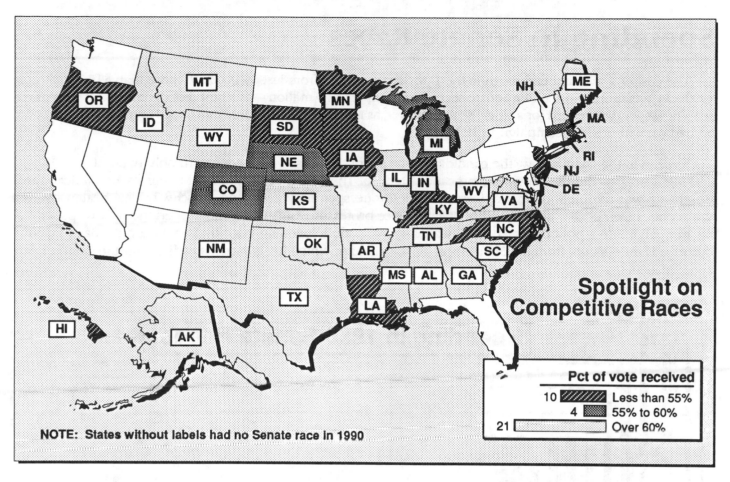

Spotlight on Competitive Races

MT
OR
ID
WY
SD
NE
MN
IA
IL
IN
MI
IL
WV
KY
VA
NH
ME
MA
RI
NJ
DE
CO
KS
OK
AR
TN
NC
SC
NM
MS
AL
GA
TX
LA
HI
AK

Pct of vote received

10		Less than 55%
4		55% to 60%
21		Over 60%

NOTE: States without labels had no Senate race in 1990

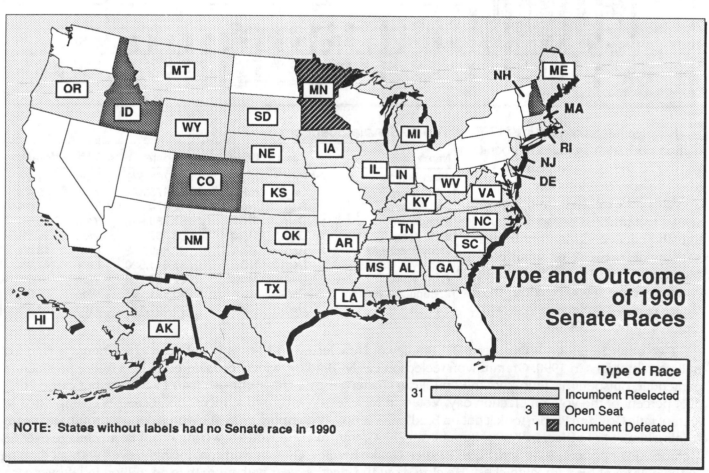

Type and Outcome of 1990 Senate Races

MT
OR
ID
WY
SD
NE
MN
IA
MI
IL
IN
WV
KY
VA
NH
ME
MA
RI
NJ
DE
CO
KS
OK
AR
TN
NC
SC
NM
MS
AL
GA
TX
LA
HI
AK

Type of Race

31		Incumbent Reelected
3		Open Seat
1		Incumbent Defeated

NOTE: States without labels had no Senate race in 1990

Spending in Senate Races

The cost of a winning campaign in the U.S. Senate ranged from just $533,000 to more than $17.7 million in 1990. On average, the price of a Senate seat was just under $3.9 million — a slight drop from 1988. The year did see a new spending record for a single seat, however, as North Carolina Republican Jesse Helms broke the record he had set with his last campaign in 1984.

As seen in the chart below, the candidates who spent the most won the most. In only two states — Hawaii and Minnesota — did the top-spending candidate lose. The defeat of incumbent Minnesota Republican Rudy Boschwitz was the most dramatic. Despite a six-to-one spending advantage, Boschwitz was beaten by Paul Wellstone, a Democratic activist and political science professor who successfully turned the relative poverty of his campaign into a political asset. In Hawaii, a more modest spending edge by Republican Pat Saiki failed to dislodge Daniel Akaka from the Senate seat he was first appointed to six months earlier after the death of Sen. Spark Matsunaga.

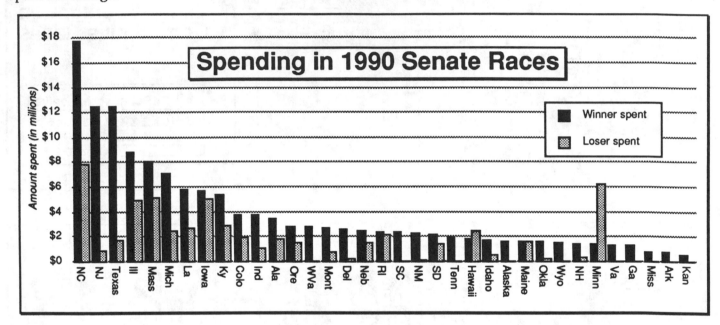

Jesse Helms' record-setting $17.7 million campaign against Democrat Harvey Gantt started gearing up long before election day. Helms operates an extensive (and *expensive*) direct mail operation that continually solicits contributions from a nationwide network of small contributors. The mailings will no doubt continue long after election day; Helms closed the election year with a deficit of over $900,000.

Top 10 Senate Spenders

Name	Party	State	Spent	W/L	Vote Pct
Jesse Helms	Rep	NC	$17,761,579	Won	52.6%
Bill Bradley	Dem	NJ	$12,475,527	Won	50.4%
Phil Gramm	Rep	Texas	$12,474,887	Won	60.2%
Paul Simon	Dem	Ill	$8,739,940	Won	65.1%
John Kerry	Dem	Mass	$8,067,033	Won	57.1%
Rudy Boschwitz	Rep	Minn	$7,866,343	Lost	48.0%
Harvey B. Gantt	Dem	NC	$7,811,520	Lost	47.0%
Carl Levin	Dem	Mich	$7,082,164	Won	57.5%
J. Bennett Johnston	Dem	La	$5,811,105	Won	53.9%
Tom Harkin	Dem	Iowa	$5,661,171	Won	54.5%

Two other Senators — Democrat Bill Bradley of New Jersey and Texas Republican Phil Gramm — ran $12 million campaigns in 1990. Gramm won reelection easily. Bradley, widely considered to be a future presidential contender, outspent his little-known Republican challenger by a factor of more than 15-to-one, but carried only 50.4 percent of the vote on election day. Voters in New Jersey, incensed at recent tax increases championed by Democratic Gov. Jim Florio, took it out on Bradley — seriously chipping away at his presidential profile and nearly turning him out of office. In Texas, Republican Phil Gramm also enjoyed a towering financial advantage over his Democratic opponent, State Sen. Hugh Parmer. Unlike Bradley, Gramm won convincingly, even without dipping to the bottom of his campaign chest. He closed out the election year with more than $4 million in leftover cash.

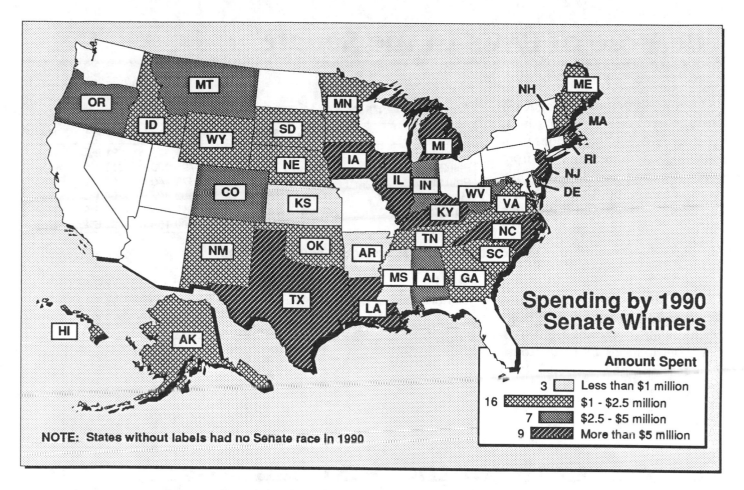

Spending by 1990 Senate Winners

Amount Spent		
3	☐	Less than $1 million
16	▦	$1 - $2.5 million
7	▨	$2.5 - $5 million
9	▧	More than $5 million

NOTE: States without labels had no Senate race in 1990

On the low end of the spectrum, Republican Nancy Kassebaum spent little more than half a million dollars to retain her Senate seat from Kansas. She was actually outspent by one of the state's U.S. House candidates, but she had little difficulty winning another six-year Senate term. On election day she captured over 73 percent of the votes.

Lowest Spending Senate Winners

Name	Party	State	Spent	Vote Pct
Nancy L. Kassebaum	Rep	Kan	$533,632	73.6%
David Pryor	Dem	Ark	$673,620	99.8%
Thad Cochran	Rep	Miss	$693,907	100.0%
Sam Nunn	Dem	Ga	$1,245,052	100.0%
John W. Warner	Rep	Va	$1,311,131	80.9%
Paul Wellstone	Dem	Minn	$1,340,708	50.4%

Senate Candidates Who Spent $100,000 or More of Their Own Money

Name	Party	State	Personal Funds	W/L	Vote Pct
James W. Rappaport	Rep	Mass	$4,220,138	Lost	43.0%
Neil Rolde	Dem	Maine	$1,518,222	Lost	39.0%
Harry Lonsdale	Dem	Ore	$743,152	Lost	46.0%
Bill Schuette	Rep	Mich	$245,000	Lost	41.0%
Josie Heath	Dem	Colo	$203,295	Lost	42.0%
Christine Todd Whitman	Rep	NJ	$163,348	Lost	47.0%
John Durkin	Dem	NH	$121,100	Lost	31.0%
Ron J. Twilegar	Dem	Idaho	$114,419	Lost	39.0%
Bill Cabaniss	Rep	Ala	$111,292	Lost	39.0%

As the list to the left shows, spending large amounts of one's own money in a U.S. Senate race is no guarantee of success. In fact, all nine Senate candidates who spent $100,000 or more of their personal funds in 1990 lost at the polls. A number of current U.S. Senators did use their own fortunes to finance their first elections. In 1988, for example, Wisconsin Democrat Herb Kohl spent over $7 million of his own money to win an open-seat race for the Senate.

23

The Role of PACs in the Senate

In contrast to their colleagues in the House of Representatives, Senators rely on contributions from individuals far more than those from political action committees. Only three Senate candidates — all incumbents — collected more than half their campaign funds from PACs in 1990. On the other hand, the much higher budgets of Senate campaigns mean they tend to collect many more dollars from PACs than do House members. The average Senate winner drew $978,000 in PAC contributions in 1990; House winners averaged $209,000 from PACs.

Top Recipients of PAC Funds

Name	Party	State	PAC rcpts	PAC Pct	W/L
Tom Harkin	Dem	Iowa	$1,814,595	31.8%	Won
Phil Gramm	Rep	Texas	$1,795,970	11.0%	Won
Paul Simon	Dem	Ill	$1,679,740	17.4%	Won
Max Baucus	Dem	Mont	$1,663,317	54.1%	Won
Jim Exon	Dem	Neb	$1,519,494	57.6%	Won
Howell Heflin	Dem	Ala	$1,506,155	37.6%	Won

Highest Percentage of PAC Funds

Name	Party	State	PAC Pct	PAC rcpts	W/L
Jim Exon	Dem	Neb	57.6%	$1,519,494	Won
Max Baucus	Dem	Mont	54.1%	$1,663,317	Won
Ted Stevens	Rep	Alaska	51.9%	$869,349	Won

Leftover Cash for the Next Campaign

The reelection races of Republican Senators Phil Gramm of Texas and Jesse Helms of North Carolina were two of the most expensive in 1990. But the wide variance in their year-end cash balances illustrates the widely differing sense of urgency with which they were conducted. Helms' record-setting campaign ended the year with a deficit of more than $900,000 — indicating a fiercely competitive race in which every dollar that could be found was put to use. Phil Gramm in Texas had an easier time of it. The campaign raised more than $16 million, but spent only $12 million, leaving Gramm with a $4 million head start on his next election, six years in the future. (Under federal campaign laws, candidates with leftover cash in their campaigns can transfer it to new campaign committees if they decide to seek other office.)

Largest Post-Election Campaign Treasuries

Name	Party	State	Net cash*	Vote Pct
Phil Gramm	Rep	Texas	$4,147,378	60.2%
Sam Nunn	Dem	Ga	$1,550,058	100.0%
Howell Heflin	Dem	Ala	$1,036,023	60.6%
David Pryor	Dem	Ark	$1,005,464	99.8%
J. Bennett Johnston	Dem	La	$945,371	53.9%

Senate Winners with Biggest Campaign Deficits

Name	Party	State	Net cash*	Vote pct
Jesse Helms	Rep	NC	-$901,962	52.6%
Daniel K. Akaka	Dem	Hawaii	-$92,062	54.0%
John Kerry	Dem	Mass	-$80,710	57.1%
Paul Wellstone	Dem	Minn	-$55,013	50.4%
Mark O. Hatfield	Rep	Ore	-$20,891	53.7%

End-of-election year balances are not nearly as significant for Senators, however, as they are for House members. With six years between elections, most Senators tend to take a break from serious fundraising — at least for a little while. For House members, who must run every two years, fundraising can be a permanent preoccupation.

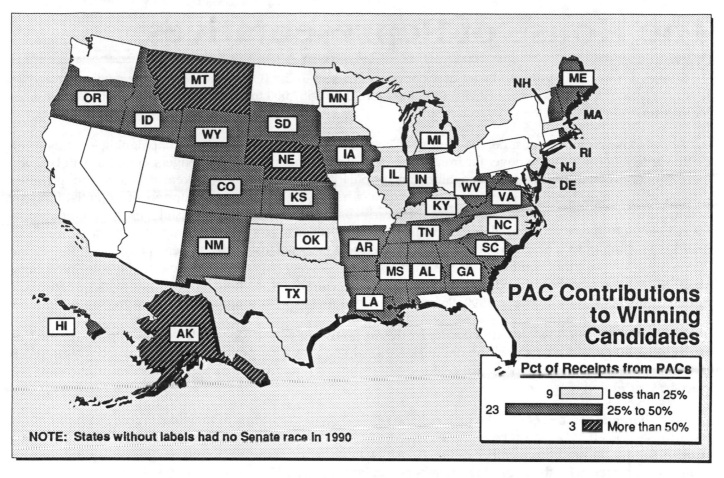

PAC Contributions to Winning Candidates

Pct of Receipts from PACs

9		Less than 25%
23		25% to 50%
3		More than 50%

NOTE: States without labels had no Senate race in 1990

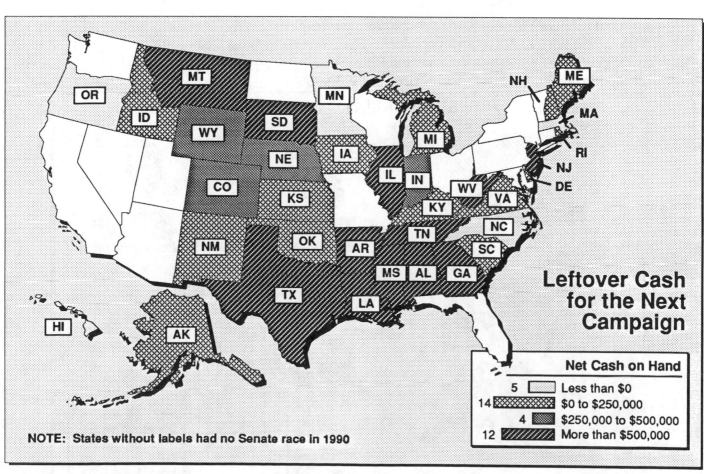

Leftover Cash for the Next Campaign

Net Cash on Hand

5		Less than $0
14		$0 to $250,000
4		$250,000 to $500,000
12		More than $500,000

NOTE: States without labels had no Senate race in 1990

25

The House of Representatives

It takes a strong campaign and a lot of money to win a seat in the U.S. House of Representatives these days — an average of $407,000 in the last election, and more than $557,000 for those winning a seat in Congress for the first time.

Since House members must defend their seats every two years, the pressures of campaigning — and raising the funds to pay for it — are never far from sight, even for incumbents. For challengers the effort can be even more daunting. Matching the name recognition and popularity of incumbent lawmakers is difficult enough when dealing with voters; it can be even more problematic when trying to attract the support of potential funders. Political action committees — the source of nearly half the funds for successful House candidates — overwhelmingly dispense their dollars to incumbents. In 1990, challengers collected only 10.6 percent of the more than $150 million in PAC donations. Candidates in open seat races got just under 12 percent. All the rest — some 77.5 percent — went to incumbents. As the charts on the following pages indicate, few challengers even came close to matching either the dollars or the votes of current office-holders. Despite widespread voter disenchantment with Congress in 1990, 96 percent of incumbents who sought reelection were successful.

The sections that follow provide a district-by-district portrait of what it took in 1990 to win election to the U.S. House. The maps and charts give the national, regional and statewide perspectives on a variety of campaign indicators, from the winners' percentage of the November vote to the size of their political war chests as the election year ended.

Overall trends can be seen in the national and regional maps. Closeups of individual races can be found in the state sections that begin on page 52. The average costs and ranking of each state are shown on the facing page. A full listing of every member of the House, with an index showing how their 1990 campaign finance statistics compared with those of other members, begins on page 149.

Nationwide, Democrats outnumbered Republicans by a margin of 267 to 167 seats in the U.S. House after the 1990 election, with one seat held by an independent. Thirty-one states had a Democratic majority in their House delegation. Eleven states — mostly in the West and Midwest — had Republican majorities. Eight states had evenly split delegations, while Vermont sent an Independent to Congress.

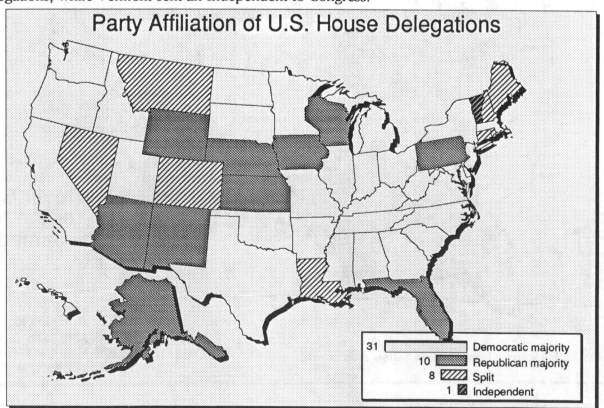

Party Affiliation of U.S. House Delegations

31	Democratic majority
10	Republican majority
8	Split
1	Independent

State-by-State Averages

The following table gives average figures and national rankings of five key campaign statistics for U.S. House winners in each state. **Vote Pct** is the average vote percentage received by the winning candidates in that state during the general election. **Spent** is the average spent by House winners in that state. **PAC Rcpts** shows the average amount winners received from political action committees. **PAC Pct** shows what percentage of winners' total revenues came from PACs. **Net Cash on Hand** gives the average winner's campaign fund balance at the end of 1990, minus any outstanding debts. Following each figure is a rank, showing how the candidates in that state compared with those in other states.

State	VotePct	Rank	PAC Rcpts	Rank	PAC Pct	Rank	Spent	Rank	Net Cash on Hand	Rank
Ala	79.2%	5	$179,277	37	56.3%	8	$302,087	44	$221,255	6
Alaska	51.7%	50	$277,725	6	49.5%	30	$564,759	6	-$94,576	48
Ariz	69.6%	20	$148,487	46	53.6%	16	$270,772	47	$121,403	28
Ark	66.9%	26	$297,088	4	55.0%	13	$512,566	12	$183,308	12
Calif	62.4%	35	$195,552	31	39.1%	41	$481,511	17	$246,538	3
Colo	63.3%	31	$180,795	36	57.6%	7	$334,170	40	$69,816	31
Conn	64.3%	30	$228,387	19	39.1%	42	$560,476	7	$30,634	39
Del	65.5%	28	$203,720	29	37.1%	43	$521,336	11	$53,814	37
Fla	73.6%	10	$187,866	35	43.0%	38	$436,052	26	$145,169	21
Ga	62.9%	34	$243,252	14	51.0%	26	$545,846	9	$139,203	22
Hawaii	63.1%	32	$145,692	47	26.6%	49	$541,624	10	-$92,444	47
Idaho	58.3%	41	$252,728	10	59.5%	5	$427,057	29	-$42,639	44
Ill	72.9%	13	$211,891	26	51.3%	23	$355,070	36	$178,929	14
Ind	60.1%	40	$259,791	9	51.9%	19	$433,814	27	$67,195	35
Iowa	81.1%	3	$153,975	45	44.1%	35	$282,750	45	$90,176	30
Kan	63.1%	33	$192,826	33	51.0%	25	$358,439	35	$67,820	33
Ky	76.2%	8	$132,618	49	40.3%	39	$245,582	50	$187,494	11
La	70.8%	16	$156,181	43	43.2%	37	$347,440	37	$67,333	34
Maine	55.5%	47	$170,564	39	35.0%	45	$499,727	14	-$47,224	46
Md	70.5%	18	$230,623	18	45.0%	34	$440,330	24	$168,111	16
Mass	77.7%	7	$137,198	48	32.9%	47	$452,795	21	$216,913	7
Mich	68.6%	22	$243,524	13	51.4%	22	$386,544	32	$191,777	9
Minn	66.9%	25	$221,920	23	57.8%	6	$405,142	31	$168,168	15
Miss	82.2%	1	$166,665	40	53.6%	15	$267,052	48	$134,856	26
Mo	56.7%	44	$268,833	8	60.2%	4	$441,804	23	$135,132	25
Mont	62.0%	36	$218,695	24	56.0%	11	$328,120	42	$145,418	20
Neb	57.9%	42	$318,374	2	51.8%	20	$592,574	3	-$44,703	45
Nev	60.2%	39	$191,741	34	34.5%	46	$573,056	4	-$19,094	42
NH	53.9%	49	$159,051	42	26.7%	48	$694,764	2	-$189,800	50
NJ	66.0%	27	$222,516	21	45.9%	32	$490,493	16	$226,535	5
NM	81.6%	2	$226,040	20	53.5%	18	$346,639	38	$181,357	13
NY	71.1%	15	$195,287	32	51.1%	24	$334,300	39	$256,274	2
NC	61.6%	37	$240,752	15	53.8%	14	$448,330	22	$59,489	36
ND	65.2%	29	$449,050	1	75.0%	1	$504,800	13	$237,008	4
Ohio	67.8%	23	$166,250	41	55.1%	12	$272,934	46	$122,522	27
Okla	70.2%	19	$154,638	44	40.0%	40	$429,847	28	$69,811	32
Ore	70.5%	17	$273,952	7	50.7%	27	$497,244	15	$211,145	8
Pa	73.2%	12	$201,662	30	53.5%	17	$365,817	34	$136,178	24
RI	57.2%	43	$317,453	3	36.1%	44	$888,344	1	-$105,566	49
SC	78.8%	6	$215,829	25	62.3%	3	$315,157	43	$137,470	23
SD	67.6%	24	$251,800	11	48.7%	31	$463,625	19	$104,643	29
Tenn	73.3%	11	$239,090	16	56.1%	9	$256,724	49	$327,674	1
Texas	80.6%	4	$237,161	17	50.4%	29	$419,075	30	$161,124	17
Utah	56.0%	45	$248,928	12	51.5%	21	$469,673	18	-$10,439	40
Vt	56.0%	46	$72,250	50	12.6%	50	$569,772	5	-$21,940	43
Va	72.0%	14	$222,053	22	50.6%	28	$461,076	20	$38,118	38
Wash	60.7%	38	$283,629	5	56.1%	10	$549,225	8	$152,139	19
WVa	68.7%	21	$211,292	27	65.1%	2	$331,577	41	$157,200	18
Wis	74.0%	9	$210,847	28	45.2%	33	$380,133	33	$190,312	10
Wyo	55.1%	48	$174,995	38	43.3%	36	$437,772	25	-$15,469	41
Natl Avg	**69.2%**		**$209,581**		**48.9%**		**$407,556**		**$156,821**	

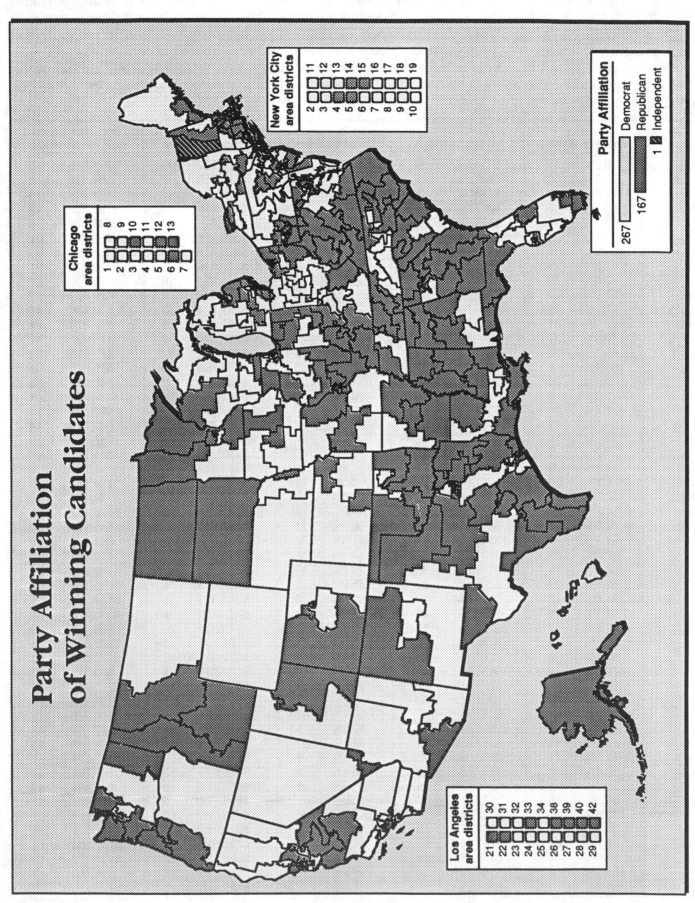

Party Affiliation
of Winning Candidates

New York City area districts

11	12	13	14	15	16	17	18	19
2	3	4	5	6	7	8	9	10

Chicago area districts

8	9	10	11	12	13
1	2	3	4	5	6	7

Los Angeles area districts

30	31	32	33	34	38	39	40	42
21	22	23	24	25	26	27	28	29

Party Affiliation

267	Democrat
167	Republican
1	Independent

Party Affiliation

The Democratic Party, which has dominated the House of Representatives since 1954, strengthened its already powerful hold on that body in 1990, emerging from the elections with a 100-seat majority. This represents a gain of 15 seats in the two years since the 1988 election.

The exact size of that majority will ebb and flow slightly during the course of the 102nd Congress, as vacancies in the 435-seat body are filled through special elections. Unlike the Senate, where vacancies can be filled by appointment, House members can only be elected by a vote of the people. As vacancies arise — through death, resignation, or in rare cases, expulsion — special elections are scheduled to select the new representative.

The 1990 election did bring one new wrinkle to the balance between the parties; the election of Independent candidate Bernie Sanders of Vermont. Sanders, the former socialist mayor of Burlington, was the first third-party candidate elected to the House since 1972.

The fact that the Democratic party has lost five of the last six presidential contests has not weakened its strong majority in the House of Representatives. Even with the GOP's biggest gains in the 1972 Nixon landslide, the Republicans still had 50 fewer seats than the Democrats. At its widest point, after the 1964 Lyndon Johnson landslide, the gap between the two parties was 155 seats.

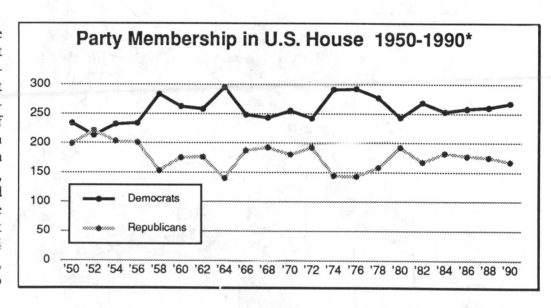

Regionally, the Democrats remain strongest in the South, where they outnumber House Republicans by a margin of more than two-to-one. The parties are most closely matched in the West, where the Democrats hold an 11-seat edge.

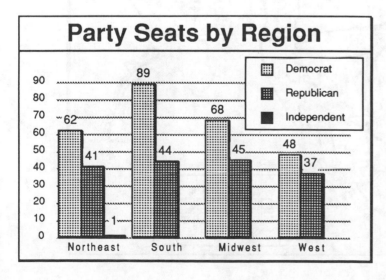

29

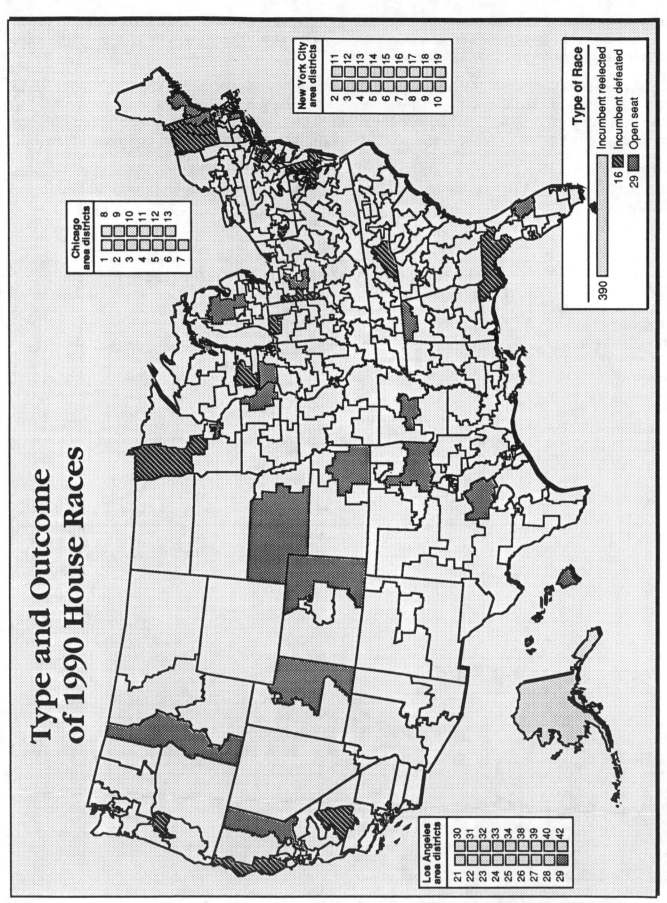

Type and Outcome of 1990 House Races

Chicago area districts
1 8
2 9
3 10
4 11
5 12
6 13
7

New York City area districts
2 11
3 12
4 13
5 14
6 15
7 16
8 17
9 18
10 19

Los Angeles area districts
21 30
22 31
23 32
24 33
25 34
26 38
27 39
28 40
29 42

Type of Race

390 ☐ Incumbent reelected
16 ▨ Incumbent defeated
29 ▦ Open seat

Type of Race

In the overwhelming majority of congressional districts across the country, voters found their incumbent representatives running for reelection. In 78 districts, the incumbents coasted to reelection without even facing a major-party opponent. In all, of the 406 incumbents seeking new terms, 390 were successful — for a reelection rate of 96 percent. That rate, though slightly lower than the 98.5 percent rate set in 1988, was typical of the pattern in recent years. The last time the House reelection rate dipped below 90 percent was in 1974, and even then it dropped only to 88 percent (see chart on page 13).

Twenty-nine districts had open seat elections in 1990, with no incumbents running. Of those, 18 were won by Democrats and 11 by Republicans.

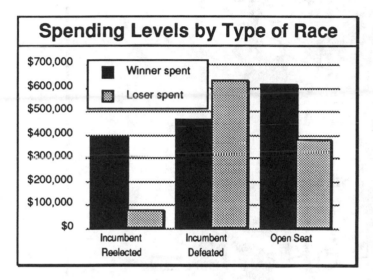

Spending Levels by Type of Race

Spending levels in U.S. House races varied widely, depending on the type of race. Incumbents who were reelected spent $390,047 on average, versus $75,360 by their opponents. The 16 incumbents who lost their seats on election day averaged more than $631,025 in campaign expenditures; their successful challengers spent an average $462,546. Only two of the 16 successful challengers actually outspent the incumbent.

In open-seat races, winning candidates spent an average $612,682 versus $388,366 for the losers. Of the 29 open seat races across the nation, 20 were won by the candidate who spent the most. The race-by-race spending comparisons can be seen in the chart below.

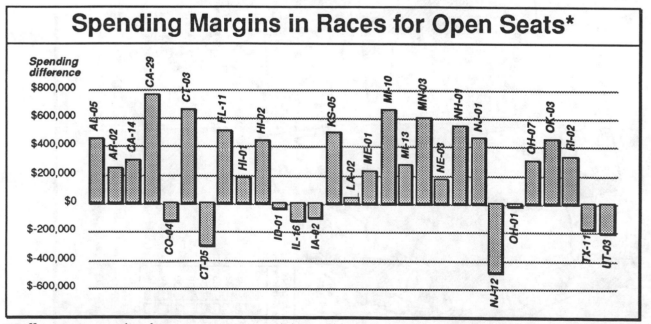

Spending Margins in Races for Open Seats*

* Difference in spending between winning candidate and losing candidate. In races with a negative value, the loser spent more than the winner.

Spotlight on Competitive Races

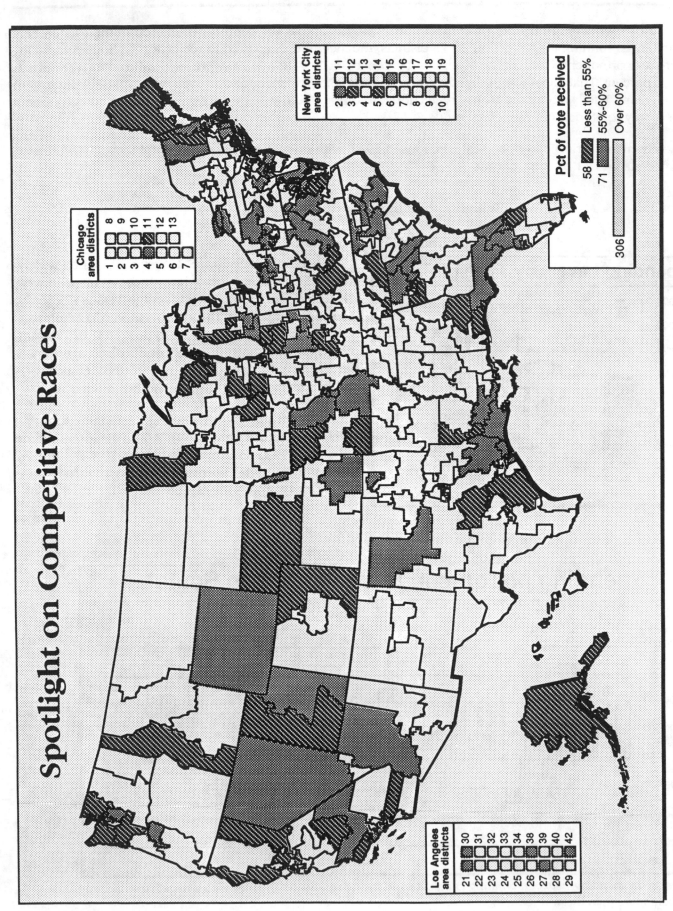

Chicago area districts

1	2	3	4	5	6	7
8	9	10	11	12	13	

New York City area districts

2	3	4	5	6	7	8	9	10
11	12	13	14	15	16	17	18	19

Los Angeles area districts

21	22	23	24	25	26	27	28	29
30	31	32	33	34	38	39	40	42

Pct of vote received

58	Less than 55%
71	55%–60%
306	Over 60%

Competition in House Races

While 96 percent of House incumbents were safely reelected in 1990, their margin of victory was not as comfortable as it was two years earlier. The comparative pie charts below tell the story — the number of close and marginal races increased, the average voter percentage of winning candidates declined. But overall, most races were still decided by wide margins. Once again in 1990, challengers rarely prevailed over incumbents. In open seat races, the candidates who spent the most won the most.

What the pie charts do not show is that voter dissatisfaction with Congress was unusually high as election day drew near. The disarray of the long-running budget talks with the White House played up the seeming inability of Congress to take hard stands on the nation's problems — and this cut into the vote totals of incumbents. But by election day, many incumbents had already sewn up their reelections. In the months leading up to the election few challengers were able to attract serious funding, while other potentially serious challengers eyed the odds of unseating incumbents and simply stayed out of the race.

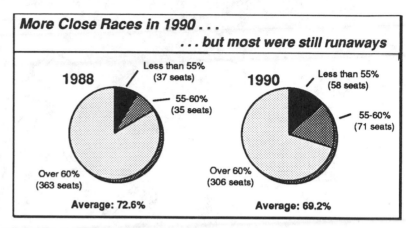

Closest House Races

Name	District	Party	Race type	Vote pct	Vote margin
Joan Kelly Horn	Mo 2	Dem	Beat incumb	50.0	54
Newt Gingrich	Ga 6	Rep	Reelected	50.3	974
Jim Nussle	Iowa 2	Rep	Open seat	49.8	1,642
Randy "Duke" Cunningham	Calif 44	Rep	Beat incumb	46.3	1,665
Carl C. Perkins	Ky 7	Dem	Reelected	50.8	1,953

The closest race in the nation in 1990 saw newcomer Joan Kelly Horn unseat Republican incumbent Jack Buechner in Missouri's 2nd congressional district, west of St. Louis, by a margin of 54 votes. An even greater upset almost befell Republican Newt Gingrich in suburban Atlanta. Gingrich, a member of the Republican House leadership and one of the nation's most visible conservatives, barely held onto his seat — despite spending $1.5 million in his reelection effort against Democrat David Worley's $333,000 campaign. Worley's message, that Gingrich was paying too much attention to grooming his national profile while ignoring his district, came close to costing Gingrich his seat.

As is clear from the chart at right, the closest races were those where challengers spent substantial sums of money. The spending gap between winners and losers was narrowest in races where the winner got less than 55 percent of the vote. Most of the races where the winner got 90 percent or more were contests where the incumbent was unopposed, or faced token opposition from third-party candidates. A total of 137 candidates (133 of whom were incumbents) ran unopposed, or faced candidates in the general election who did not report spending any money on their campaign.

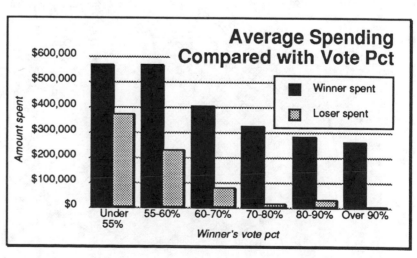

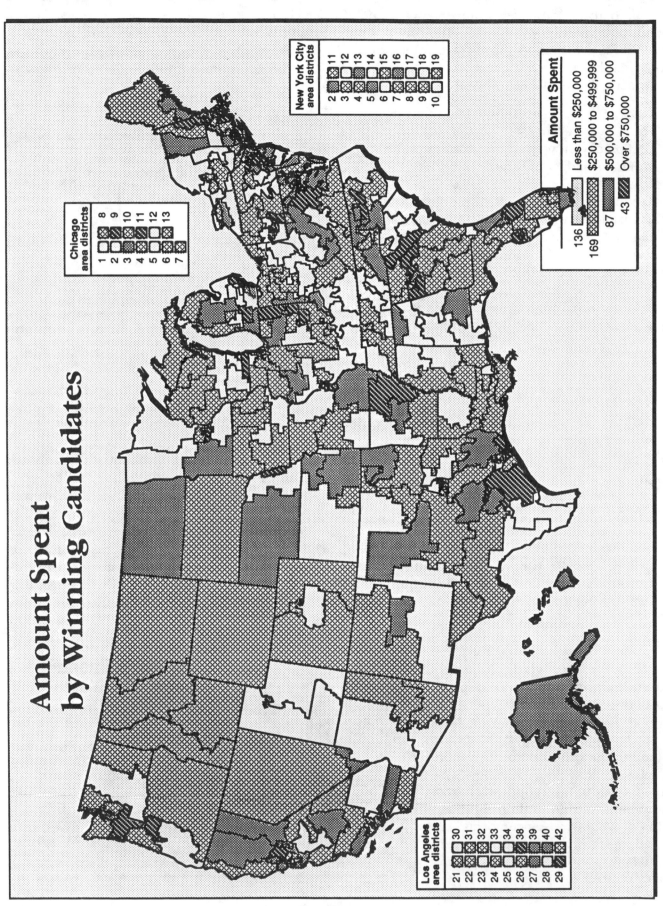

Amount Spent by Winning Candidates

New York City area districts
11, 12, 13, 14, 15, 16, 17, 18, 19
2, 3, 4, 5, 6, 7, 8, 9, 10

Chicago area districts
8, 9, 10, 11, 12, 13
1, 2, 3, 4, 5, 6, 7

Amount Spent
136 — Less than $250,000
169 — $250,000 to $499,999
87 — $500,000 to $750,000
43 — Over $750,000

Los Angeles area districts
30, 31, 32, 33, 34, 38, 39, 40, 42
21, 22, 23, 24, 25, 26, 27, 28, 29

Spending in House Races

The average price of admission for a seat in the U.S. House of Representatives was $407,556 in 1990 — up from slightly over $390,000 in 1988. That figure can be misleading, however, since the great majority of the races were won by wide margins by incumbents with plenty of cash to spare and no seriously-financed opposition.

In 252 of the 435 races, the winner spent at least *ten times* the amount spent by the loser. In 85 percent of the races, the winner outspent the loser by a margin of two-to-one or more.

Those candidates elected for the first time in 1990 spent an average of nearly $560,000 in their campaigns; of that, an average $57,000 came from their own pockets.

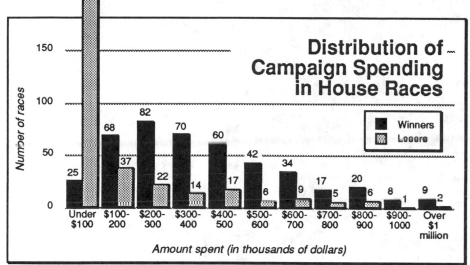

As seen graphically in the chart on the left, a great disparity could be seen in spending by winners and losers. Only about one loser in four spent more than $100,000, while winners — predominantly incumbents — typically spent between $100,000 and $500,000 in their campaigns. Included in the "under $100,000" losers category were 143 races in which the incumbent ran unopposed or the challenger spent no money at all.

Top Spenders in 1990 House Campaigns

Spent	Name	Dist	Party	Vote Pct	Outcome
$1,707,539	Marguerite Chandler	NJ 12	Dem	31.0%	Lost
$1,538,945	*Newt Gingrich*	Ga 6	Rep	50.3%	Won
$1,455,794	*Richard A. Gephardt*	Mo 3	Dem	56.8%	Won
$1,445,577	*Robert K. Dornan*	Calif 38	Rep	58.1%	Won
$1,279,382	*Jolene Unsoeld*	Wash 3	Dem	53.8%	Won
$1,224,626	Dick Zimmer	NJ 12	Rep	64.0%	Won
$1,218,178	*David E. Bonior*	Mich 12	Dem	64.7%	Won
$1,097,107	*John P. Murtha*	Pa 12	Dem	61.7%	Won
$1,083,427	*Wayne Owens*	Utah 2	Dem	57.6%	Won
$1,067,366	Reid Hughes	Fla 4	Dem	44.0%	Lost
$1,029,304	*Vic Fazio*	Calif 4	Dem	54.7%	Won

Incumbents are shown in italics

Lowest Spenders Among 1990 House Winners

Spent	Winner	Dist	Party	VotePct	Race Type
$6,766	*William H. Natcher*	Ky 2	Dem	66.0%	Reelected
$14,816	*Andrew Jacobs Jr.*	Ind 10	Dem	66.4%	Reelected
$40,698	*Bill Goodling*	Pa 19	Rep	100.0%	Reelected
$49,935	*Sid Morrison*	Wash 4	Rep	70.7%	Reelected
$53,137	*Bob Wise*	WVa 3	Dem	100.0%	Reelected
$56,903	*Neal Smith*	Iowa 4	Dem	97.9%	Reelected
$56,922	*Jim Cooper*	Tenn 4	Dem	67.4%	Reelected
$59,112	*David O'B Martin*	NY 26	Rep	100.0%	Reelected
$71,181	*G. V. Sonny Montgomery*	Miss 3	Dem	100.0%	Reelected
$75,367	*Clarence E. Miller*	Ohio 10	Rep	63.2%	Reelected

Eleven House candidates mounted million-dollar campaigns in 1990, with the open-seat race in New Jersey's 12th district attracting the biggest purse of all — $2.9 million in combined spending by the top two candidates. Georgia's Newt Gingrich, who pumped more than $1.5 million into his reelection campaign, barely survived at the polls. His opponent, David Worley, spent just $333,000.

Bucking the national trend toward bigger and more expensive campaigns were a relative handful of House incumbents who glided to reelection without spending a lot of money. Leading the list once again in 1990 was William Natcher (D-Ky), who spent less than $7,000 defending the seat he has held since 1953.

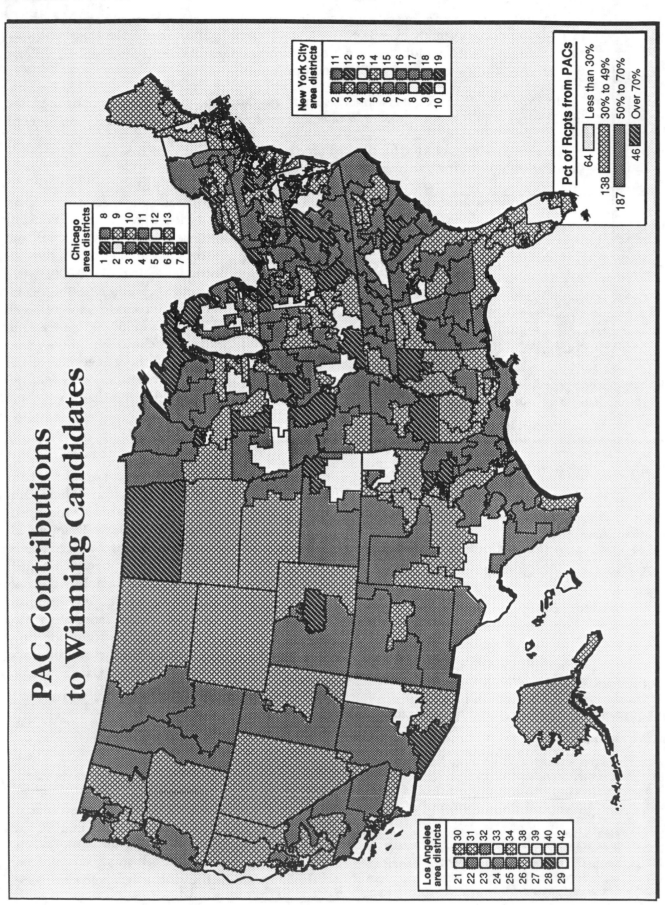

PAC Contributions
to Winning Candidates

New York City area districts

11	12	13	14	15	16	17	18	19	
2	3	4	5	6	7	8	9	10	

Chicago area districts

8	9	10	11	12	13	
1	2	3	4	5	6	7

Los Angeles area districts

30	31	32	33	34	38	39	40	42
21	22	23	24	25	26	27	28	29

Pct of Rcpts from PACs

64	Less than 30%
138	30% to 49%
187	50% to 70%
46	Over 70%

PAC Contributions in House Campaigns

If "money is the mother's milk of politics," as California power broker Jesse Unruh once proclaimed, then PACs — political action committees — are the mother's milk of House incumbents. Contributions from PACs accounted for nearly half the campaign dollars raised by winning House members in 1990. With each election, the proportion of PAC dollars in House members' campaign coffers continues to inch higher. In a total of 233 House races (out of 435), the winning candidate collected 50 percent or more of his or her funds from PACs. Only nine House incumbents won office without them.

An extensive study of PAC contributions by the Center for Responsive Politics after the 1988 congressional elections found that PAC dollars commonly follow committee assignments. While no single PAC can give more than $10,000 in an election cycle (and most give only $1,000 or so at a time), it is common practice for PACs of a feather to flock together. Members sitting on committees important to a particular interest group routinely receive contributions not from one or two PACs from that industry, but a dozen or more.

Top PAC Recipients in 1990 House Elections

PAC rcpts	Name	Dist	Party	VotePct	Outcome
$761,537	*Richard A. Gephardt*	Mo 3	Dem	56.8%	Won
$732,737	*David E. Bonior*	Mich 12	Dem	64.7%	Won
$624,248	*Jolene Unsoeld*	Wash 3	Dem	53.8%	Won
$621,927	*John D. Dingell*	Mich 16	Dem	66.6%	Won
$614,287	*Peter Hoagland*	Neb 2	Dem	57.9%	Won
$576,758	*Robert T. Matsui*	Calif 3	Dem	60.3%	Won
$542,039	*Butler Derrick*	SC 3	Dem	58.0%	Won
$540,732	*Wayne Owens*	Utah 2	Dem	57.6%	Won
$516,953	*William H. Gray III*	Pa 2	Dem	92.1%	Won
$497,561	*Robert H. Michel*	Ill 18	Rep	98.4%	Won

Incumbents are shown in italics

House Majority Leader Dick Gephardt led the list of PAC recipients in the House during 1990. In all, nine of the top 10 PAC recipients in 1990 were Democrats — reflecting the fact that PAC dollars flow most heavily to the party that holds the balance of power, as well as all committee and subcommittee chairmanships.

A growing number of House members have come to rely on PACs as their primary source of campaign funds. Forty-six House members collected 70 percent or more of their money from PACs in 1990. The only challenger on the list at right was John Wayne Caton, a Texas Democrat who collected only $15,000 in his run for the seat — $13,600 of which came from PACs.

Highest Percentage of PAC Receipts

PAC pct	Name	Dist	Party	VotePct	Outcome
90.4%	*William J. Coyne*	Pa 14	Dem	71.8%	Won
89.9%	John Wayne Caton	Texas 26	Dem	30.0%	Lost
88.2%	*Morris K. Udall*	Ariz 2	Dem	65.9%	Won
85.6%	*Bernard J. Dwyer*	NJ 6	Dem	50.5%	Won
85.3%	*William L. Clay*	Mo 1	Dem	60.9%	Won
84.9%	*Jim McDermott*	Wash 7	Dem	72.3%	Won
84.7%	*Joel Hefley*	Colo 5	Rep	66.4%	Won
83.9%	*Mary Rose Oakar*	Ohio 20	Dem	73.3%	Won
82.6%	*Joseph M. Gaydos*	Pa 20	Dem	65.6%	Won
82.5%	*Cardiss Collins*	Ill 7	Dem	79.9%	Won

Incumbents are shown in italics

1990 House Incumbents Who Took No PAC Funds

PAC rcpts	Name	Dist	Party	Vote pct	Outcome
$0	Bill Archer	Texas 7	Rep	100.0%	Won
$0	Anthony C. Beilenson	Calif 23	Dem	61.7%	Won
$0	Philip M. Crane	Ill 12	Rep	82.2%	Won
$0	Bill Goodling	Pa 19	Rep	100.0%	Won
$0	Bill Gradison	Ohio 2	Rep	64.4%	Won
$0	Andrew Jacobs Jr.	Ind 10	Dem	66.4%	Won
$0	Jim Leach	Iowa 1	Rep	99.8%	Won
$0	Edward J. Markey	Mass 7	Dem	99.9%	Won
$0	William H. Natcher	Ky 2	Dem	66.0%	Won
$0	Ralph Regula	Ohio 16	Rep	58.9%	Won

The list of holdouts from the wave of PAC spending dropped to just nine in 1990 — down from 11 in the 1988 elections. All won by comfortable margins.

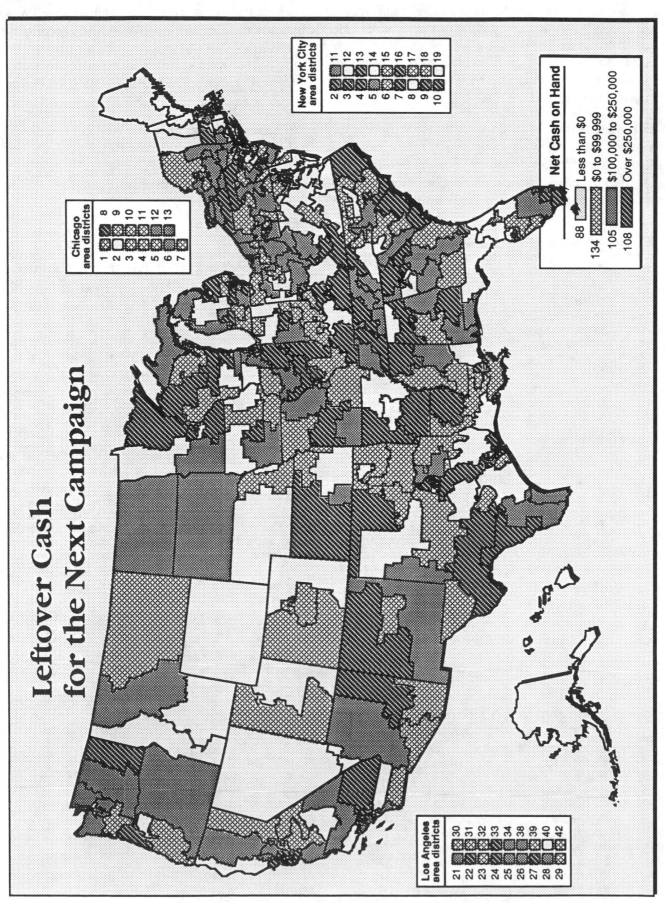

Leftover Cash
for the Next Campaign

Net Cash on Hand

Less than $0
$0 to $99,999
$100,000 to $250,000
Over $250,000

88
134
105
108

New York City area districts

2 11
3 12
4 13
5 14
6 15
7 16
8 17
9 18
10 19

Chicago area districts

1 8
2 9
3 10
4 11
5 12
6 13
7

Los Angeles area districts

21 30
22 31
23 32
24 33
25 34
26 38
27 39
28 40
29 42

Leftover Cash for the Next Campaign

The cost of winning a seat in the U.S. House of Representatives hit a new high in 1990, but so did congressional fundraising — and the amount of money left over in campaign accounts at the close of the election year. As of Dec. 31, 1990, the average House winner had $156,821 in the bank.

This significant head start in fundraising puts incumbents at an enormous advantage for the next election. That edge will be of particular use to incumbents in 1992, since congressional reapportionment (based on the 1990 census) will mandate the redrawing of nearly every congressional district in the nation.

In all, some 213 House incumbents ended the 1990 election year with more than $100,000 in the bank. Twenty-eight had balances exceeding half a million dollars.

Not all winning candidates, of course, were so fortunate — particularly those who won their seats for the first time. The average newly-elected member of Congress faced an end-of-the-year deficit of more than $73,000.

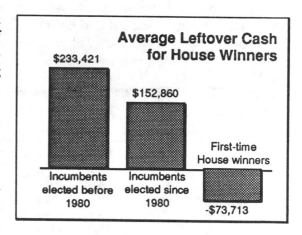

Average Leftover Cash for House Winners

$233,421 — Incumbents elected before 1980
$152,860 — Incumbents elected since 1980
-$73,713 — First-time House winners

But with incumbency comes a vastly enhanced ability to raise political funds. By setting aside large sums well in advance of the next election, incumbents can often dissuade potential challengers from entering the race at all.

Largest Campaign Treasuries at the End of 1990

Net cash	Name	Dist	Party	Vote Pct
$1,859,603	Stephen J. Solarz	NY 13	Dem	80.4%
$1,714,807	Mel Levine	Calif 27	Dem	58.2%
$1,669,915	David Dreier	Calif 33	Rep	63.7%
$1,580,475	Charles E. Schumer	NY 10	Dem	80.4%
$1,128,637	Robert T. Matsui	Calif 3	Dem	60.3%
$1,114,068	Dan Rostenkowski	Ill 8	Dem	79.1%
$1,044,255	James H. Quillen	Tenn 1	Rep	99.9%
$967,326	Matthew J. Rinaldo	NJ 7	Rep	74.6%
$811,742	Robert G. Torricelli	NJ 9	Dem	57.0%
$811,150	Michael A. Andrews	Texas 25	Dem	100.0%

Largest 1990 Year-End Deficts by Current House Members

Net cash	Name	Dist	Party	Vote Pct
-$433,924	Charles H. Taylor	NC 11	Rep	50.7%
-$407,788	Pete Geren	Texas 12	Dem	71.3%
-$374,532	Bill Zeliff	NH 1	Rep	55.1%
-$307,774	Dick Nichols	Kan 5	Rep	59.3%
-$293,151	James H. Scheuer	NY 8	Dem	72.3%
-$213,125	John F. Reed	RI 2	Dem	59.2%
-$205,159	Dick Zimmer	NJ 12	Rep	64.0%
-$190,967	Patsy T. Mink	Hawaii 2	Dem	66.3%
-$186,381	John A. Boehner	Ohio 8	Rep	61.1%
-$158,300	William J. Jefferson	La 2	Dem	52.5%

One other factor may have contributed to the record-high levels of leftover cash. A key stipulation in the pay raise bill that the House passed in 1989 was an end to the so-called "grandfather clause" in House rules that allows Congressmen elected before 1980 to convert their campaign cash to personal use when they retire. Under the pay raise agreement, senior members may only take advantage of the grandfather clause *if they retire at the end of their current terms.* If they run for re-election in 1992, they will no longer be able to convert their campaign cash to their personal use. That fact could well contribute to an unusually high number of retirements in 1992, and a correspondingly large number of open seat races in the coming election.

The Regions

The maps on the following eight pages give a breakdown of campaign spending and party affiliations of winning House candidates in four major regions of the United States — the Northeast, South, Midwest and West. The maps are divided into congressional districts. Accompanying each one is a combination legend and bar chart that explains the categories and shows how many districts fall within each category.

Also included in the spending maps are lists of the five most expensive House races in each region, as well as the five least expensive winning campaigns.

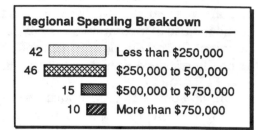

Regional Spending Breakdown

42		Less than $250,000
46		$250,000 to 500,000
15		$500,000 to $750,000
10		More than $750,000

Most Expensive Campaigns

Name	Party	District	W/L	Spent
Richard A. Gephardt	Dem	Mo 3	W	$1,455,794
David E. Bonior	Dem	Mich	W	$1,218,178
Jim Ramstad	Rep	Minn 3	W	$935,454
Peter Hoagland	Dem	Neb 2	W	$929,247
Frank Annunzio	Dem	Ill 11	W	$855,952

Least Expensive Winning Campaigns

Name	Party	District	Spent
Andrew Jacobs Jr.	Dem	Ind 10	$14,816
Neal Smith	Dem	Iowa 4	$56,903
Clarence E. Miller	Rep	Ohio 10	$75,367
William S. Broomfield	Rep	Mich 18	$78,205
James A. Traficant Jr.	Dem	Ohio 17	$79,064

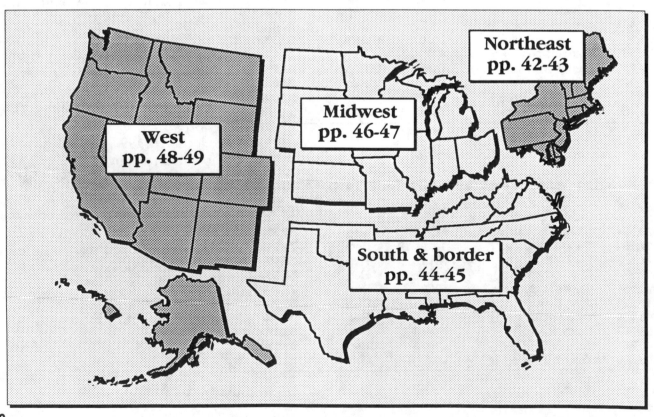

West pp. 48-49

Midwest pp. 46-47

Northeast pp. 42-43

South & border pp. 44-45

While most differences in campaign finances between regions were relatively minor, the Western region was the most expensive in the nation for running congressional campaigns in 1990 — just as it was two years earlier. Successful House candidates spent an average of nearly $460,000 in their campaigns in Western states — more than $52,000 above the national average. The cost of losing was also highest in the West; an average of more than $128,000. Western House winners also led the nation in total receipts for their 1990 campaigns (over $515,000).

Midwestern congressmen drew the most in contributions from political action committees — an average of more than $219,000. The Midwest was also the least expensive region for running for the House; the average winning campaign there cost just under $370,000.

Northeastern congressmen had the highest year-end cash reserves after the 1990 election, an average of nearly $176,000. Close behind was the Western region.

House winners in the South enjoyed the highest average vote percentage — 73.4 percent — while those in the West won by an average of just over 63 percent.

Though the regional differences in most cases were fairly slight, they did show a remarkable consistency with the elections of 1988. In every one of the seven categories listed below, the regional leaders in 1990 were the same as in 1988.

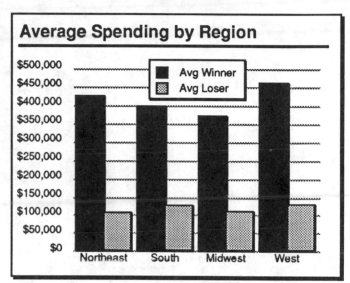

Winners' Averages in Different Regions of the Country

	Northeast	South	Midwest	West	Natl Avg
Amount spent	$420,864	$396,289	$369,137	$459,977	$407,556
Total receipts	$473,095	$431,179	$412,767	$515,334	$452,862
PAC receipts	$198,921	$210,137	$219,209	$208,955	$209,581
PAC pct	46.3%	50.2%	52.6%	45.1%	48.9%
Leftover cash	$175,753	$144,099	$141,552	$173,861	$156,821
Vote pct	70.0%	73.4%	68.0%	63.3%	69.2%
Loser spent*	$106,408	$123,358	$109,205	$128,659	$116,665

* Average spent by second-highest vote getter in the November election

Northeast
Party Affiliation of House Winners

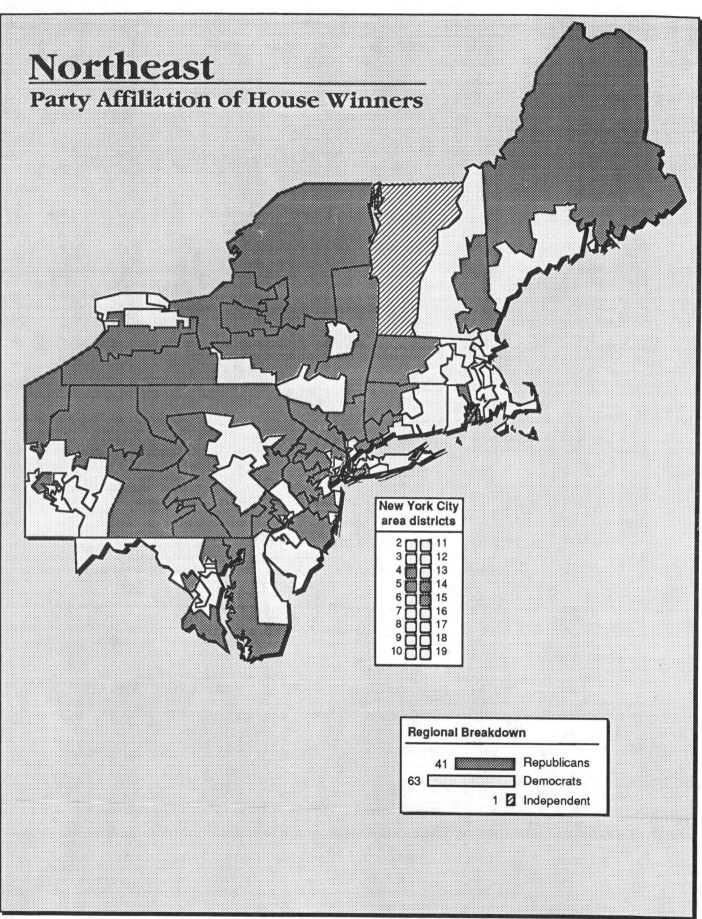

New York City area districts

2		11	
3		12	
4		13	
5		14	
6		15	
7		16	
8		17	
9		18	
10		19	

Regional Breakdown

41		Republicans
63		Democrats
1		Independent

Northeast
Amount Spent by Winning Candidates

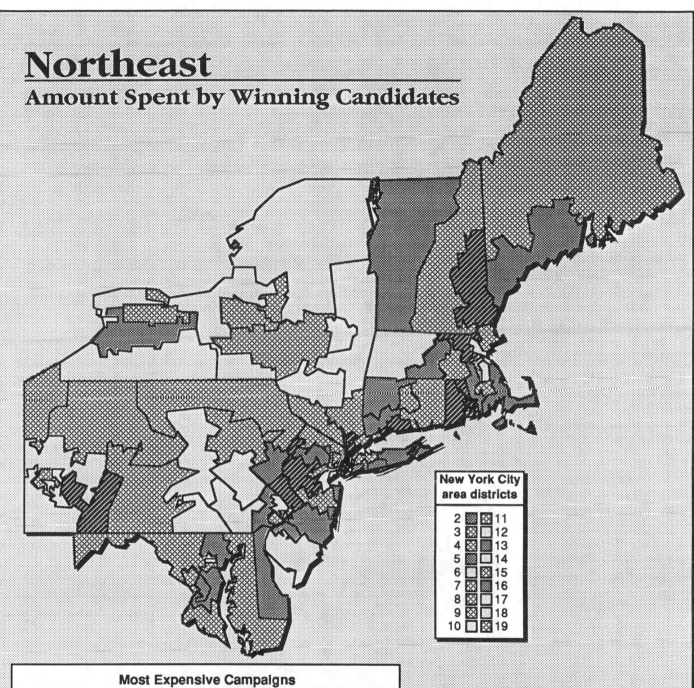

New York City area districts

2		11
3		12
4		13
5		14
6		15
7		16
8		17
9		18
10		19

Most Expensive Campaigns

Name	Party	District	W/L	Spent
Marguerite Chandler	Dem	NJ 12	L	$1,707,539
Dick Zimmer	Rep	NJ 12	W	$1,224,626
John P. Murtha	Dem	Pa 12	W	$1,097,107
Rosa DeLauro	Dem	Conn 3	W	$957,982
Bill Zeliff	Rep	NH 1	W	$924,367

Least Expensive Winning Campaigns

Name	Party	District	Spent
Bill Goodling	Rep	Pa 19	$40,698
David O'B Martin	Rep	NY 26	$59,112
Henry J. Nowak	Dem	NY 33	$93,158
George W. Gekas	Rep	Pa 17	$93,331
Charles E. Schumer	Dem	NY 10	$97,082

Regional Spending Breakdown

31		Less than $250,000
39		$250,000 to $499,999
24		$500,000 to $750,000
11		Over $750,000

South & Border States
Party Affiliation of House Winners

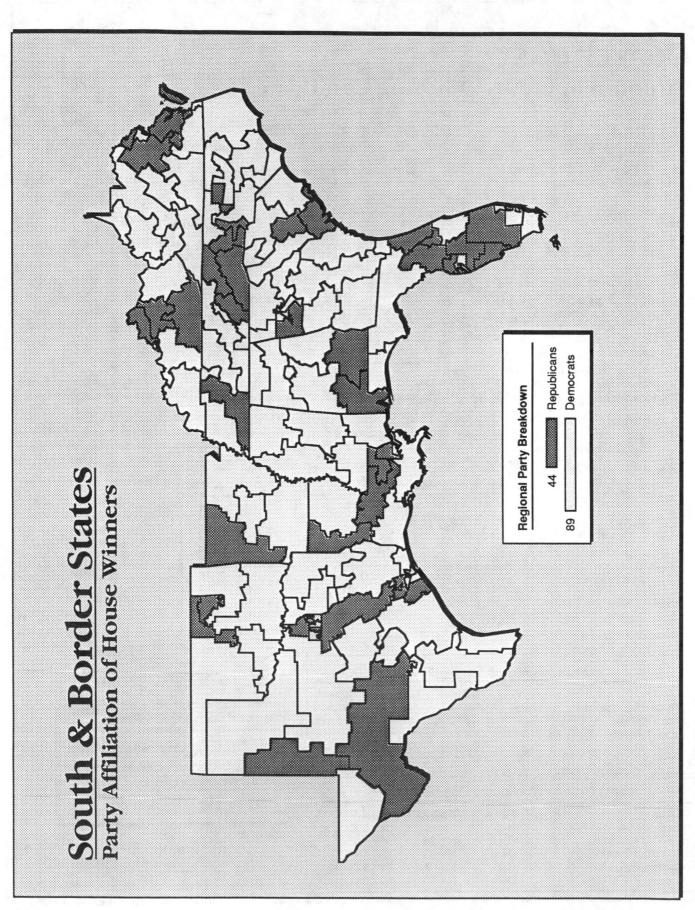

Regional Party Breakdown

44 Republicans

89 Democrats

44

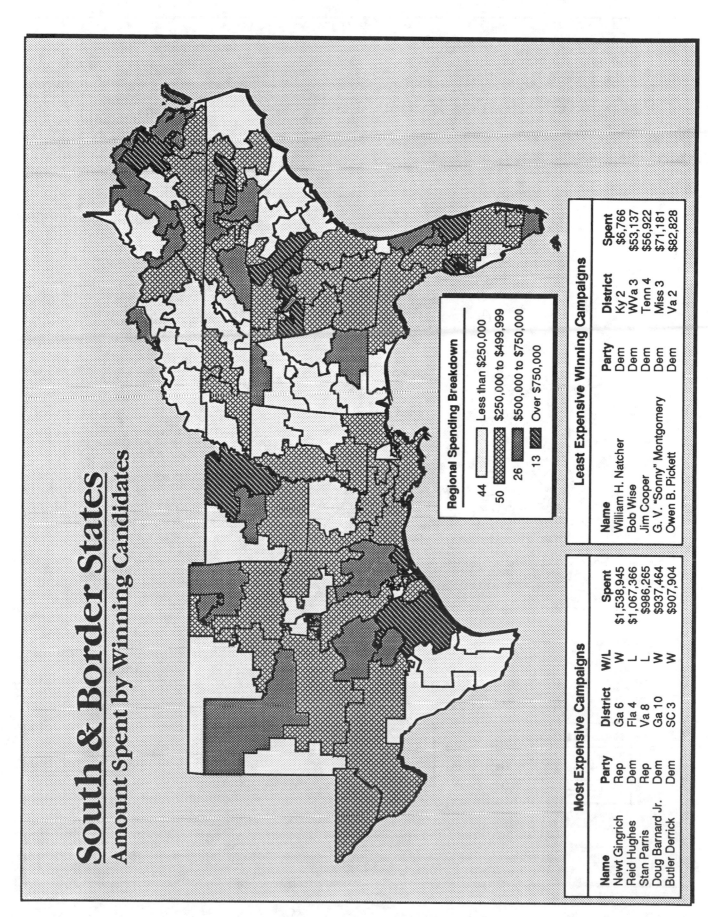

South & Border States
Amount Spent by Winning Candidates

Regional Spending Breakdown

44	Less than $250,000
50	$250,000 to $499,999
26	$500,000 to $750,000
13	Over $750,000

Most Expensive Campaigns

Name	Party	District	W/L	Spent
Newt Gingrich	Rep	Ga 6	W	$1,538,945
Reid Hughes	Dem	Fla 4	L	$1,067,366
Stan Parris	Rep	Va 8	L	$986,265
Doug Barnard Jr.	Dem	Ga 10	W	$937,464
Butler Derrick	Dem	SC 3	W	$907,904

Least Expensive Winning Campaigns

Name	Party	District	Spent
William H. Natcher	Dem	Ky 2	$6,766
Bob Wise	Dem	WVa 3	$53,137
Jim Cooper	Dem	Tenn 4	$56,922
G. V. "Sonny" Montgomery	Dem	Miss 3	$71,181
Owen B. Pickett	Dem	Va 2	$82,828

Midwest
Party Affiliation of House Winners

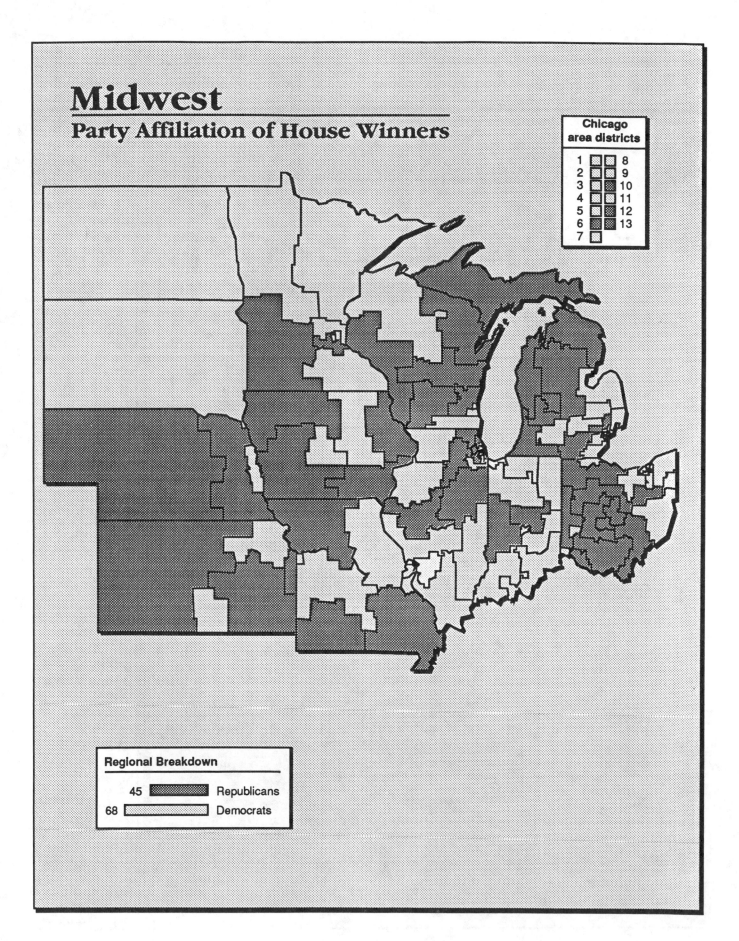

Chicago area districts

1 □□ 8
2 □□ 9
3 □ 10
4 □□ 11
5 □□ 12
6 □□ 13
7 □

Regional Breakdown

45 ▨▨▨ Republicans

68 □□□ Democrats

Midwest
Amount Spent by Winning Candidates

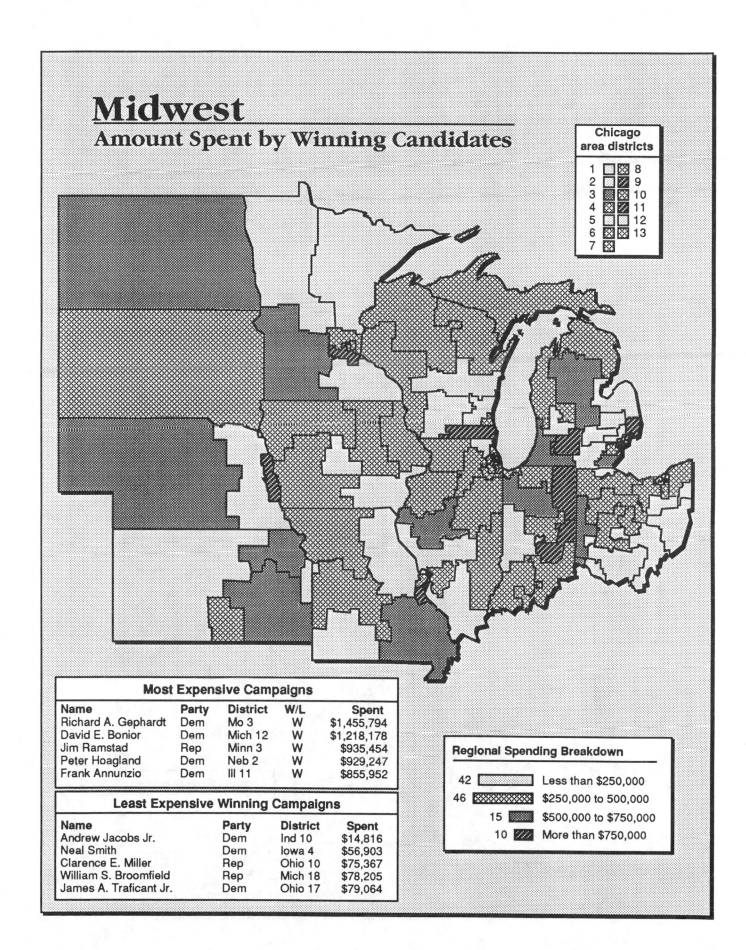

Chicago area districts

1	8
2	9
3	10
4	11
5	12
6	13
7	

Most Expensive Campaigns

Name	Party	District	W/L	Spent
Richard A. Gephardt	Dem	Mo 3	W	$1,455,794
David E. Bonior	Dem	Mich 12	W	$1,218,178
Jim Ramstad	Rep	Minn 3	W	$935,454
Peter Hoagland	Dem	Neb 2	W	$929,247
Frank Annunzio	Dem	Ill 11	W	$855,952

Least Expensive Winning Campaigns

Name	Party	District	Spent
Andrew Jacobs Jr.	Dem	Ind 10	$14,816
Neal Smith	Dem	Iowa 4	$56,903
Clarence E. Miller	Rep	Ohio 10	$75,367
William S. Broomfield	Rep	Mich 18	$78,205
James A. Traficant Jr.	Dem	Ohio 17	$79,064

Regional Spending Breakdown

42	Less than $250,000
46	$250,000 to 500,000
15	$500,000 to $750,000
10	More than $750,000

Western States
Party Affiliation of House Winners

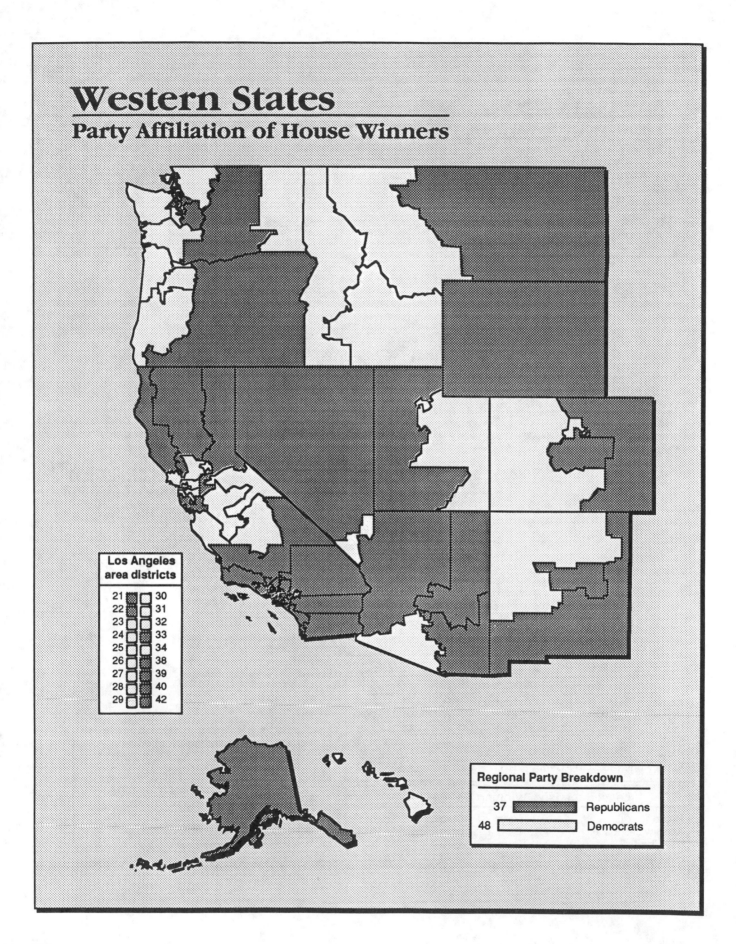

Los Angeles
area districts

21	30
22	31
23	32
24	33
25	34
26	38
27	39
28	40
29	42

Regional Party Breakdown

37 Republicans
48 Democrats

Western States
Amount Spent by Winning Candidates

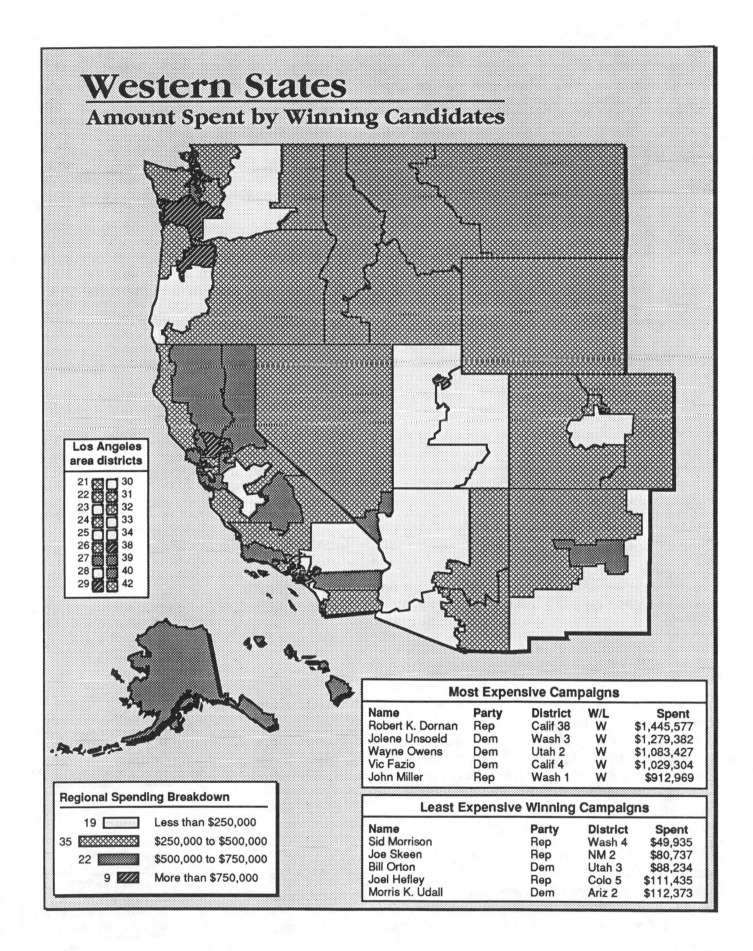

Los Angeles area districts

21		30	
22		31	
23		32	
24		33	
25		34	
26		38	
27		39	
28		40	
29		42	

Most Expensive Campaigns

Name	Party	District	W/L	Spent
Robert K. Dornan	Rep	Calif 38	W	$1,445,577
Jolene Unsoeld	Dem	Wash 3	W	$1,279,382
Wayne Owens	Dem	Utah 2	W	$1,083,427
Vic Fazio	Dem	Calif 4	W	$1,029,304
John Miller	Rep	Wash 1	W	$912,969

Least Expensive Winning Campaigns

Name	Party	District	Spent
Sid Morrison	Rep	Wash 4	$49,935
Joe Skeen	Rep	NM 2	$80,737
Bill Orton	Dem	Utah 3	$88,234
Joel Hefley	Rep	Colo 5	$111,435
Morris K. Udall	Dem	Ariz 2	$112,373

Regional Spending Breakdown

19		Less than $250,000
35		$250,000 to $500,000
22		$500,000 to $750,000
9		More than $750,000

The States

The following 96 pages show state-by-state analyses of campaign finances in the 1990 elections. On the right-hand page are maps identifying each congressional district. The states are arranged alphabetically and each state, or group of states, has four maps:

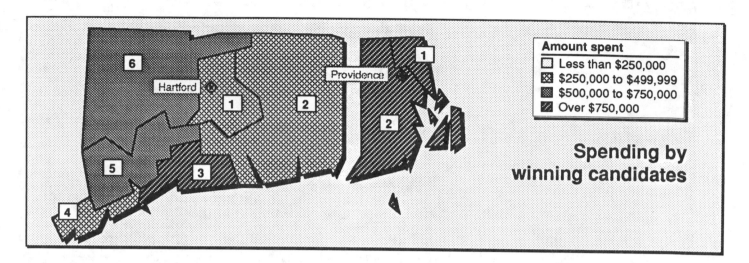

Amount spent
- ☐ Less than $250,000
- ▨ $250,000 to $499,999
- ▩ $500,000 to $750,000
- ▧ Over $750,000

Spending by winning candidates

• **Spotlight on competitive races**, showing the winners' vote percentage in each district. Like the maps in the previous sections, these maps show at a glance which races were close (where the winner drew less than 55 percent of the vote), which were marginal (where the winner got 55-60 percent), and which were not close (where the winner got more than 60 percent of the vote).

Pct of vote received
- ▧ Less than 55%
- ▩ 55% to 60%
- ☐ Over 60%

• **Amount spent by winning candidate**. Again, like the national and regional maps, these divide all House races into four spending categories: campaigns which cost under $250,000, those which cost $250,000 to $500,000, those costing $500,000 to $750,000, and those costing more than $750,000.

Amount spent
- ☐ Less than $250,000
- ▨ $250,000 to $499,999
- ▩ $500,000 to $750,000
- ▧ Over $750,000

• **PAC contributions to winning candidates**, which shows what percentage of the winners' total receipts came from political action committees. It should be noted that these maps highlight the *proportion* of funds received from PACs, not the total dollar amounts. The maps are divided into four categories: candidates who received less than 30 percent of their funds from PACs, those who got 30 to 50 percent, those with 50 to 70 percent, and those who received more than 70 percent of their campaign revenues from political action committees.

Pct of receipts from PACs
- ☐ Less than 30%
- ▨ 30% to 49%
- ▩ 50% to 70%
- ▧ Over 70%

• **Leftover cash for the next campaign**, which indicates the winners' campaign bank balances as of December 31, 1990, minus outstanding debts. The categories here show candidates with a net deficit; those with surpluses up to $100,000; those with surpluses between $100,000 and $250,000, and those who closed the year with more than $250,000 in their campaign accounts.

Net cash on hand
- ☐ Less than $0
- ▨ $0 to $99,999
- ▩ $100,000 to $250,000
- ▧ Over $250,000

On the facing page are further details of that state's election finances, including a **vital statistics** chart listing the name, party, vote percentage and key campaign finance statistics for each congressional winner in the 1990 elections from that state. Included among the statistics are:

Vital Statistics of 1990 Winners

Dist	Name	Party	Vote Pct	Race Type	Total Receipts	PAC Receipts	PAC Pct	Spent	Net cash on Hand
Connecticut									
1	Barbara B. Kennelly	Dem	71.4%	Reelected	$483,041	$296,400	61.4%	$406,138	$176,983
2	Sam Gejdenson	Dem	59.7%	Reelected	$458,980	$185,950	40.5%	$464,500	-$32,079
3	Rosa DeLauro	Dem	52.1%	Open	$973,625	$401,805	41.3%	$957,982	-$84,359
4	Christopher Shays	Rep	76.5%	Reelected	$447,327	$55,500	12.4%	$395,892	$74,546
5	Gary Franks	Rep	51.7%	Open	$587,045	$177,927	30.3%	$581,625	-$68,947
6	Nancy L. Johnson	Rep	74.4%	Reelected	$517,724	$252,737	48.8%	$556,718	$117,662

Vote percentage. This is the percentage of the vote that the winner received in the November general election. Figures shown are from the official state-by-state tabulations.

Race type. Three types of races are noted: those where incumbents were reelected, those where incumbents were defeated, and open seat races, where no incumbent was running.

Total receipts include funds received from individual contributions, PAC receipts, and contributions or loans from the candidate. The figure does not include money given by political parties.

PAC receipts show the total received from political action committees, minus any refunds to those PACs.

PAC percentage is the percentage of total receipts that came from political action committees.

Spent shows the actual amount spent on the campaign. Expenditures for other purposes, such as contributions to other candidates' campaigns, are not included.

Net cash on hand shows the campaign's total amount of cash on hand as of December 31, 1990, minus any outstanding debts.

A **campaign spending graph** shows the spending of the winning and losing candidates in each district. In races with more than two candidates, the spending total of the loser who got the highest vote percentage is shown. This spending chart provides an instant picture of the level of financial competition in each district.

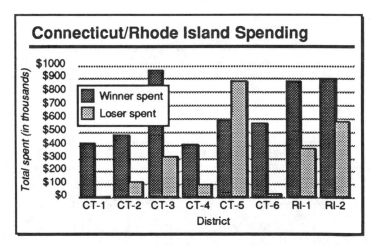

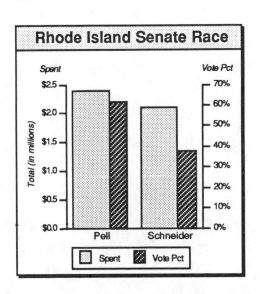

In states that had a contested U.S. Senate election in 1990, a **Senate election chart** is also included. This chart shows the level of spending by each candidate, as well as the final tally of votes received. Three states — Arkansas, Georgia and Mississippi — have no charts, since the incumbent Senators in those states ran unopposed on the November ballot.

Alabama

Vital Statistics of 1990 Winners

Dist	Name	Party	Vote Pct	Race Type	Total Receipts	PAC Receipts	PAC Pct	Spent	Net cash on Hand
1	Sonny Callahan	Rep	99.6%	Reelected	$318,680	$169,350	53.1%	$183,910	$236,511
2	Bill Dickinson	Rep	51.3%	Reelected	$425,127	$218,921	51.5%	$596,096	$250,325
3	Glen Browder	Dem	73.7%	Reelected	$280,234	$190,058	67.8%	$176,550	$119,913
4	Tom Bevill	Dem	99.7%	Reelected	$220,907	$105,550	47.8%	$168,054	$566,499
5	Bud Cramer	Dem	67.1%	Open	$662,457	$246,932	37.3%	$638,361	-$66,229
6	Ben Erdreich	Dem	92.8%	Reelected	$237,722	$172,819	72.7%	$113,168	$364,025
7	Claude Harris	Dem	70.5%	Reelected	$237,577	$151,307	63.7%	$238,466	$77,742
Sen	Howell Heflin	Dem	60.6%	Reelected	$4,005,473	$1,506,155	37.6%	$3,453,983	$1,036,023

The spending patterns in Alabama's 1990 congressional elections reflected trends that could be found in nearly every state in the union: most incumbents seeking reelection ran fairly modestly-funded campaigns against nominal opponents, while open seat races and the occasional vulnerable incumbent caused spending in a handful of districts to rise dramatically.

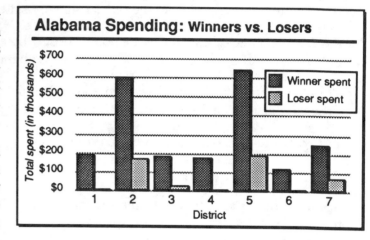

In Alabama's case, the one tight race was in the 2nd district, where 13-term Congressman Bill Dickinson had to fight off not only a serious challenger — former state Human Resources Commissioner Faye Baggiano — but ethics charges concerning his involvement in a $300,000 business venture with a Montgomery constituent. Dickinson eventually won the race, collecting just 51.3 percent of the vote, after spending nearly $600,000 on the campaign — more than triple what Baggiano spent.

The one other expensive House race in Alabama was upstate in the 5th district, where Democrat Bud Cramer vastly outspent and outpolled Republican Albert McDonald. The seat came open after former Congressman Ronnie Flippo filed to run (unsuccessfully) for the Democratic nomination for governor.

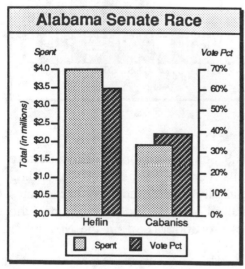

In the race for Senate, two-term incumbent Howell Heflin maintained a sizeable lead — both in votes and fundraising — over Republican state Senator Bill Cabaniss. Heflin outspent Cabaniss two-to-one and carried home just over 60 percent of the vote on election day.

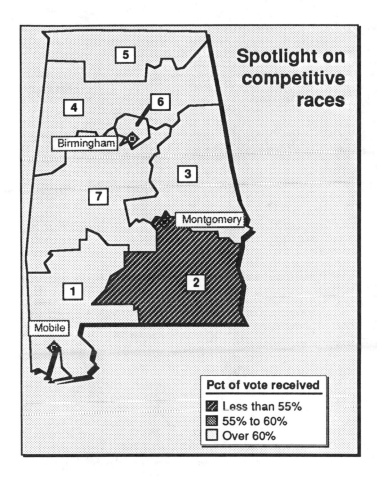

Spotlight on competitive races

Pct of vote received
▨ Less than 55%
▩ 55% to 60%
☐ Over 60%

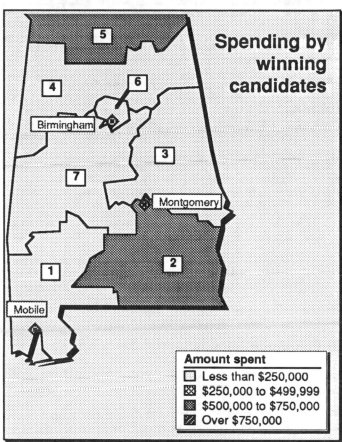

Spending by winning candidates

Amount spent
☐ Less than $250,000
▨ $250,000 to $499,999
▩ $500,000 to $750,000
▨ Over $750,000

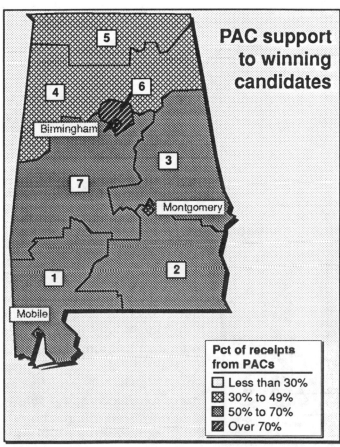

PAC support to winning candidates

Pct of receipts from PACs
☐ Less than 30%
▨ 30% to 49%
▩ 50% to 70%
▨ Over 70%

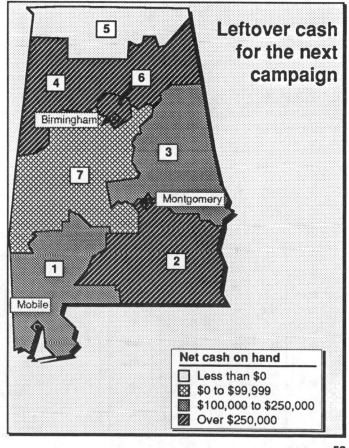

Leftover cash for the next campaign

Net cash on hand
☐ Less than $0
▨ $0 to $99,999
▩ $100,000 to $250,000
▨ Over $250,000

Alaska & Hawaii

Vital Statistics of 1990 Winners

Dist	Name	Party	Vote Pct	Race Type	Total Receipts	PAC Receipts	PAC Pct	Spent	Net cash on Hand
Alaska									
1	Don Young	Rep	51.7%	Reelected	$560,908	$277,725	49.5%	$564,759	-$94,576
Sen	Ted Stevens	Rep	66.2%	Reelected	$1,674,716	$869,349	51.9%	$1,633,790	$234,997
Hawaii									
1	Neil Abercrombie	Dem	60.0%	Open	$476,231	$143,600	30.1%	$442,211	$6,079
2	Patsy T. Mink	Dem	66.3%	Reelected*	$641,324	$147,784	23.0%	$641,037	-$190,967
Sen	Daniel K. Akaka	Dem	54.0%	Reelected†	$1,764,875	$850,514	48.2%	$1,760,839	-$92,062

* Mink was elected in a special election in Sept. 1990, then ran again in November.
† Akaka was appointed to the seat in May 1990. This was his first Senate election.

The nation's two farthest-flung states were the scenes of spirited election contests in 1990. The Hawaiian congressional delegation underwent a complete reshuffling from its 1988 lineup. In Alaska, veteran congressman Don Young faced his tightest race since first winning the seat in 1973.

The death of Sen. Spark Matsunaga in April 1990 set the wheels of change in motion in Hawaii. Congressman Daniel Akaka was named to fill the vacancy through the fall election, when the remaining four years of Matsunaga's term would be up for grabs. His opponent in November was Patricia Saiki, the state's lone Republican in Congress. Akaka eventually won the senate race, edging out Saiki with 54 percent of the vote, despite being outspent.

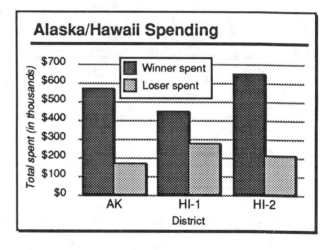

The Senate contest, meanwhile, created vacancies in both of Hawaii's U.S. House seats. Into that vacuum came two former Democratic members of Congress: Patsy Mink, who served six terms in the 1960s and 70s; and Neil Abercrombie, who served briefly in 1986-87. Mink was elected in a September special election, then ran and won again in November. Both Abercrombie and Mink won by relatively comfortable margins in a state that has been overwhelmingly Democratic since achieving statehood in 1959. Both were also able to raise considerably more money in campaign contributions than their opponents.

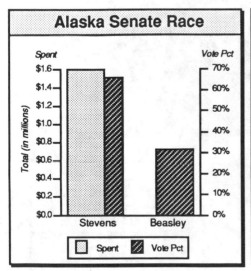

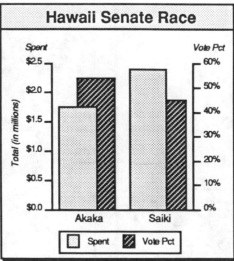

The lineup in Alaska stayed the same as in 1988. Sen. Ted Stevens won easy reelection to his fifth term in the U.S. Senate, spending $1.6 million against an opponent who spent only $1,000. The race for the U.S. House was much closer; incumbent Republican Don Young had to spent more than half a million dollars to retain the seat he has held since 1973. His opponent, Valdez Mayor John Devens, was able to raise only $168,000, but he collected 48 percent of the vote.

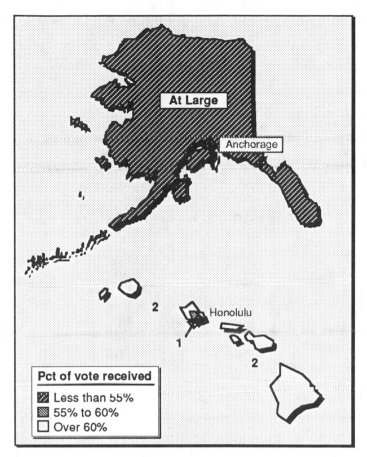

Pct of vote received
- ▨ Less than 55%
- ▩ 55% to 60%
- ☐ Over 60%

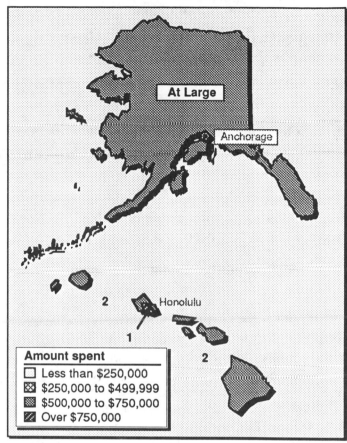

Amount spent
- ☐ Less than $250,000
- ▦ $250,000 to $499,999
- ▩ $500,000 to $750,000
- ▨ Over $750,000

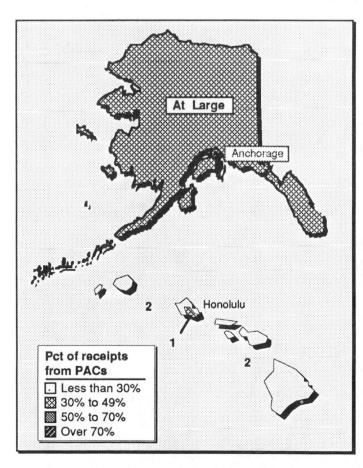

Pct of receipts from PACs
- ⊡ Less than 30%
- ▦ 30% to 49%
- ▩ 50% to 70%
- ▨ Over 70%

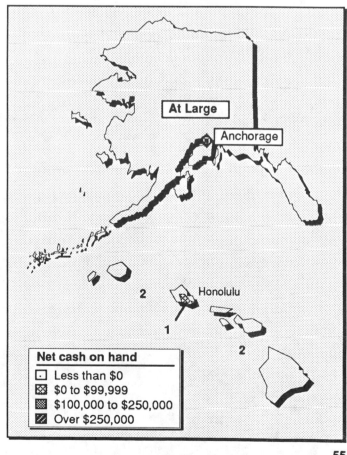

Net cash on hand
- ☐ Less than $0
- ▦ $0 to $99,999
- ▩ $100,000 to $250,000
- ▨ Over $250,000

Arizona

Vital Statistics of 1990 Winners

Dist	Name	Party	Vote Pct	Race Type	Total Receipts	PAC Receipts	PAC Pct	Spent	Net cash on Hand
1	John J. Rhodes III	Rep	99.5%	Reelected	$326,640	$170,339	52.1%	$323,328	$9,621
2	Morris K. Udall	Dem	65.9%	Reelected	$153,320	$135,250	88.2%	$112,373	$73.749
3	Bob Stump	Rep	56.6%	Reelected	$231,127	$132,850	57.5%	$225,149	$113,651
4	Jon Kyl	Rep	61.3%	Reelected	$588,180	$170,389	29.0%	$442,366	$328,905
5	Jim Kolbe	Rep	64.8%	Reelected	$325,457	$133,605	41.0%	$250,642	$81,087

Arizona's five incumbent House members faced only nominal opposition in the 1990 elections. None faced seriously financed challengers, all were re-elected, and only Bob Stump in the 3rd district failed to collect at least 60 percent of the vote.

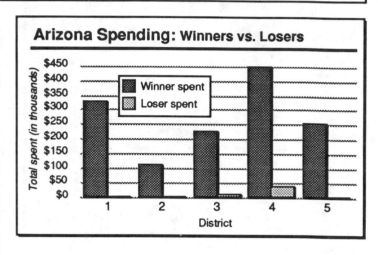

The 1992 elections may be more interesting, however, as incumbent Republican Sen. John McCain faces reelection. McCain was one of the so-called "Keating Five" senators whose efforts on behalf of Arizona-based S&L operator Charles Keating were investigated by the Senate ethics committee. The comittee cleared McCain (as well as his Democratic colleague, Arizona Sen. Dennis DeConcini) of charges that they acted improperly, but voters in the state may be especially sensitive to the ethics issue — particularly after a series of political scandals in the state involving alleged illegal payoffs to several state legislators. DeConcini faces reelection in 1994.

One change in the state's U.S. House delegation is guaranteed before the next election. Longtime congressman Morris Udall resigned his office in May 1991 due to deteriorating health. Udall's successor was chosen in a special election in September 1991.

Boundaries of the state's congressional districts will also be shifting considerably in 1992, and Arizona will gain one additional U.S. House seat due to reapportionment following the 1990 census.

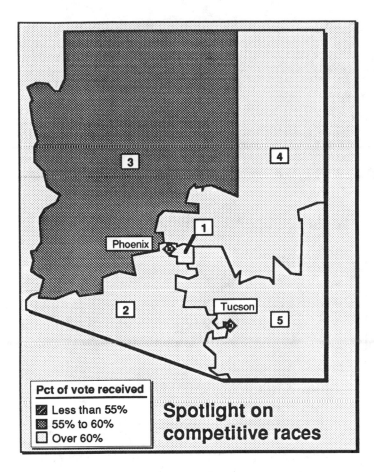

Pct of vote received
- ▦ Less than 55%
- ▨ 55% to 60%
- ☐ Over 60%

Spotlight on competitive races

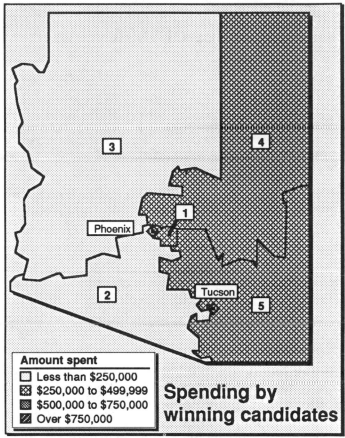

Amount spent
- ☐ Less than $250,000
- ▨ $250,000 to $499,999
- ▦ $500,000 to $750,000
- ▧ Over $750,000

Spending by winning candidates

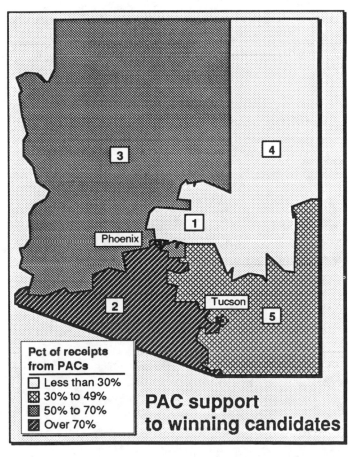

Pct of receipts from PACs
- ☐ Less than 30%
- ▨ 30% to 49%
- ▦ 50% to 70%
- ▧ Over 70%

PAC support to winning candidates

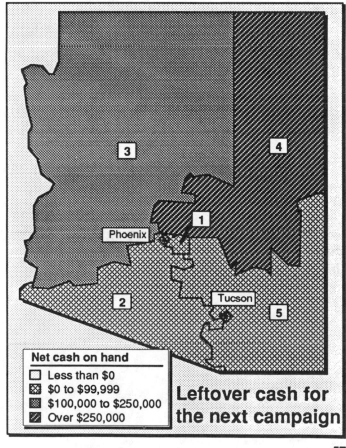

Net cash on hand
- ☐ Less than $0
- ▨ $0 to $99,999
- ▦ $100,000 to $250,000
- ▧ Over $250,000

Leftover cash for the next campaign

57

Arkansas

Vital Statistics of 1990 Winners

Dist	Name	Party	Vote Pct	Race Type	Total Receipts	PAC Receipts	PAC Pct	Spent	Net cash on Hand
1	Bill Alexander	Dem	64.3%	Reelected	$773,016	$405,150	52.4%	$785,626	-$108,071
2	Ray Thornton	Dem	60.4%	Open	$697,067	$242,400	34.8%	$678,429	-$24,045
3	John Paul Hammerschmidt	Rep	70.5%	Reelected	$266,438	$166,500	62.5%	$105,354	$500,684
4	Beryl Anthony Jr.	Dem	72.4%	Reelected	$530,662	$374,300	70.5%	$480,853	$364,662
Sen	David Pryor	Dem	99.8%	Reelected	$1,500,936	$589,099	39.2%	$673,620	$1,005,464

Arkansas voters found two competitive congressional races on their 1990 ballots: one open seat race to replace a congressman who ran instead for governor, and a hard-fought primary battle between two Democrats. The open seat was in the 2nd congressional district, where Republican incumbent Tommy Robinson filed for governor instead of reelection to the U.S. House. (He later lost in the Republican primary). The battle to fill the seat was eventually won by Ray Thornton, a former congressman and longtime Arkansas political figure. Thornton substantially outspent his Republican opponent, State Rep. Jim Keet, and carried 60 percent of the vote on election day.

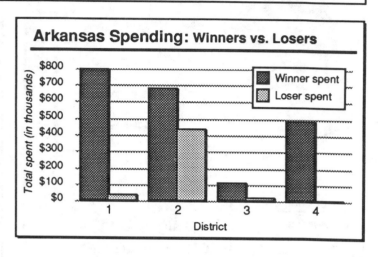

Veteran Democrat Bill Alexander in the 1st district spent nearly $800,000 to ensure his reelection — more than 20 times the spending of his Republican opponent in the general election. But the real spending in that race came in the May primary, when Alexander faced a well-financed challenge by fellow Democrat Mike Gibson. Gibson came close to matching the incumbent's spending dollar for dollar in that contest, but came up just a bit short on election day with 46 percent of the primary vote. The general election, by contrast, was a cakewalk for Alexander, but his overall election-year spending forced him to close the year with a deficit of more than $100,000.

The state's two other House incumbents won decisively in November, though their levels of campaign spending varied widely. In the 4th district, Beryl Anthony spent $480,000 against a Republican challenger who spent just $511 on his campaign. Republican John Paul Hammerschmidt in the 3rd district won by nearly as wide a margin, but spent only $105,000 in the campaign. Both Hammerschmidt and Anthony closed the election year with well-stocked campaign accounts of $500,000 and $364,000 respectively.

The reelection race for Sen. David Pryor turned out not to be a race at all. No Republicans filed to oppose him, and Pryor became one of four U.S. Senators in 1990 to win reelection without a major-party opponent. Since he had no opposition, Pryor's campaign was the second least expensive among Senate winners in 1990. He spent less than half of the $1.5 million he had collected, and closed out the year with just over $1 million in the bank.

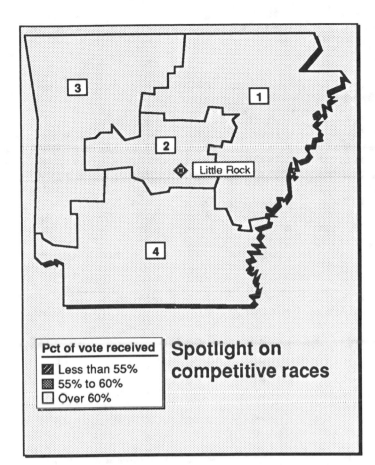

Pct of vote received

- ▨ Less than 55%
- ▩ 55% to 60%
- ☐ Over 60%

Spotlight on competitive races

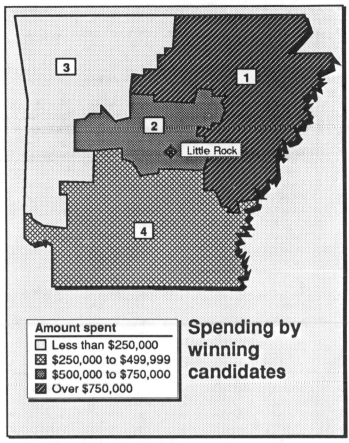

Amount spent

- ☐ Less than $250,000
- ▨ $250,000 to $499,999
- ▦ $500,000 to $750,000
- ▨ Over $750,000

Spending by winning candidates

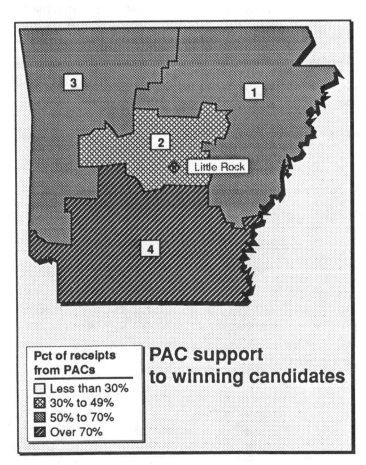

Pct of receipts from PACs

- ☐ Less than 30%
- ▨ 30% to 49%
- ▦ 50% to 70%
- ▨ Over 70%

PAC support to winning candidates

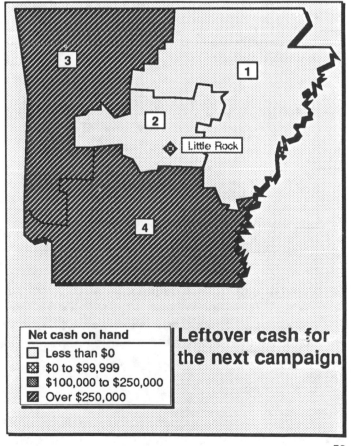

Net cash on hand

- ☐ Less than $0
- ▨ $0 to $99,999
- ▦ $100,000 to $250,000
- ▨ Over $250,000

Leftover cash for the next campaign

California

Vital Statistics of 1990 Winners

Dist	Name	Party	Vote Pct	Race Type	Total Receipts	PAC Receipts	PAC Pct	Spent	Net cash on Hand
1	Frank Riggs	Rep	43.3%	Beat Incumb	$257,745	$8,000	3.1%	$251,662	-$141,378
2	Wally Herger	Rep	63.7%	Reelected	$616,075	$212,749	34.5%	$515,020	$114,862
3	Robert T. Matsui	Dem	60.3%	Reelected	$1,207,843	$576,758	47.8%	$734,005	$1,128,637
4	Vic Fazio	Dem	54.7%	Reelected	$845,622	$450,445	53.3%	$1,029,304	$194,402
5	Nancy Pelosi	Dem	77.2%	Reelected	$462,664	$255,400	55.2%	$440,973	$97,689
6	Barbara Boxer	Dem	68.1%	Reelected	$922,666	$335,234	36.3%	$655,402	$499,349
7	George Miller	Dem	60.5%	Reelected	$469,400	$262,657	56.0%	$448,026	$438,229
8	Ronald V. Dellums	Dem	61.3%	Reelected	$790,386	$71,935	9.1%	$840,029	$37,629
9	Pete Stark	Dem	58.4%	Reelected	$525,271	$270,170	51.4%	$300,996	$362,004
10	Don Edwards	Dem	62.7%	Reelected	$224,999	$170,800	75.9%	$209,243	$55,464
11	Tom Lantos	Dem	65.9%	Reelected	$788,298	$120,550	15.3%	$620,782	$637,734
12	Tom Campbell	Rep	60.8%	Reelected	$1,286,200	$249,581	19.4%	$658,135	$632,835
13	Norman Y. Mineta	Dem	58.0%	Reelected	$666,915	$361,274	54.2%	$644,962	$342,701
14	John T. Doolittle	Rep	51.5%	Open	$529,813	$234,764	44.3%	$517,668	$2,275
15	Gary Condit	Dem	66.2%	Reelected	$234,423	$74,970	32.0%	$212,430	-$19,566
16	Leon E. Panetta	Dem	74.2%	Reelected	$295,399	$129,250	43.8%	$272,710	$204,599
17	Calvin Dooley	Dem	54.5%	Beat Incumb	$547,763	$171,985	31.4%	$538,354	-$52,731
18	Richard H. Lehman	Dem	100.0%	Reelected	$302,473	$201,780	66.7%	$299,728	$96,145
19	Robert J. Lagomarsino	Rep	54.6%	Reelected	$643,444	$145,517	22.6%	$658,365	-$19,480
20	Bill Thomas	Rep	59.8%	Reelected	$430,525	$235,447	54.7%	$496,845	$157,392
21	Elton Gallegly	Rep	58.4%	Reelected	$599,454	$156,611	26.1%	$449,668	$209,540
22	Carlos J. Moorhead	Rep	60.0%	Reelected	$444,157	$231,350	52.1%	$400,109	$666,684
23	Anthony C. Beilenson	Dem	61.7%	Reelected	$231,386	$0	0.0%	$201,404	$45,449
24	Henry A. Waxman	Dem	68.9%	Reelected	$500,847	$315,400	63.0%	$287,505	$468,893
25	Edward R. Roybal	Dem	70.0%	Reelected	$144,260	$79,877	55.4%	$190,702	$196,852
26	Howard L. Berman	Dem	61.1%	Reelected	$510,538	$181,500	35.5%	$450,401	$200,471
27	Mel Levine	Dem	58.2%	Reelected	$1,496,790	$239,207	16.0%	$587,961	$1,714,807
28	Julian C. Dixon	Dem	72.7%	Reelected	$161,900	$124,145	76.7%	$113,669	$136,981
29	Maxine Waters	Dem	79.4%	Open	$740,793	$211,172	28.5%	$759,538	$27,717
30	Matthew G. Martinez	Dem	58.2%	Reelected	$209,495	$93,803	44.8%	$186,130	$43,205
31	Mervyn M. Dymally	Dem	67.1%	Reelected	$434,143	$167,716	38.6%	$418,232	$25,795
32	Glenn M. Anderson	Dem	61.5%	Reelected	$411,845	$256,766	62.4%	$462,503	$31,783
33	David Dreier	Rep	63.7%	Reelected	$591,313	$100,276	17.0%	$172,451	$1,669,915
34	Esteban E. Torres	Dem	60.7%	Reelected	$241,635	$87,788	36.3%	$217,810	$148,388
35	Jerry Lewis	Rep	60.6%	Reelected	$452,381	$291,014	64.3%	$211,940	$338,797
36	George E. Brown Jr.	Dem	52.7%	Reelected	$818,181	$452,635	55.3%	$822,686	-$53,910
37	Al McCandless	Rep	49.7%	Reelected	$551,789	$179,600	32.5%	$602,444	-$14,400
38	Robert K. Dornan	Rep	58.1%	Reelected	$1,615,282	$35,234	2.2%	$1,445,577	$168,200
39	William E. Dannemeyer	Rep	65.3%	Reelected	$594,692	$129,250	21.7%	$627,842	$97,744
40	C. Christopher Cox	Rep	67.6%	Reelected	$688,836	$178,516	25.9%	$682,365	-$56,509
41	Bill Lowery	Rep	49.2%	Reelected	$485,964	$204,915	42.2%	$575,637	$14,915
42	Dana Rohrabacher	Rep	59.3%	Reelected	$423,924	$119,075	28.1%	$398,963	$49,366
43	Ron Packard	Rep	68.1%	Reelected	$167,017	$99,716	59.7%	$147,249	$174,589
44	Randy "Duke" Cunningham	Rep	46.3%	Beat Incumb	$539,721	$214,547	39.8%	$534,167	-$25,207
45	Duncan Hunter	Rep	72.8%	Reelected	$368,560	$110,465	30.0%	$376,408	$6,229

Though the lion's share of attention — and dollars — in California's 1990 elections was focused on the wide-open race for governor, the election proved to be contentious in a number of congressional districts across the state as well. Three incumbents were toppled from office, while four others spent more than $1 million each to retain their seats. Several others escaped with uncomfortably close calls. In no fewer than nine districts, the winning candidate collected less than 55 percent of the votes.

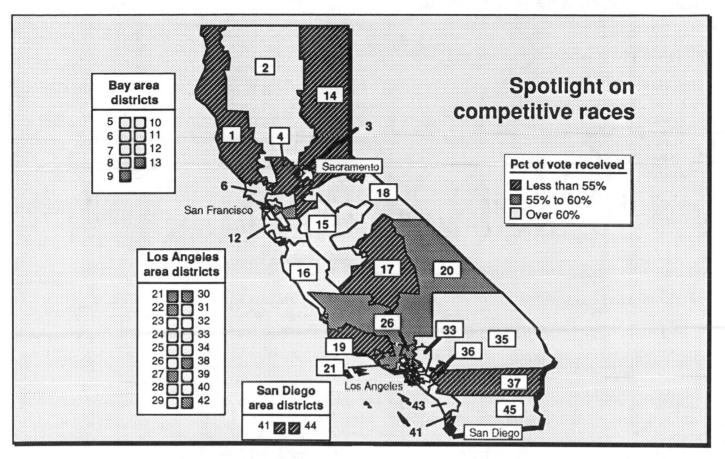

Spotlight on competitive races

Bay area districts

San Francisco

Sacramento

Pct of vote received
- Less than 55%
- 55% to 60%
- Over 60%

Los Angeles area districts

Los Angeles

San Diego area districts

San Diego

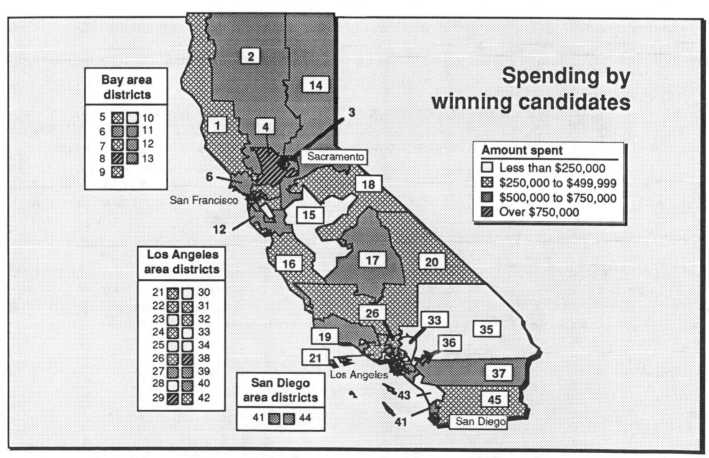

Spending by winning candidates

Bay area districts

San Francisco

Sacramento

Amount spent
- Less than $250,000
- $250,000 to $499,999
- $500,000 to $750,000
- Over $750,000

Los Angeles area districts

Los Angeles

San Diego area districts

San Diego

California *(cont'd)*

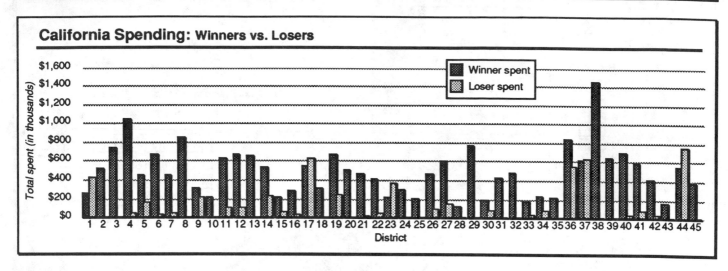

California Spending: Winners vs. Losers

Winner spent
Loser spent

Total spent *(in thousands)*

$1,600 $1,400 $1,200 $1,000 $800 $600 $400 $200 $0

District

The three upsets were all connected to scandals or ethical questions. In the 1st district, along the northern coast, four-term Democrat Douglas Bosco was edged out of his seat by Republican newcomer Frank Riggs — despite the fact that the incumbent outspent Riggs by more than $160,000. What likely turned the trick was Riggs' persistent attempt to tie Bosco to the national Savings & Loan scandal. Riggs eventually won the seat by a 1.4 percent margin in a three-way race.

The S&L scandal also proved a fatal liability for Republican Chip Pashayan in the San Joaquin Valley's 17th district. Among other things, the six-term incumbent was blasted by Democrat Calvin Dooley for contributions he received in 1986 from S&L magnate Charles Keating. Though slightly outspent, Dooley did manage to raise and spend more than $500,000 in his campaign — enough to topple the incumbent.

Downstate in the 44th district in San Diego, Democrat Jim Bates survived a testy primary challenge, but could not survive the ethical charges of sexual harassment levelled against him both in the primary and the general election. The ultimate beneficiary was Republican Randy "Duke" Cunningham, a former navy pilot and newcomer to politics. Cunningham spent $200,000 less than Bates, but beat him at the polls by 1,665 votes.

However tumultuous California's 1990 contests, they will likely seem tame in comparison to what's ahead in 1992, when California voters will face two U.S. Senate contests, a statewide redistricting, and seven new U.S. House seats. When former GOP Senator Pete Wilson won the governor's race in 1990, he appointed little-known Republican John Seymour to fill the vacancy — but Seymour will have to defend that seat in a special election in 1992 to fill the final two years of Wilson's term. At the same time, longtime Democratic Senator Alan Cranston, beset by health problems and heavy fallout from the Keating Five S&L scandal, has announced he will retire, opening up a second U.S. Senate seat in 1992. The addition of seven new House districts ensure that at least that many open seat races in the next election. And the prime candidates moving to contest those seats are likely to come from the state's legislature — a body where senate seats have been known to cost upwards of $1 million. Adding everything up, California in 1992 should offer the most expensive election contests in the nation's history — a prospect that could have national repercussions, since California is currently the nation's largest exporter of campaign funds to other states. So many in-state races could keep most of the Golden State's campaign dollars within its boundaries, freezing out candidates in other states who have come more and more to rely on big-league California donors.

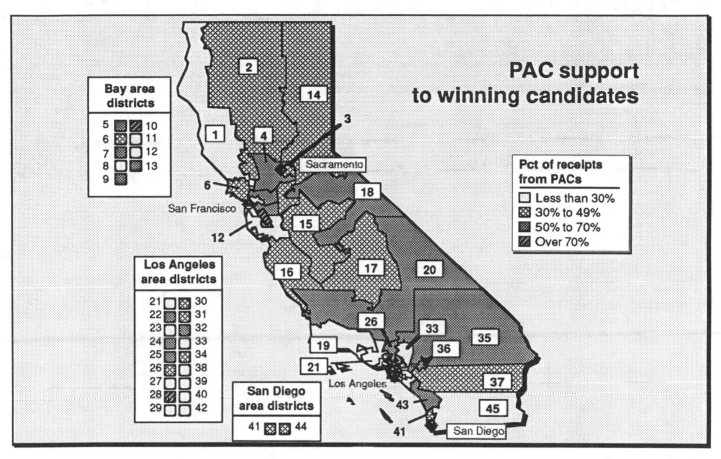

PAC support to winning candidates

Bay area districts

5		10
6		11
7		12
8		13
9		

Pct of receipts from PACs
- Less than 30%
- 30% to 49%
- 50% to 70%
- Over 70%

Los Angeles area districts

21		30
22		31
23		32
24		33
25		34
26		38
27		39
28		40
29		42

San Diego area districts

41   44

Sacramento
San Francisco
Los Angeles
San Diego

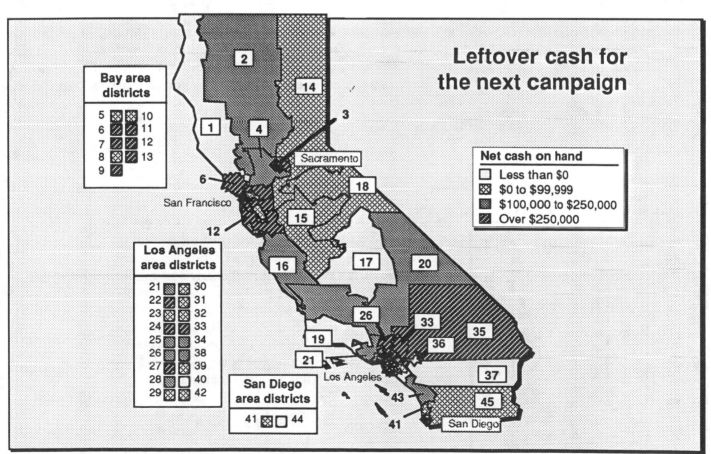

Leftover cash for the next campaign

Bay area districts

5		10
6		11
7		12
8		13
9		

Net cash on hand
- Less than $0
- $0 to $99,999
- $100,000 to $250,000
- Over $250,000

Los Angeles area districts

21		30
22		31
23		32
24		33
25		34
26		38
27		39
28		40
29		42

San Diego area districts

41   44

Sacramento
San Francisco
Los Angeles
San Diego

Colorado

Vital Statistics of 1990 Winners

Dist	Name	Party	Vote Pct	Race Type	Total Receipts	PAC Receipts	PAC Pct	Spent	Net cash on Hand
1	Patricia Schroeder	Dem	63.7%	Reelected	$441,609	$113,588	25.7%	$521,500	$192,156
2	David E. Skaggs	Dem	60.7%	Reelected	$415,235	$242,070	58.3%	$396,017	$22,172
3	Ben Nighthorse Campbell	Dem	70.2%	Reelected	$310,176	$210,480	67.9%	$335,760	$13,513
4	Wayne Allard	Rep	54.1%	Open	$363,633	$174,550	48.0%	$360,206	-$6,572
5	Joel Hefley	Rep	66.4%	Reelected	$135,707	$114,981	84.7%	$111,435	$85,219
6	Dan Schaefer	Rep	64.5%	Reelected	$375,683	$229,103	61.0%	$280,103	$122,410
Sen	Hank Brown	Rep	55.7%	Open	$4,179,746	$1,388,784	33.2%	$3,723,911	$443,184

The retirement of Colorado's senior senator, Republican Bill Armstrong, prompted two changes in the state's congressional delegation. Republican Congressman Hank Brown left his House seat to move up to the Senate, and Wayne Allard, a Republican state senator from Loveland, took over Brown's former seat in the 4th district.

The open-seat race in the 4th district was the only one where both candidates raised roughly comparable amounts. Allard, the Republican winner, actually raised $120,000 less than Democrat Dick Bond. Both candidates in that race collected about half their campaign dollars from PACs.

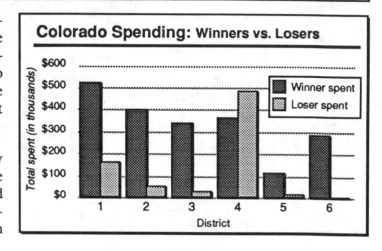

Colorado Spending: Winners vs. Losers

Aside from the open seat races, Colorado's congressional elections in 1990 were short on drama. The state's five incumbent House members had little difficulty winning reelection in 1990. All won with more than 60 percent of the vote, and only Pat Schroeder in the 1st district faced an opponent able to muster more than $100,000. Schroeder's own spending topped half a million dollars — triple the amount spent by Republican challenger Gloria Gonzales Roemer.

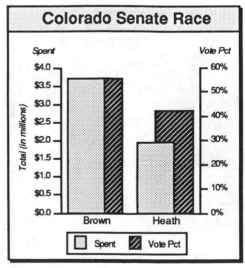

Colorado Senate Race

In his pursuit of a seat in the U.S. Senate, Hank Brown brought with him a valuable asset: a seat on the tax-writing House Ways and Means Committee that put him in good stead with an array of political action committees. In all, Brown collected nearly $1.4 million from PACs. Included in that total was nearly $134,000 from insurance industry PACs, making him the number one recipient of insurance PAC dollars in the U.S. Congress during 1990. Brown's Democratic opponent, Josie Heath, collected only $314,000 from PACs — predominantly from labor and ideological groups.

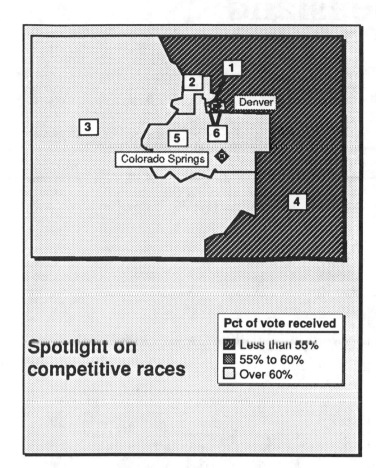

**Spotlight on
competitive races**

Pct of vote received
- Less than 55%
- 55% to 60%
- Over 60%

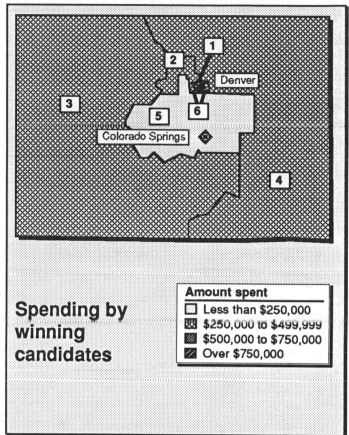

**Spending by
winning
candidates**

Amount spent
- Less than $250,000
- $250,000 to $499,999
- $500,000 to $750,000
- Over $750,000

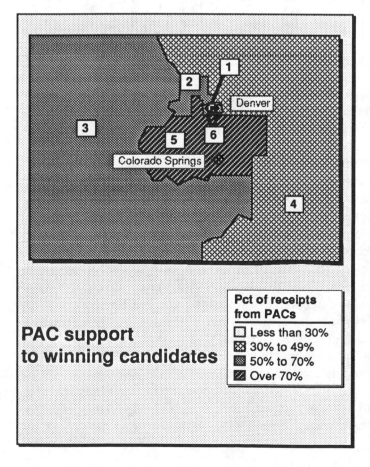

**PAC support
to winning candidates**

Pct of receipts
from PACs
- Less than 30%
- 30% to 49%
- 50% to 70%
- Over 70%

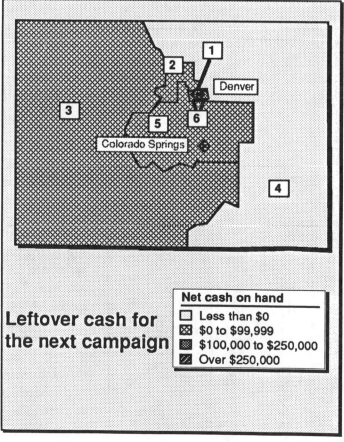

**Leftover cash for
the next campaign**

Net cash on hand
- Less than $0
- $0 to $99,999
- $100,000 to $250,000
- Over $250,000

Connecticut/Rhode Island

Vital Statistics of 1990 Winners

Dist	Name	Party	Vote Pct	Race Type	Total Receipts	PAC Receipts	PAC Pct	Spent	Net cash on Hand
Connecticut									
1	Barbara B. Kennelly	Dem	71.4%	Reelected	$483,041	$296,400	61.4%	$406,138	$176,983
2	Sam Gejdenson	Dem	59.7%	Reelected	$458,980	$185,950	40.5%	$464,500	-$32,079
3	Rosa DeLauro	Dem	52.1%	Open	$973,625	$401,805	41.3%	$957,982	-$84,359
4	Christopher Shays	Rep	76.5%	Reelected	$447,327	$55,500	12.4%	$395,892	$74,546
5	Gary Franks	Rep	51.7%	Open	$587,045	$177,927	30.3%	$581,625	-$68,947
6	Nancy L. Johnson	Rep	74.4%	Reelected	$517,724	$252,737	48.8%	$556,718	$117,662
Rhode Island									
1	Ronald K. Machtley	Rep	55.2%	Reelected	$857,775	$332,689	38.8%	$879,464	$1,994
2	John F. Reed	Dem	59.2%	Open	$902,877	$302,216	33.5%	$897,224	-$213,125
Sen	Claiborne Pell	Dem	61.8%	Reelected	$2,261,423	$882,583	39.0%	$2,383,170	$216,256

As in many other states during 1990, the races for governor dominated voter attention in southern New England — particularly in Connecticut, where the contest was eventually won by maverick Republican-turned-independent Lowell Weicker, the state's former Senator. Gubernatorial politics in Connecticut also shook up the state's congressional delegation, as two House members — Bruce Morrison in the 3rd district and John Rowland in the 5th — chose to compete (unsuccessfully) for governor rather than seek reelection to Congress. That opened up two House seats and a flurry of spending to fill the vacancies. Democrat Rosa DeLauro was the winner in the 3rd district, capturing the election on the strength of a campaign

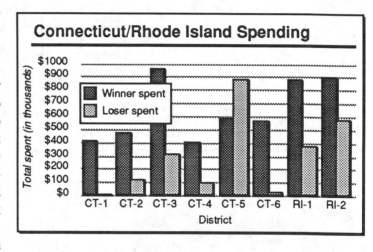

Connecticut/Rhode Island Spending

that cost nearly a million dollars — three times the spending of her Republican opponent. In the 5th district, money didn't matter as much, as black conservative Gary Franks carved out a narrow victory despite being outspent by former congressman Toby Moffett by nearly $300,000. Franks thus became the only black Republican in Congress.

Next door in Rhode Island, where voters dumped incumbent governor Edward D. DiPrete by a three-to-one margin, they reelected Democrat Claiborne Pell to his sixth full term in the U.S. Senate. Pell's opponent was Republican congresswoman Claudine Schneider, who gave up her House seat to challenge the veteran incumbent. Schneider was able to raise a respectable $2 million campaign war chest, but was only able to capture 38 percent of the vote. Replacing her in the House was Democratic State Sen. John Reed, who spent just under $900,000 to defeat Republican Trudy Coxe. The state's 1st district was also a magnet for campaign cash. Freshman Republican Ronald Machtley won the seat in 1988, upsetting the powerful (but scandal-plagued) Fernand St Germain. He won the seat then despite being significantly outspent, but in 1990 he was taking no chances. Machtley spent nearly $880,000 defending the seat — more than double the amount raised by his Democratic opponent. The combined spending of the state's two winning congressmen gave Rhode Island the distinction of being the most expensive state in the nation in spending by House winners.

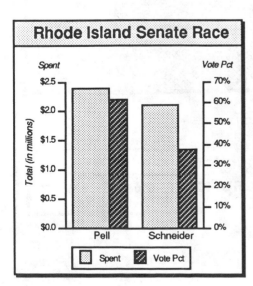

Rhode Island Senate Race

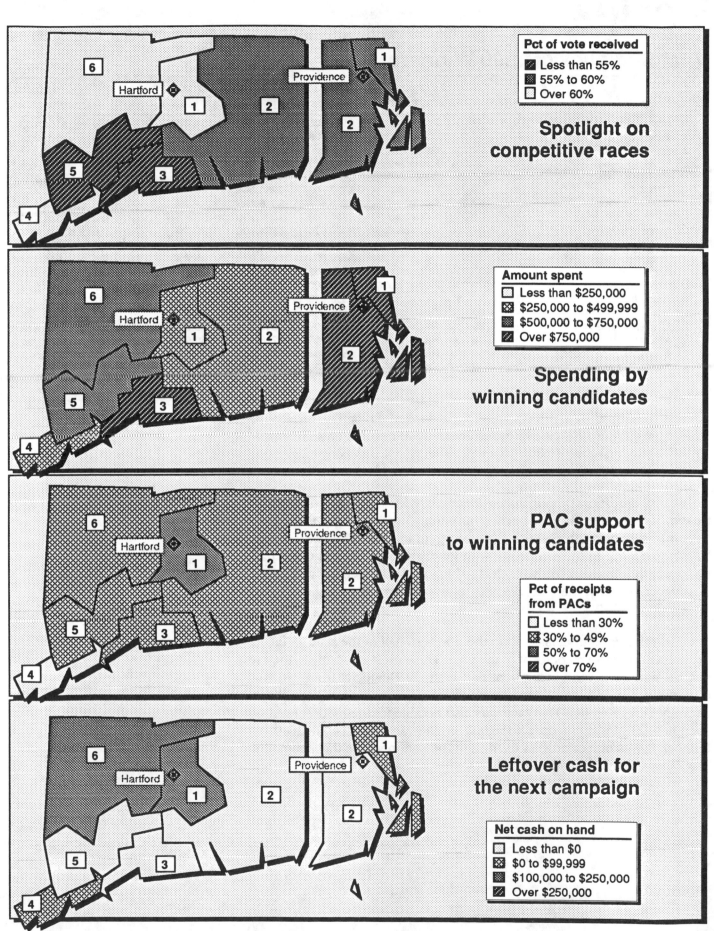

Pct of vote received
- Less than 55%
- 55% to 60%
- Over 60%

Spotlight on competitive races

Amount spent
- Less than $250,000
- $250,000 to $499,999
- $500,000 to $750,000
- Over $750,000

Spending by winning candidates

PAC support to winning candidates

Pct of receipts from PACs
- Less than 30%
- 30% to 49%
- 50% to 70%
- Over 70%

Leftover cash for the next campaign

Net cash on hand
- Less than $0
- $0 to $99,999
- $100,000 to $250,000
- Over $250,000

67

Florida

Vital Statistics of 1990 Winners

Dist	Name	Party	Vote Pct	Race Type	Total Receipts	PAC Receipts	PAC Pct	Spent	Net cash on Hand
1	Earl Hutto	Dem	52.2%	Reelected	$184,405	$95,307	51.7%	$158,280	$109,103
2	Pete Peterson	Dem	56.9%	Beat Incumb	$306,429	$131,670	43.0%	$306,104	-$61,818
3	Charles E. Bennett	Dem	72.7%	Reelected	$87,580	$28,950	33.1%	$108,953	$276,917
4	Craig T. James	Rep	55.9%	Reelected	$643,579	$211,951	32.9%	$634,891	-$143,474
5	Bill McCollum	Rep	59.9%	Reelected	$427,325	$148,050	34.6%	$564,994	$101,264
6	Cliff Stearns	Rep	59.2%	Reelected	$497,703	$200,346	40.2%	$462,925	-$10,439
7	Sam M. Gibbons	Dem	67.6%	Reelected	$492,517	$316,125	64.2%	$825,795	$278,960
8	C. W. Bill Young	Rep	100.0%	Reelected	$231,400	$129,750	56.1%	$201,188	$341,773
9	Michael Bilirakis	Rep	58.1%	Reelected	$600,670	$234,430	39.0%	$815,366	-$2,383
10	Andy Ireland	Rep	100.0%	Reelected	$410,468	$169,683	41.3%	$384,555	$98,267
11	Jim Bacchus	Dem	51.9%	Open	$877,500	$410,073	46.7%	$875,386	-$15,274
12	Tom Lewis	Rep	100.0%	Reelected	$338,253	$80,425	23.8%	$405,471	$121,358
13	Porter J. Goss	Rep	100.0%	Reelected	$303,600	$121,825	40.1%	$244,740	$64,847
14	Harry A. Johnston	Dem	66.0%	Reelected	$508,525	$252,919	49.7%	$469,101	$42,284
15	E. Clay Shaw Jr.	Rep	97.8%	Reelected	$413,387	$242,760	58.7%	$120,632	$306,224
16	Lawrence J. Smith	Dem	100.0%	Reelected	$527,994	$246,935	46.8%	$275,873	$413,843
17	William Lehman	Dem	78.3%	Reelected	$425,117	$216,350	50.9%	$369,764	$275,781
18	Ileana Ros-Lehtinen*	Rep	60.4%	Reelected	$575,234	$168,784	29.3%	$560,847	$14,387
19	Dante B. Fascell	Dem	62.0%	Reelected	$459,789	$163,116	35.5%	$500,117	$546,593

For the most part, voters in Florida looked favorably on House incumbents in the 1990 elections, reelecting 17 of the 18 who sought new terms. But the margins of victory were not always solid, and one incumbent — Republican Bill Grant in the 2nd district — lost his seat.

Grant's defeat, by Democrat Pete Peterson, was a particularly sweet one for the Democrats, as Grant switched his party affiliation from Democrat to Republican shortly after winning his last term in 1988. The party switch became an issue in the campaign, with Peterson charging that Grant had broken faith with the voters who elected him. Peterson eventually captured nearly 57 percent of the vote, despite being outspent by a margin of more than $500,000.

Five other incumbents — all in the northern half of the state — failed to attract more than 60 percent of the vote. The closest call came in the 1st district, where six-term incumbent Earl Hutto, a Democrat from Panama City, drew a surprisingly low 52 percent of the vote against Republican attorney Terry Ketchel. That race was also notable for the modest level of spending: Hutto spent only $158,000 in the race, versus $182,000 by Ketchel. It was one of only 14 districts in the nation where the incumbent was outspent by a challenger.

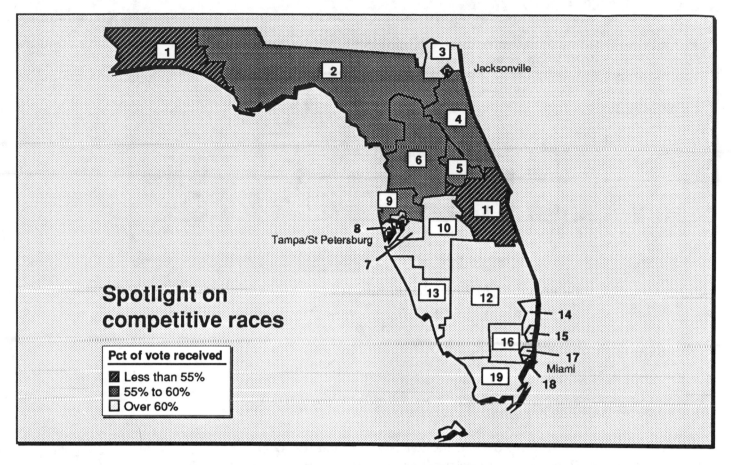

Spotlight on competitive races

Pct of vote received
- Less than 55%
- 55% to 60%
- Over 60%

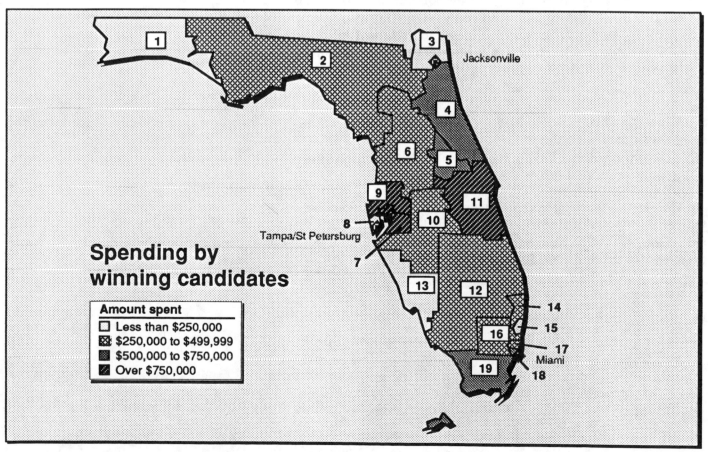

Spending by winning candidates

Amount spent
- Less than $250,000
- $250,000 to $499,999
- $500,000 to $750,000
- Over $750,000

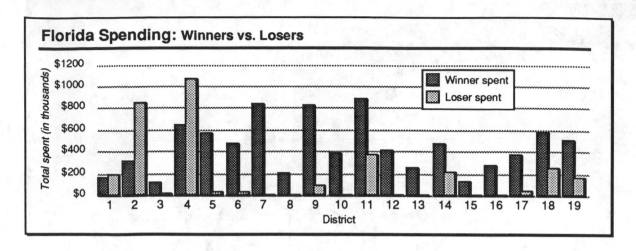

Florida Spending: Winners vs. Losers

Total spent (in thousands) — Winner spent / Loser spent

District

Across the state in the 4th district, freshman congressman Craig T. James fared slightly better — though the outcome was in doubt right up to election day. James, a Republican, first won the seat in 1988, ousting scandal-plagued Bill Chappell, the Democratic incumbent. James' challenger in 1990 was Reid Hughes, a millionaire oil distributor who poured over $800,000 of his own money into a campaign that eventually cost more than a million dollars. James spent $634,000 defending the seat; on election day he collected just under 56 percent of the vote.

Just to the south, in the 11th district, the state's only open-seat race paired Democrat Jim Bacchus against Republican Bill Tolley. The seat's former occupant, Bill Nelson, ran for governor instead of reelection. (Nelson lost in the Democratic primary to Lawton Chiles, who was eventually elected). Bacchus vastly outspent his Republican opponent ($875,000 to $364,000), but carried the district win a slim 52 percent of the vote.

While incumbent lawmakers in the northern half of the state were struggling, their colleagues to the south had an easier time of it. Six of them were reelected without having to face a major party opponent and none of the others dropped below 60 percent at the polls.

Florida's burgeoning population growth during the 1980s made it a big winner in congressional reapportionment. In the 1992 elections, voters will elect a total of 23 U.S. House members — an increase of four new seats in Congress for the Sunshine State.

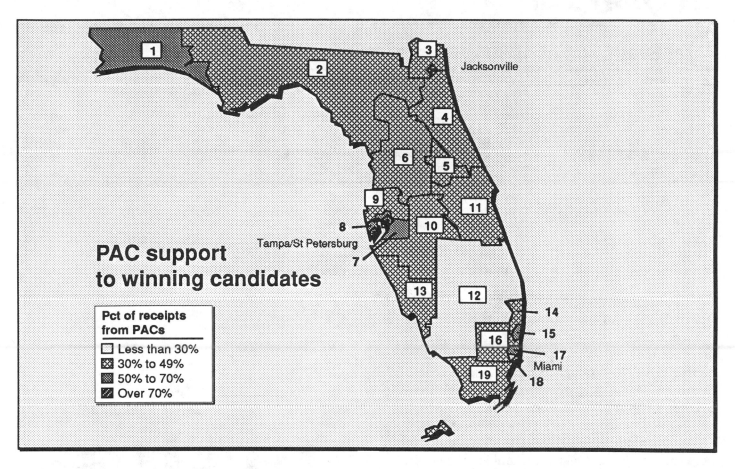

PAC support
to winning candidates

**Pct of receipts
from PACs**
- ☐ Less than 30%
- ▨ 30% to 49%
- ▦ 50% to 70%
- ▩ Over 70%

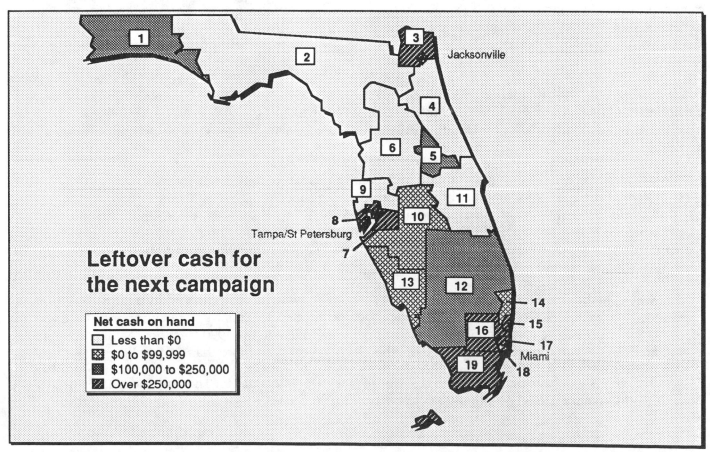

Leftover cash for
the next campaign

Net cash on hand
- ☐ Less than $0
- ▨ $0 to $99,999
- ▦ $100,000 to $250,000
- ▩ Over $250,000

Georgia

Vital Statistics of 1990 Winners

Dist	Name	Party	Vote Pct	Race Type	Total Receipts	PAC Receipts	PAC Pct	Spent	Net cash on Hand
1	Lindsay Thomas	Dem	71.2%	Reelected	$378,206	$166,665	44.1%	$399,035	$67,690
2	Charles Hatcher	Dem	73.0%	Reelected	$328,506	$211,150	64.3%	$296,470	$20,533
3	Richard Ray	Dem	63.2%	Reelected	$369,264	$155,950	42.2%	$378,774	$150,654
4	Ben Jones	Dem	52.4%	Reelected	$707,046	$416,033	58.8%	$711,015	-$30,356
5	John Lewis	Dem	75.6%	Reelected	$271,450	$175,510	64.7%	$108,118	$260,822
6	Newt Gingrich	Rep	50.3%	Reelected	$1,538,827	$433,421	28.2%	$1,538,945	-$108,836
7	George "Buddy" Darden	Dem	60.1%	Reelected	$389,661	$198,536	51.0%	$404,874	$100,737
8	J. Roy Rowland	Dem	68.7%	Reelected	$368,200	$228,050	61.9%	$365,513	$210,642
9	Ed Jenkins	Dem	55.8%	Reelected	$302,029	$184,500	61.1%	$318,247	$448,273
10	Doug Barnard Jr.	Dem	58.3%	Reelected	$778,139	$262,701	33.8%	$937,464	$271,869
Sen	Sam Nunn	Dem	100.0%	Reelected	$2,118,911	$622,750	29.4%	$1,245,052	$1,550,058

Georgia's 6th congressional district, stretching from suburban Atlanta to the Alabama border, was the scene of one of the closest and most surprising races in the nation in 1990, as the outspoken conservative Newt Gingrich nearly lost his seat to Democrat David Worley. It was the second encounter in as many elections between Gingrich and Worley, a 32-year-old attorney who collected 41 percent of the vote in 1988. Gingrich seemed to be taking no chances with a $1.5 million reelection campaign — vastly larger than Worley's $333,000 — but on election day he managed only a bare majority of the vote, 50.3 percent.

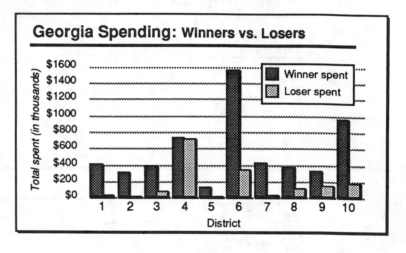

Georgia Spending: Winners vs. Losers

It was not the only close race in the Peach State. Next door in the 4th district freshman Democrat Ben Jones had his hands full with Republican state Rep. John Linder. Jones was one of only six challengers to upset incumbents in 1988, when he ousted scandal-plagued Pat Swindall. In 1990, Jones' $700,000 war chest was matched nearly dollar for dollar by Linder, and Jones captured a slim 52.4 percent of the vote.

Two other incumbents — Ed Jenkins in the 9th district and Doug Barnard in the 10th — also won reelection with less than 60 percent of the vote. Barnard in particular was hit for his connection with the growing Savings & Loan scandal (he is a senior member of the House banking subcommittee that oversees S&L regulation). But Barnard's financial cushion was considerable. He spent $937,000 to ensure his reelection, versus the $157,000 spent by his opponent, Republican Sam Jones. Ed Jenkins' 9th district reelection race was slightly closer in votes (he won less than 56 percent of the vote) and much closer in dollars (Jenkins spent $318,000 — about double what his challenger spent).

Elsewhere in the state, incumbents had an easier time of it, winning reelection easily against under-funded opponents. The easiest race of all wasn't even a race. Democratic Senator Sam Nunn ran unopposed. He was one of four U.S. Senators to be reelected without a major party opponent in the 1990 elections. Nunn, thought to be eyeing an eventual run for president, closed out the election year with more than $1.5 million in the bank.

In 1992, voters will have one additional U.S. House race to look forward to. The state picked up an extra seat from reapportionment, based on population gains in the 1990 census.

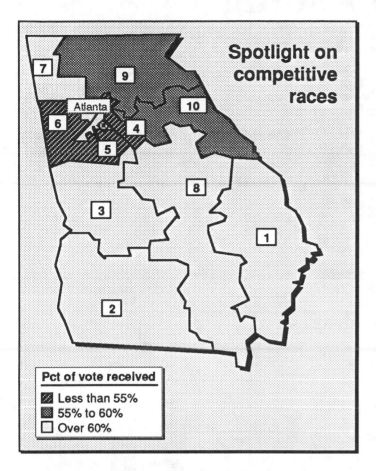

Spotlight on competitive races

Pct of vote received
- Less than 55%
- 55% to 60%
- Over 60%

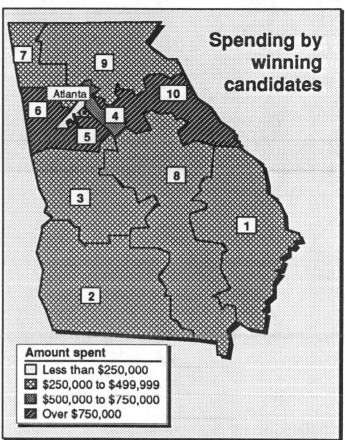

Spending by winning candidates

Amount spent
- Less than $250,000
- $250,000 to $499,999
- $500,000 to $750,000
- Over $750,000

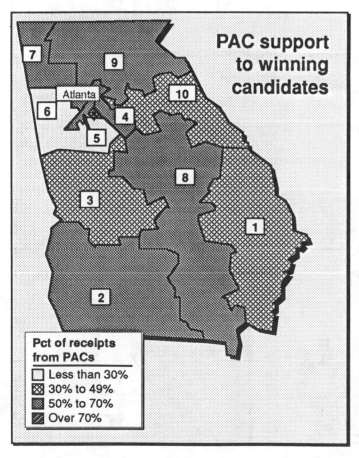

PAC support to winning candidates

Pct of receipts from PACs
- Less than 30%
- 30% to 49%
- 50% to 70%
- Over 70%

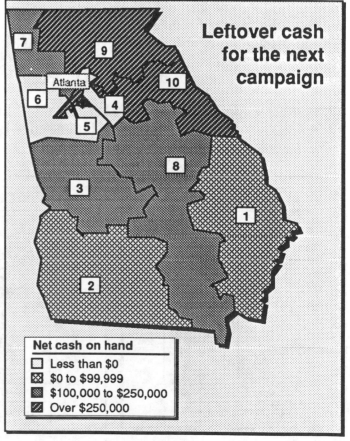

Leftover cash for the next campaign

Net cash on hand
- Less than $0
- $0 to $99,999
- $100,000 to $250,000
- Over $250,000

Idaho/Montana/Wyoming

Vital Statistics of 1990 Winners

Dist	Name	Party	Vote Pct	Race Type	Total Receipts	PAC Receipts	PAC Pct	Spent	Net cash on Hand
Idaho									
1	Larry LaRocco	Dem	53.0%	Open	$449,419	$238,753	53.1%	$447,895	-$69,794
2	Richard Stallings	Dem	63.6%	Reelected	$405,115	$266,702	65.8%	$406,219	-$15,484
Sen	Larry E. Craig	Rep	61.3%	Open	$1,734,617	$807,126	46.5%	$1,652,532	$91,834
Montana									
1	Pat Williams	Dem	61.1%	Reelected	$458,293	$296,640	64.7%	$345,258	$214,350
2	Ron Marlenee	Rep	63.0%	Reelected	$297,771	$140,750	47.3%	$310,981	$76,486
Sen	Max Baucus	Dem	68.1%	Reelected	$3,075,422	$1,663,317	54.1%	$2,607,552	$505,883
Wyoming									
1	Craig Thomas	Rep	55.1%	Reelected	$404,308	$174,995	43.3%	$437,772	-$15,469
Sen	Alan K. Simpson	Rep	63.9%	Reelected	$1,670,927	$800,723	47.9%	$1,443,298	$425,328

The only change in congressional lineups in the northern Rocky Mountain states in 1990 came in Idaho, where three-term incumbent Sen. James McClure retired from office, leaving an open seat in the U.S. Senate. Republican Congressman Larry Craig, the early favorite to succeed him, lived up to expectations and won the seat, easily outpolling (and out-fundraising) Democrat Ron Twilegar, a former state legislator.

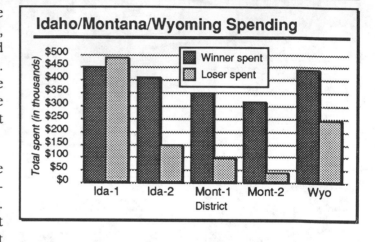

The race to fill Craig's vacated House seat was more contentious. The eventual winner was Boise stockbroker and longtime Democratic activist Larry LaRocco. Though slightly outspent, LaRocco managed to defeat Republican State Sen. Skip Smyser, returning Idaho's 1st congressional district to Democrat hands for the first time since 1966.

All other seats in the region stayed safely in the hands of incumbents. The only close race was in Wyoming, where Republican Craig Thomas successfully defended the seat he won in a 1989 special election. The seat became vacant early that year when former Congressman Dick Cheney was appointed Secretary of Defense.

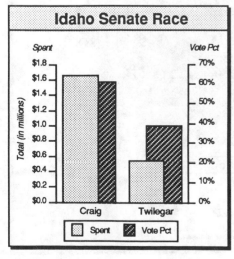

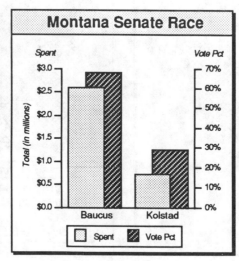

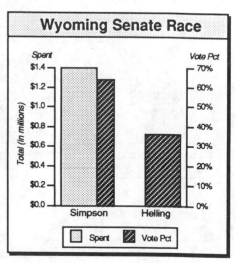

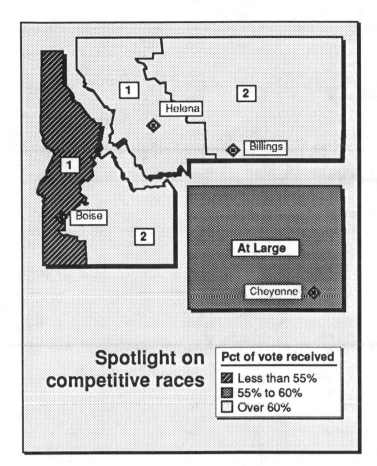

Spotlight on competitive races

Pct of vote received
- Less than 55%
- 55% to 60%
- Over 60%

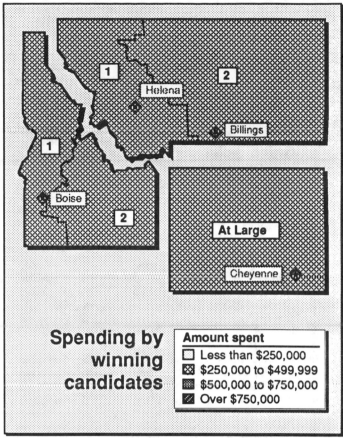

Spending by winning candidates

Amount spent
- Less than $250,000
- $250,000 to $499,999
- $500,000 to $750,000
- Over $750,000

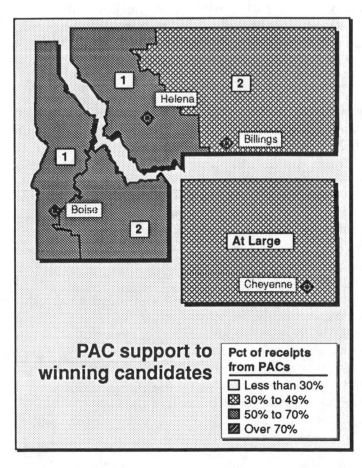

PAC support to winning candidates

Pct of receipts from PACs
- Less than 30%
- 30% to 49%
- 50% to 70%
- Over 70%

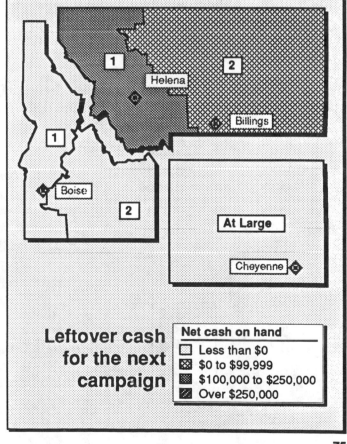

Leftover cash for the next campaign

Net cash on hand
- Less than $0
- $0 to $99,999
- $100,000 to $250,000
- Over $250,000

Illinois

Vital Statistics of 1990 Winners

Dist	Name	Party	Vote Pct	Race Type	Total Receipts	PAC Receipts	PAC Pct	Spent	Net cash on Hand
1	Charles A. Hayes	Dem	93.8%	Reelected	$110,665	$85,250	77.0%	$125,509	$19,130
2	Gus Savage	Dem	78.2%	Reelected	$196,926	$57,800	29.4%	$190,685	-$55,589
3	Marty Russo	Dem	70.9%	Reelected	$547,782	$380,466	69.5%	$541,279	$6,168
4	George E. Sangmeister	Dem	59.2%	Reelected	$477,551	$356,393	74.6%	$472,757	$17,142
5	William O. Lipinski	Dem	66.3%	Reelected	$183,213	$137,317	75.0%	$171,746	$19,110
6	Henry J. Hyde	Rep	66.7%	Reelected	$302,541	$130,648	43.2%	$270,435	$187,768
7	Cardiss Collins	Dem	79.9%	Reelected	$278,392	$229,648	82.5%	$399,748	$90,094
8	Dan Rostenkowski	Dem	79.1%	Reelected	$378,282	$197,700	52.3%	$298,653	$1,114,068
9	Sidney R. Yates	Dem	71.2%	Reelected	$779,125	$267,746	34.4%	$839,106	$53,828
10	John Porter	Rep	67.7%	Reelected	$255,970	$110,025	43.0%	$313,498	$71,996
11	Frank Annunzio	Dem	53.6%	Reelected	$723,159	$472,891	65.4%	$855,952	$35,719
12	Philip M. Crane	Rep	82.2%	Reelected	$163,442	$0	0.0%	$163,376	$115,919
13	Harris W. Fawell	Rep	65.8%	Reelected	$336,789	$119,570	35.5%	$271,913	$103,808
14	Dennis Hastert	Rep	66.9%	Reelected	$461,002	$181,074	39.3%	$312,555	$191,061
15	Edward Madigan	Rep	100.0%	Reelected	$432,247	$269,587	62.4%	$277,802	$542,570
16	John W. Cox Jr.	Dem	54.6%	Open	$377,421	$191,216	50.7%	$371,114	-$7,012
17	Lane Evans	Dem	66.5%	Reelected	$417,626	$228,598	54.7%	$390,401	$30,911
18	Robert H. Michel	Rep	98.4%	Reelected	$705,878	$497,561	70.5%	$579,258	$241,996
19	Terry L. Bruce	Dem	66.3%	Reelected	$471,745	$306,491	65.0%	$258,093	$574,423
20	Richard J. Durbin	Dem	66.2%	Reelected	$338,066	$204,928	60.6%	$209,360	$307,371
21	Jerry F. Costello	Dem	66.0%	Reelected	$654,131	$231,550	35.4%	$394,896	$273,831
22	Glenn Poshard	Dem	83.7%	Reelected	$68,078	$5,150	7.6%	$103,396	$2,136
Sen	Paul Simon	Dem	65.1%	Reelected	$9,643,884	$1,679,740	17.4%	$8,739,940	$843,731

The congressional race that overshadowed all others in Illinois during 1990 was the Senate contest between incumbent Democrat Paul Simon and his Republican challenger, Congresswoman Lynn Martin. But while the race early on looked to be a close one, as the months wore on Martin's chances of pulling an upset seemed to fade. One reason was the considerable war chest that Simon was able to build. He eventually raised close to $10 million and outspent Martin two-to-one. The returns on election day followed roughly the same pattern, with Simon winning nearly two-thirds of the vote.

Simon entered the race with an impressive advantage: not only was he a popular incumbent within the state, but his name recognition — both inside and outside Illinois — was greatly enhanced by his 1988 run for the Democratic nomination for president. That national profile translated into a considerable fundraising ability. Of the $3 million he collected from individuals giving $200 or more, just over 50 percent came from outside Illinois.

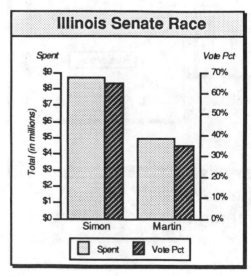

Illinois Senate Race

Simon's success was mirrored by congressional incumbents throughout the state. All 21 of the U.S. House members who ran for reelection were successful. The only change in the Illinois delegation came in the 16th district, where the vacancy opened by Lynn Martin's bid for the Senate was filled by Democrat John Cox.

Cox's victory was a surprise. An attorney from Galena, he defeated Republican State Representative John Hallock in a district that was considered to be solidly Republican. Hallock enjoyed a moderate fundraising advantage as well, eventually spending nearly half a million dollars to Cox's $371,000. But the Republican's built-in advantages were counterbalanced by a sometimes stumbling campaign, and Cox was the victor on election day with almost 55 percent of the vote.

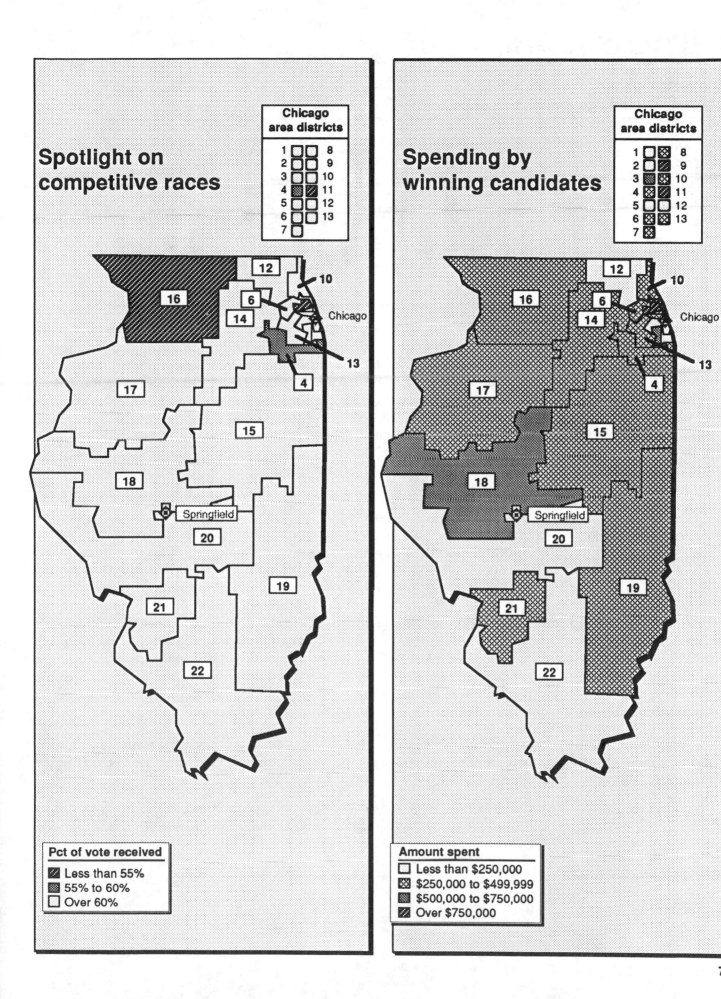

Spotlight on competitive races

Chicago area districts
1, 2, 3, 4, 5, 6, 7, 8, 9, 10, 11, 12, 13

12
10
16
6
14
Chicago
13
4
17
15
18
Springfield
20
19
21
22

Pct of vote received
- Less than 55%
- 55% to 60%
- Over 60%

Spending by winning candidates

Chicago area districts
1, 2, 3, 4, 5, 6, 7, 8, 9, 10, 11, 12, 13

12
10
16
6
14
Chicago
13
4
17
15
18
Springfield
20
19
21
22

Amount spent
- Less than $250,000
- $250,000 to $499,999
- $500,000 to $750,000
- Over $750,000

Illinois (cont'd)

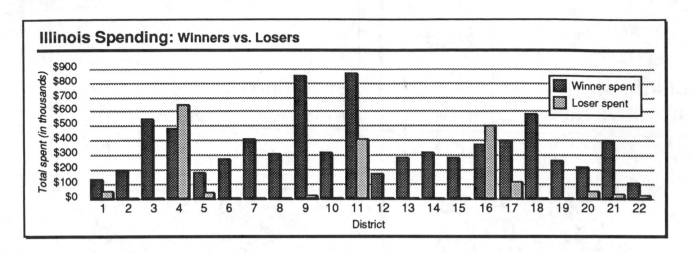

Illinois Spending: Winners vs. Losers

Total spent (in thousands) — Winner spent / Loser spent — District

The one Illinois incumbent who did have a difficult time of it in 1990 was Frank Annunzio, the chairman of the House subcommittee that overseas supervision of financial institutions. Annunzio's opponent, Republican State Senator Walter Dudycz, accused the 13-term incumbent of turning a blind eye to scandals within the savings and loan industry, while accepting thousands of dollars in campaign contributions from S&L PACs and executives. The charges helped focus wide attention on the contest, and forced Annunzio to vastly increase his spending in what should have been an easy reelection contest. By the time the 1990 campaign was over, Annunzio had spent $855,000 to defend his seat — more than three and a half times what he spent in 1988. On election day, he polled just 53.6 percent of the vote — his closest race since 1972.

One other Chicago area incumbent dramatically increased his spending in the 1990 elections — veteran Democrat Sidney Yates of the 9th district. For Yates, the battle came not in the general election, but in the Democratic primary, where Edwin Eisendrath, a wealthy Chicago alderman, threatened to launch a top-dollar campaign to unseat him. Eisendrath spent $640,000 in the primary, but Yates, taking no chances, pushed his own fundraising efforts into high gear to more than match the challenger's budget. He carried the primary easily and won the general election with a comfortable 71 percent of the vote.

Just south of Chicago, in the 4th district, Illinois Republicans saw a chance to regain a seat they had lost in the last election. The Democratic incumbent, George Sangmeister, had barely won the seat in 1988, upsetting one-term Republican congressman Jack Davis with just 50.3 percent of the vote. In 1990, Sangmeister's challenger was Manny Hoffman, the mayor of suburban Homewood. Hoffman was able to raise a sizeable campaign fund of more than $640,000 — well above the $472,000 spent by Sangmeister. But the Democrat prevailed on election day, winning reelection with 59 percent of the vote.

In other House districts around the state, incumbents had few problems. As illustrated by the chart above, challengers had an all but impossible time raising funds to compete with current office-holders. Except in a handful of races, incumbents had little difficulty at the polls.

The 1992 elections could be more difficult. Illinois will lose two U.S. House seats to reapportionment in the next Congress, setting up the possibility that some incumbents will either have to retire or face off against each other.

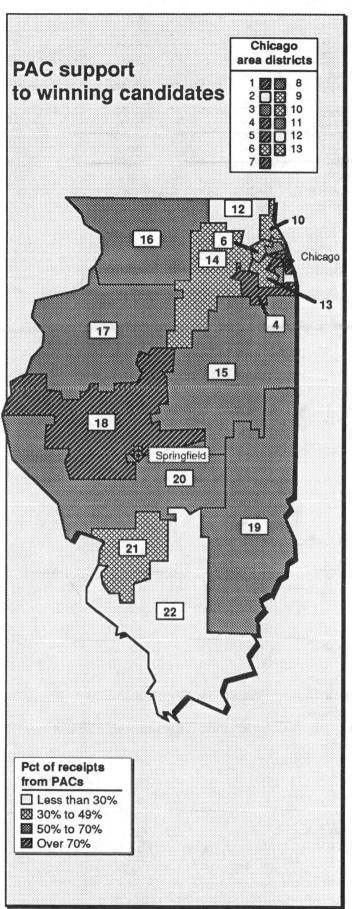

PAC support to winning candidates

Chicago area districts

1		8
2		9
3		10
4		11
5		12
6		13
7		

Chicago

Pct of receipts from PACs

- Less than 30%
- 30% to 49%
- 50% to 70%
- Over 70%

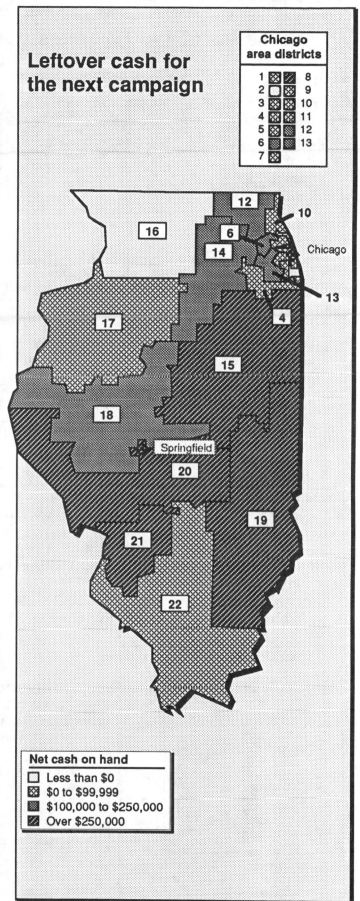

Leftover cash for the next campaign

Chicago area districts

1		8
2		9
3		10
4		11
5		12
6		13
7		

Chicago

Net cash on hand

- Less than $0
- $0 to $99,999
- $100,000 to $250,000
- Over $250,000

Indiana

Vital Statistics of 1990 Winners

Dist	Name	Party	Vote Pct	Race Type	Total Receipts	PAC Receipts	PAC Pct	Spent	Net cash on Hand
1	Peter J. Visclosky	Dem	66.0%	Reelected	$248,272	$168,020	67.7%	$299,280	$43,701
2	Philip R. Sharp	Dem	59.4%	Reelected	$714,491	$495,349	69.3%	$773,178	$29,944
3	Tim Roemer	Dem	50.9%	Beat Incumb	$504,884	$268,863	53.2%	$473,055	$31,826
4	Jill Long	Dem	60.7%	Reelected	$753,725	$448,381	59.5%	$752,362	-$10,610
5	Jim Jontz	Dem	53.1%	Reelected	$620,713	$405,145	65.3%	$652,280	-$40,850
6	Dan Burton	Rep	63.5%	Reelected	$526,451	$202,436	38.5%	$311,727	$400,894
7	John T. Myers	Rep	57.6%	Reelected	$198,191	$98,870	49.9%	$222,792	$102,885
8	Frank McCloskey	Dem	54.7%	Reelected	$467,981	$322,320	68.9%	$446,040	$23,382
9	Lee H. Hamilton	Dem	69.0%	Reelected	$399,758	$188,525	47.2%	$392,606	$58,592
10	Andrew Jacobs Jr.	Dem	66.4%	Reelected	$28,712	$0	0.0%	$14,816	$32,188
Sen	Daniel R. Coats	Rep	53.6%	Reelected	$4,082,803	$1,103,964	27.0%	$3,718,903	$363,900

In contrast to their counterparts in most other states, U.S. House incumbents in Indiana — at least in four of the state's 10 congressional districts — faced well-financed opponents in the 1990 elections. One incumbent, Republican John Hiler, lost his seat. All the others won reelection, though not always by comfortable margins.

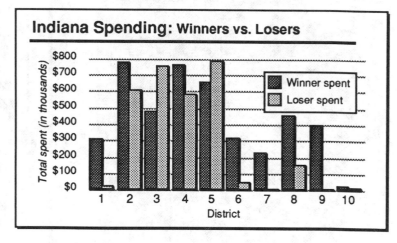

Indiana Spending: Winners vs. Losers

Hiler's hold on the seat in the 3rd congressional district had never been secure. In his five previous elections since winning the seat in 1980, he had never collected more than 55 percent of the vote. In 1988 he spent more than a million dollars defending the seat, but won with just 54 percent. His opponent in 1990, Democrat Tim Roemer, was not able to match Hiler's fundraising, but the $473,000 he eventually spent was enough to give him a narrow victory in November.

Victory did not come cheap to three other Indiana incumbents. Democrats Phil Sharp in the 2nd district and Jill Long in the 4th each spent more than $750,000 against exceptionally well-financed opponents. And fellow Democrat Jim Jontz in the 5th district was actually outspent by his Republican challenger, John A. Johnson, who poured $626,000 of his own money into a campaign that eventually cost close to $800,000. Jontz prevailed on election day, but not by much; capturing just 53 percent of the vote.

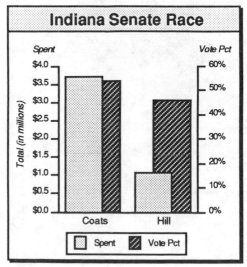

Indiana Senate Race

One district in the state did not share the trend toward top-dollar spending patterns. Democrat Andrew Jacobs spent less than $15,000 in his reelection bid; it was the second least expensive winning House campaign in the nation. Jacobs' opponent spent even less, and Jacobs outpolled his challenger two-to-one.

The Indiana Senate race was Dan Coats' first contest as a U.S. Senator. He was appointed to the seat in January 1989, filling the vacancy created by Dan Quayle's election to vice president. Though Coats went into the race with a massive lead in fundraising (he more than tripled the spending of Democratic challenger Baron Hill), the race was never a runaway and Coats settled for a narrow victory on election day. The exercise may have to be repeated again shortly. Coats' Senate term runs only through the end of Quayle's unexpired term. He'll have to run again in 1992.

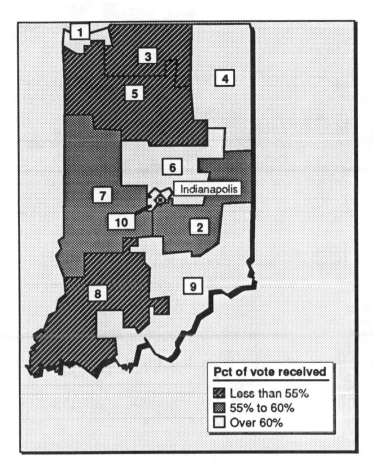

Pct of vote received

▨ Less than 55%
▦ 55% to 60%
☐ Over 60%

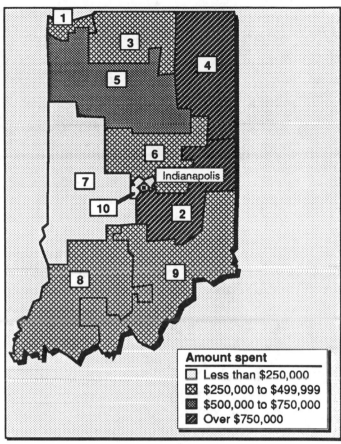

Amount spent

☐ Less than $250,000
▩ $250,000 to $499,999
▦ $500,000 to $750,000
▨ Over $750,000

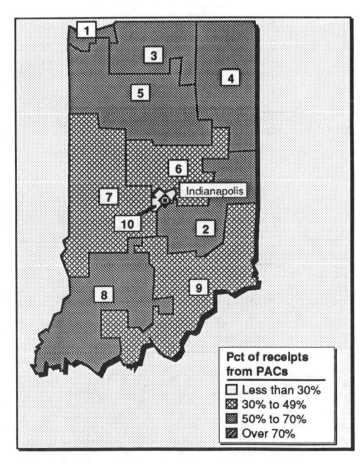

Pct of receipts from PACs

☐ Less than 30%
▩ 30% to 49%
▦ 50% to 70%
▨ Over 70%

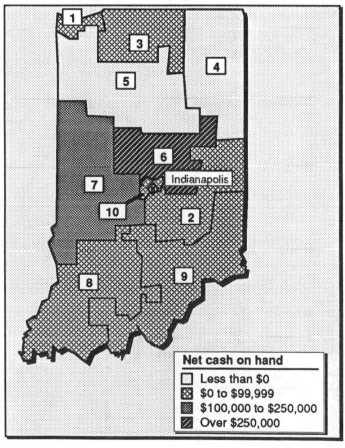

Net cash on hand

☐ Less than $0
▩ $0 to $99,999
▦ $100,000 to $250,000
▨ Over $250,000

81

Iowa

Vital Statistics of 1990 Winners

Dist	Name	Party	Vote Pct	Race Type	Total Receipts	PAC Receipts	PAC Pct	Spent	Net cash on Hand
1	Jim Leach	Rep	99.8%	Reelected	$115,051	$0	0.0%	$87,489	$46,917
2	Jim Nussle	Rep	49.8%	Open	$469,933	$146,558	31.2%	$466,259	-$28,827
3	Dave Nagle	Dem	99.2%	Reelected	$360,951	$262,405	72.7%	$345,154	$20,963
4	Neal Smith	Dem	97.9%	Reelected	$167,829	$116,970	69.7%	$56,903	$376,309
5	Jim Ross Lightfoot	Rep	68.0%	Reelected	$497,363	$146,243	29.4%	$418,134	$140,810
6	Fred Grandy	Rep	71.8%	Reelected	$409,067	$251,675	61.5%	$322,563	-$15,118
Sen	Tom Harkin	Dem	54.5%	Reelected	$5,715,839	$1,814,595	31.8%	$5,661,171	$11,222

The race of the year in Iowa during 1990 was the showdown in the Senate between incumbent Democrat Tom Harkin and Rep. Tom Tauke, the 40-year-old Republican congressman from the 2nd district. From the beginning, Harkin was seen as vulnerable, with Tauke as the challenger most likely to move the seat into the Republican column. Money from around the country poured into both candidates' campaign treasuries. In all, more than $11 million was spent on the race by Harkin and Tauke. In November, Harkin pulled out the victory, defying a local jinx by becoming the first Democrat from Iowa ever to win reelection to the U.S. Senate.

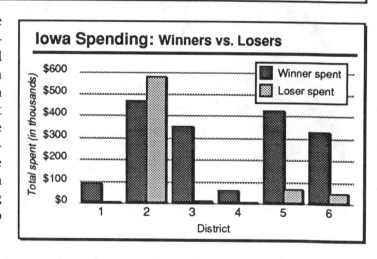

The contest to fill the vacancy left in the 2nd district was also a free-spending affair, with an outcome even closer than the Senate race. The eventual winner was Republican Jim Nussle, who won the seat by a margin of just one percent over Democrat Eric Tabor. Due to the presence of a third (independent) candidate in the race, Nussle collected just under 50 percent of the district's votes. It was the third defeat in as many elections for Tabor, despite the fact that he outspent Nussle by more than $100,000.

Incumbents in Iowa's five other congressional districts all won reelection by wide margins. Three of them — Jim Leach, Dave Nagle and Neal Smith — faced no major-party opposition. Republicans Jim Ross Lightfoot in the 5th district and Fred Grandy in the 6th both faced Democratic opponents, but both incumbents vastly outspent and outpolled their challengers.

Few of the current office-holders are likely to relax in 1992, since Iowa will be losing one of its six U.S. House seats to reapportionment — squeezing at least one incumbent out of a job.

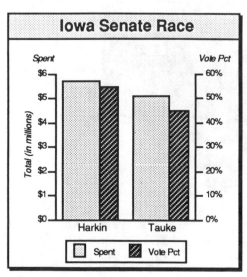

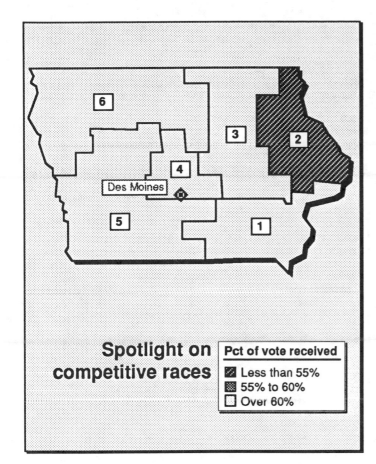

Spotlight on competitive races

	Pct of vote received
▨	Less than 55%
▥	55% to 60%
☐	Over 60%

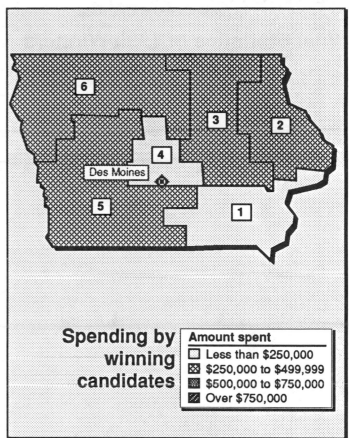

Spending by winning candidates

	Amount spent
☐	Less than $250,000
▨	$250,000 to $499,999
▦	$500,000 to $750,000
▨	Over $750,000

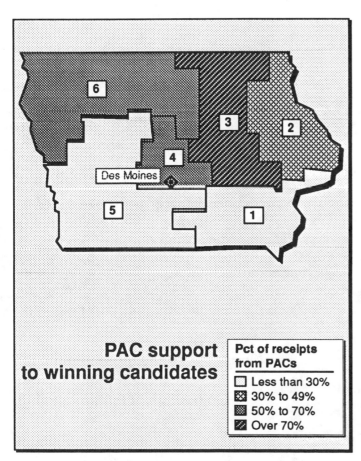

PAC support to winning candidates

	Pct of receipts from PACs
☐	Less than 30%
▨	30% to 49%
▦	50% to 70%
▨	Over 70%

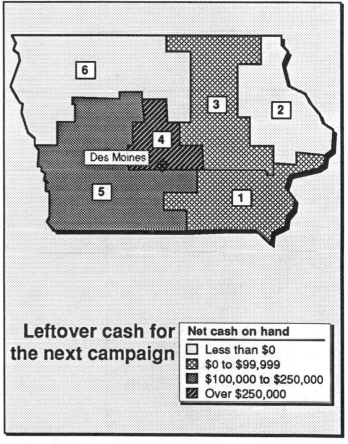

Leftover cash for the next campaign

	Net cash on hand
☐	Less than $0
▨	$0 to $99,999
▦	$100,000 to $250,000
▨	Over $250,000

Kansas

Vital Statistics of 1990 Winners

Dist	Name	Party	Vote Pct	Race Type	Total Receipts	PAC Receipts	PAC Pct	Spent	Net cash on Hand
1	Pat Roberts	Rep	62.6%	Reelected	$225,572	$133,250	59.1%	$156,356	$399,529
2	Jim Slattery	Dem	62.8%	Reelected	$467,018	$327,550	70.1%	$504,861	$52,999
3	Jan Meyers	Rep	60.1%	Reelected	$211,505	$110,641	52.3%	$209,986	$2,081
4	Dan Glickman	Dem	70.8%	Reelected	$520,945	$292,565	56.2%	$355,581	$192,262
5	Dick Nichols	Rep	59.3%	Open	$573,188	$100,125	17.5%	$565,410	-$307,774
Sen	Nancy Landon Kassebaum	Rep	73.6%	Reelected	$532,964	$179,108	33.6%	$533,632	$217,135

Kansas voters stuck with their incumbent representatives in the 1990 elections, reelecting — by comfortable margins — each member of Congress who sought a new term. All the incumbents also enjoyed healthy financial cushions for their races. Not one congressional challenger in Kansas managed to collect even $90,000 in contributions, let alone come within striking distance of the incumbents' war chests.

Even the one open-seat race was financially noncompetitive. Republican banker Dick Nichols, the early favorite in the reliably Republican district, left nothing to chance, mounting a $565,000 campaign — half of which came from his own pocket. His Democratic opponent, George Wingert, spent just $70,000. On election day, Nichols collected 59 percent of the votes.

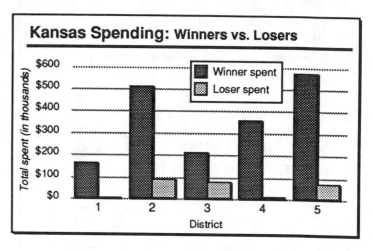

In the months before the Kansas Senate race, the only real question was whether the popular Nancy Kassebaum would seek reelection. Once she agreed to file for another term, at the urging of national Republicans, the outcome was never in question — even though Kassebaum's spending was only a fraction of the national average in Senate races. Her Democratic opponent, Wichita educator and liberal activist Dick Williams, spent only $16,000 and collected only one vote out of every four cast.

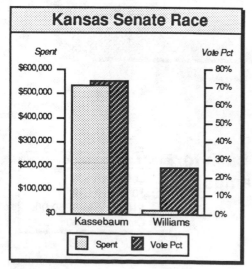

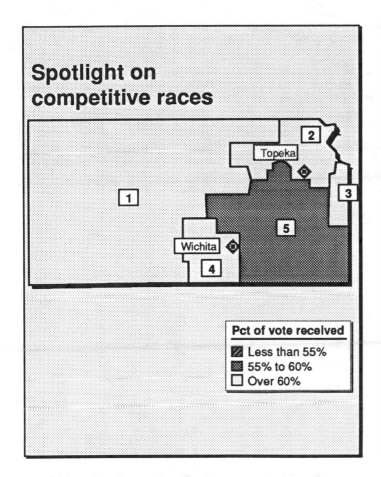

Spotlight on competitive races

Pct of vote received
- Less than 55%
- 55% to 60%
- Over 60%

Spending by winning candidates

Amount spent
- Less than $250,000
- $250,000 to $499,999
- $500,000 to $750,000
- Over $750,000

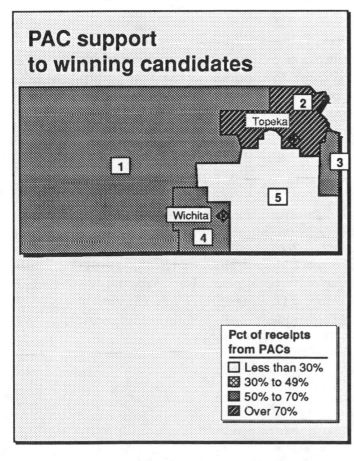

PAC support to winning candidates

Pct of receipts from PACs
- Less than 30%
- 30% to 49%
- 50% to 70%
- Over 70%

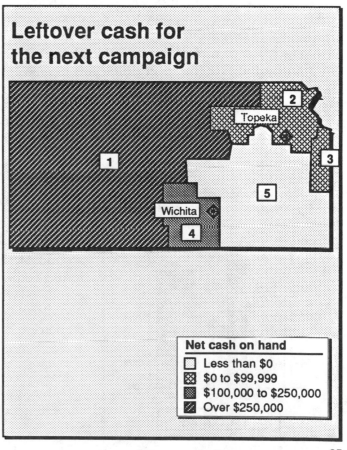

Leftover cash for the next campaign

Net cash on hand
- Less than $0
- $0 to $99,999
- $100,000 to $250,000
- Over $250,000

Kentucky

Vital Statistics of 1990 Winners

Dist	Name	Party	Vote Pct	Race Type	Total Receipts	PAC Receipts	PAC Pct	Spent	Net cash on Hand
1	Carroll Hubbard Jr.	Dem	86.9%	Reelected	$351,966	$271,327	77.1%	$239,620	$335,477
2	William H. Natcher	Dem	66.0%	Reelected	$6,768	$0	0.0%	$6,766	$0
3	Romano L. Mazzoli	Dem	60.6%	Reelected	$301,713	$300	0.1%	$333,885	-$38,384
4	Jim Bunning	Rep	69.3%	Reelected	$532,775	$225,900	42.4%	$563,409	$97,018
5	Harold Rogers	Rep	100.0%	Reelected	$183,211	$71,025	38.8%	$110,188	$266,195
6	Larry J. Hopkins	Rep	100.0%	Reelected	$203,286	$92,200	45.4%	$120,647	$691,433
7	Carl C. Perkins	Dem	50.8%	Reelected	$340,047	$267,575	78.7%	$344,561	-$39,283
Sen	Mitch McConnell	Rep	52.2%	Reelected	$5,707,726	$1,317,929	23.1%	$5,401,678	$190,373

The 1990 election produced no changes in Kentucky's congressional delegation. Seven House members and one Senator ran for reelection, and each of them won. But the election year was not without its surprises or its interesting footnotes.

One incumbent — Carl Perkins in the 7th district — nearly lost his seat after a surprisingly strong showing by Republican Will Scott. Perkins managed only 50.8 percent of the vote, even after outspending Scott two-to-one in an Appalachian coal mining district that has been reliably Democratic for generations.

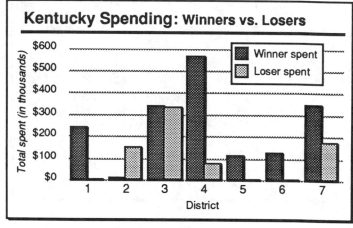

Across the state in the 2nd district, Democrat William Natcher walked easily to his 20th successive term in the U.S. House — though hardly in typical style. Natcher spent only $6,766 in his reelection campaign, less than one-twentieth the amount spent by his Republican challenger, Martin A. Tori. It was the least expensive winning House campaign in the nation, made even more unusual by the fact that every dime of it came from Natcher's own pocket. While that particular style of campaigning is unique among modern congressman, it is vintage Natcher. Since winning his first election in 1953, Natcher has never accepted a campaign contribution — nor missed a single vote on the House floor. His constituents seem to appreciate it; he outpolled his free-spending challenger nearly two-to-one.

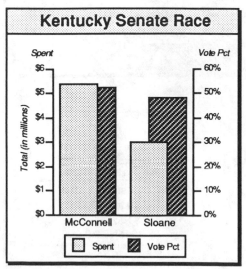

When Mitch McConnell first won his seat in the U.S. Senate in 1984, he did it on the strength of an aggressive campaign and a memorable negative TV spot attacking the incumbent, Sen. Walter Huddleston. McConnell won the race by a margin of just over 5,000 votes. This time around, McConnell was taking no chances. His Democratic opponent, former Louisville mayor Harvey Sloane, raised $3 million, but McConnell countered with a campaign costing $5.4 million. The race was competitive all the way, with McConnell finally edging out Sloane with just over 52 percent of the vote on election day.

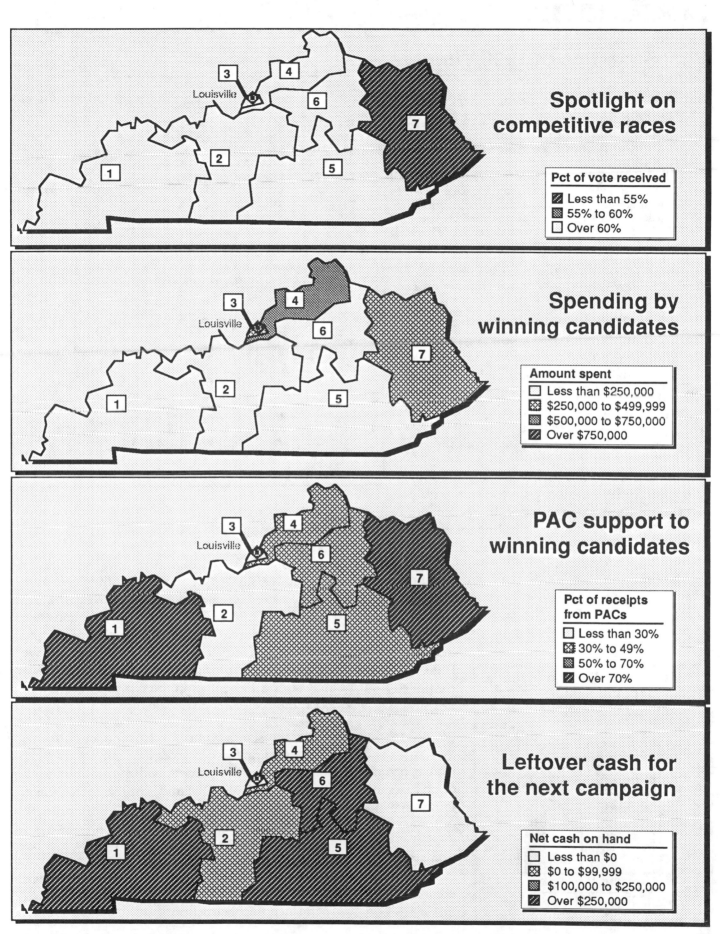

Spotlight on competitive races

Pct of vote received
- Less than 55%
- 55% to 60%
- Over 60%

Spending by winning candidates

Amount spent
- Less than $250,000
- $250,000 to $499,999
- $500,000 to $750,000
- Over $750,000

PAC support to winning candidates

Pct of receipts from PACs
- Less than 30%
- 30% to 49%
- 50% to 70%
- Over 70%

Leftover cash for the next campaign

Net cash on hand
- Less than $0
- $0 to $99,999
- $100,000 to $250,000
- Over $250,000

Louisiana

Vital Statistics of 1990 Winners

Dist	Name	Party	Vote Pct	Race Type	Total Receipts	PAC Receipts	PAC Pct	Spent	Net cash on Hand
1	Bob Livingston	Rep	83.9%	Reelected	$279,603	$140,878	50.4%	$108,207	$282,513
2	William J. Jefferson	Dem	52.5%	Open	$448,100	$104,950	23.4%	$446,743	-$158,300
3	W. J. "Billy" Tauzin	Dem	87.7%	Reelected	$460,418	$243,922	53.0%	$474,224	$48,411
4	Jim McCrery	Rep	54.7%	Reelected	$469,766	$190,623	40.6%	$481,504	$36,690
5	Jerry Huckaby	Dem	73.5%	Reelected	$218,774	$106,498	48.7%	$240,832	$273,331
6	Richard H. Baker	Rep	100.0%	Reelected	$382,622	$153,761	40.2%	$332,905	$67,056
7	Jimmy Hayes	Dem	57.7%	Reelected	$317,295	$164,550	51.9%	$309,229	-$73,151
8	Clyde C. Holloway	Rep	56.3%	Reelected	$383,701	$144,263	37.6%	$385,877	$62,110
Sen	J. Bennett Johnston	Dem	53.9%	Reelected	$4,816,299	$1,444,713	30.0%	$5,811,105	$945,371

The race that attracted the most attention in Louisiana — by far — in 1990 was the contest for the U.S. Senate seat held by Democrat Bennett Johnston, a three-term incumbent. The interest was not so much in Johnston, however, as in the man who was running to unseat him: David Duke, former Imperial Wizard of the Knights of the Ku Klux Klan. The day of reckoning came not in November, but in the October 6th Louisiana primary when Johnston garnered more than 50 percent of the vote, eliminating Duke from the race.

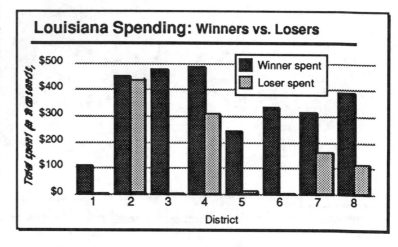

The state's election procedures are unique in the nation. Every election year, the state holds a non-partisan primary in October. If the winner in a particular race gets more than 50 percent of the vote, he or she is thereby elected without having to run again in November. If no one gets 50 percent, the two highest vote-getters face each other in the general election — even if both come from the same party.

The prospect of ex-Klansman Duke running as a Republican for the U.S. Senate stirred nationwide attention in the race. The national Republican Party publicly disowned Duke and several prominent Republicans actually went to the state to campaign against him. His fate was sealed two days before the primary, when the mainstream GOP candidate, Ben Bagert, announced he was withdrawing from the race. That made it much easier for Johnston to poll a majority of the votes, averting a November showdown with Duke. It was not likely to be the end of Duke's political career, however. He polled a surprisingly strong 44 percent in the October primary and has since set his eyes on the Louisiana governorship.

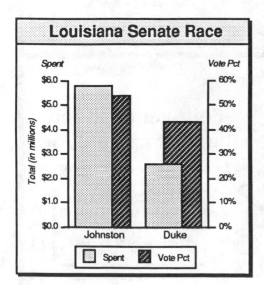

Though less dramatic, the state's eight U.S. House races also held their share of closely contested races — in votes if not in dollars. Three House incumbents polled less than 60 percent of the vote, and the one open-seat race, in the 2nd district (New Orleans), saw Democrat William Jefferson winning with just 52.5 percent of the vote over Marc Morial, son of former New Orleans mayor Dutch Morial. The seat became vacant with the retirement of Lindy Boggs, and given Louisiana's unique primary system, the only question in November was which of the competing black Democrats would suceed her. Both candidates raised comparable funds and Johnson eventually prevailed, becoming Lousiana's first black Congressman since Reconstruction.

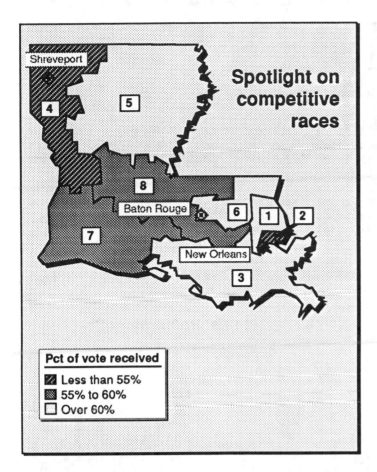

Spotlight on competitive races

Pct of vote received
- Less than 55%
- 55% to 60%
- Over 60%

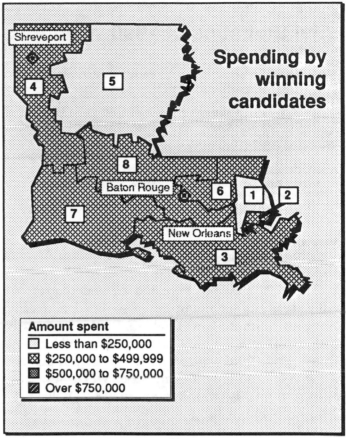

Spending by winning candidates

Amount spent
- Less than $250,000
- $250,000 to $499,999
- $500,000 to $750,000
- Over $750,000

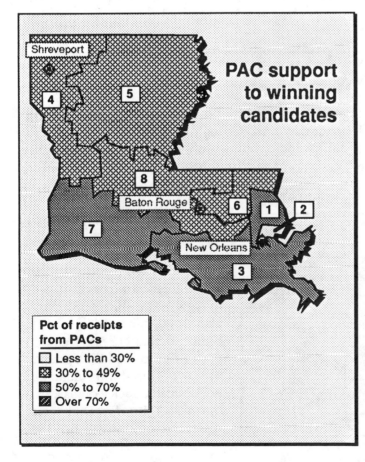

PAC support to winning candidates

Pct of receipts from PACs
- Less than 30%
- 30% to 49%
- 50% to 70%
- Over 70%

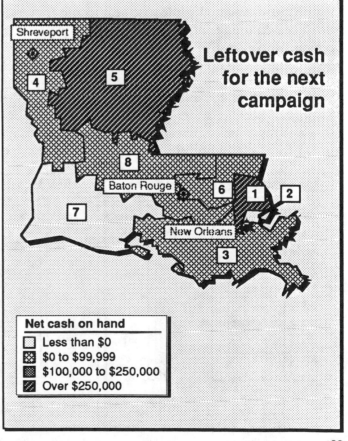

Leftover cash for the next campaign

Net cash on hand
- Less than $0
- $0 to $99,999
- $100,000 to $250,000
- Over $250,000

89

Maine/New Hampshire/Vermont

Vital Statistics of 1990 Winners

Dist	Name	Party	Vote Pct	Race Type	Total Receipts	PAC Receipts	PAC Pct	Spent	Net cash on Hand
Maine									
1	Thomas H. Andrews	Dem	60.1%	Open	$697,604	$243,473	34.9%	$693,165	-$92,283
2	Olympia J. Snowe	Rep	51.0%	Reelected	$278,223	$97,655	35.1%	$306,289	-$2,165
Sen	William S. Cohen	Rep	61.3%	Reelected	$1,511,559	$553,944	36.6%	$1,633,623	$17,906
New Hampshire									
1	Bill Zeliff	Rep	55.1%	Open	$950,621	$132,101	13.9%	$924,367	-$374,532
2	Dick Swett	Dem	52.7%	Beat Incumb	$470,252	$186,000	39.5%	$465,160	-$5,067
Sen	Robert C. Smith	Rep	65.1%	Open	$1,509,288	$663,150	43.9%	$1,420,172	$89,118
Vermont									
1	Bernard Sanders	Ind	56.0%	Beat Incumb	$571,556	$72,250	12.6%	$569,772	-$21,940

The 1990 elections revealed an undercurrent of political unrest — if not upheaval — in economically struggling northern New England. By the time it was over, two House incumbents were upended by challengers, and a third was reelected with only 51 percent of the vote. The only incumbent to win a new term fairly comfortably was Republican Sen. William S. Cohen of Maine.

Two other incumbents had already stepped down through retirement, while one — Robert Smith of New Hampshire — vacated his House seat to run for (and win) a seat in the Senate. The challengers had seen it coming. In contrast to the rest of the nation, nearly every congressional contest in the region was financially competitive.

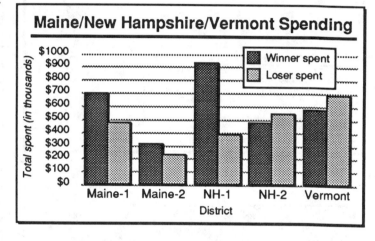

The race that spoke the loudest to the region's willingness to stir up the political pot was the election in Vermont of Bernie Sanders, the outspoken socialist (and former mayor of Burlington), who won election as an Independent. Sanders won 56 percent of the vote, vanquishing Republican incumbent Peter Smith and a little-known Democrat who carried only 3 percent of the vote on election day. Though Sanders made no attempt to disguise his socialist leanings, his campaign relied on the top-dollar techniques of modern electioneering. The campaign eventually cost nearly $570,000.

Voters just across the border in New Hampshire's 2nd district also showed they were ready for political change, as Democrat Dick Swett pulled off a dramatic upset of first-term incumbent Republican Chuck Douglas. Swett thus became the first Democrat to represent the district since 1912.

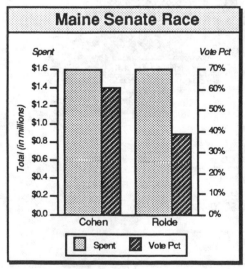

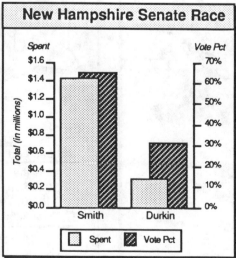

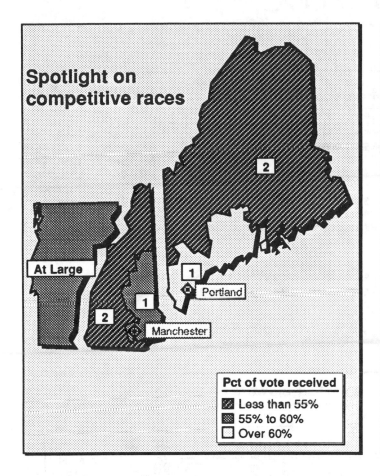

Spotlight on competitive races

At Large

Portland

Manchester

Pct of vote received
- Less than 55%
- 55% to 60%
- Over 60%

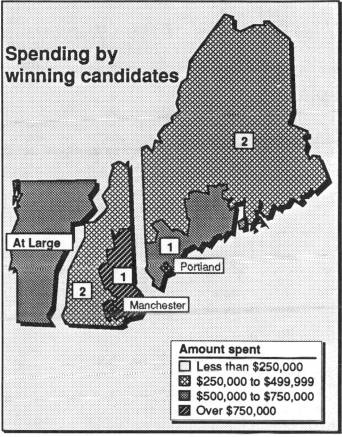

Spending by winning candidates

At Large

Portland

Manchester

Amount spent
- Less than $250,000
- $250,000 to $499,999
- $500,000 to $750,000
- Over $750,000

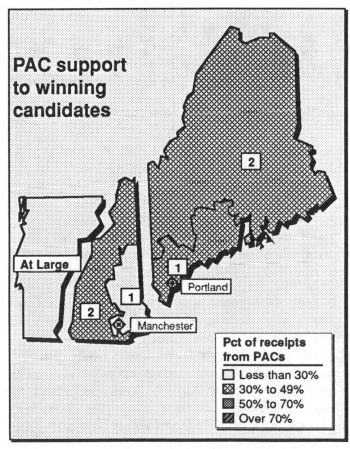

PAC support to winning candidates

At Large

Portland

Manchester

Pct of receipts from PACs
- Less than 30%
- 30% to 49%
- 50% to 70%
- Over 70%

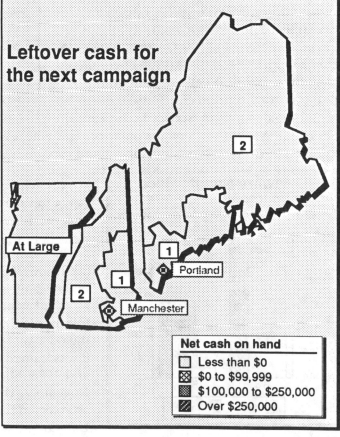

Leftover cash for the next campaign

At Large

Portland

Manchester

Net cash on hand
- Less than $0
- $0 to $99,999
- $100,000 to $250,000
- Over $250,000

Maryland/Delaware/D.C.

Vital Statistics of 1990 Winners

Dist	Name	Party	Vote Pct	Race Type	Total Receipts	PAC Receipts	PAC Pct	Spent	Net cash on Hand
Maryland									
1	Wayne T. Gilchrest	Rep	56.8%	Beat Incumb	$266,930	$60,074	22.5%	$264,932	-$2,719
2	Helen Delich Bentley	Rep	74.4%	Reelected	$781,008	$214,305	27.4%	$730,852	$127,685
3	Benjamin L. Cardin	Dem	69.7%	Reelected	$532,752	$200,790	37.7%	$363,847	$250,724
4	Tom McMillen	Dem	58.9%	Reelected	$757,145	$421,625	55.7%	$560,909	$328,285
5	Steny H. Hoyer	Dem	80.7%	Reelected	$725,418	$417,235	57.5%	$716,469	$321,405
6	Beverly B. Byron	Dem	65.3%	Reelected	$282,337	$163,245	57.8%	$325,997	$33,737
7	Kweisi Mfume	Dem	85.0%	Reelected	$224,826	$128,000	56.9%	$205,671	$84,387
8	Constance A. Morella	Rep	73.5%	Reelected	$542,961	$239,709	44.1%	$353,959	$201,384
Delaware									
1	Thomas R. Carper	Dem	65.5%	Reelected	$548,682	$203,720	37.1%	$521,336	$53,814
Sen	Joseph R. Biden Jr.	Dem	62.7%	Reelected	$2,819,488	$714,466	25.3%	$2,598,868	$141,151
District of Columbia*									
1	Eleanor Holmes Norton	Dem	62.0%	Open	$447,441	$145,205	32.5%	$446,856	-$54,537

* Non-voting delegate

In the 1988 elections, when incumbent House members were reelected to Congress at a near-record rate of 98.5 percent, one incumbent who was widely thought to have dodged a bullet was Democrat Roy Dyson of Maryland's 1st district. Dyson had been plagued with a string of scandals in 1988, but survived the election by just 1,504 votes. His opponent then was a politically unknown high school teacher, Wayne Gilchrest. In 1990 Gilchrest made another run for the seat and Dyson encountered yet another political embarrassment, that despite his strong support of defense contractors he had avoided military service in the Vietnam War by filing as a conscientious objector. This time, even though Gilchrest was outspent nearly three-to-one, he managed to overcome the incumbent and capture nearly 57 percent of the vote on election day.

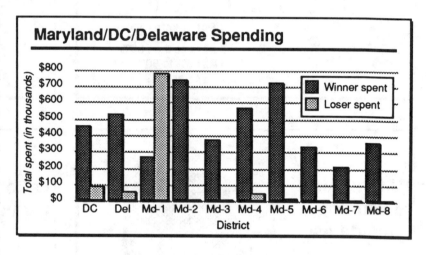

Maryland/DC/Delaware Spending

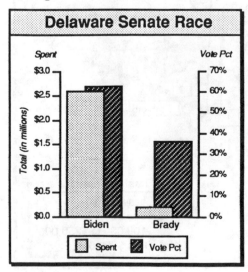

Delaware Senate Race

Elsewhere in Maryland and neighboring Delaware, all other incumbents ran for new terms and were successfully reelected. Only one, Democrat Tom McMillen in Maryland's 4th district, dipped below 60 percent of the vote. None faced serious financial opposition.

Aside from Gilchrest, the only change in the area's congressional lineup came in the District of Columbia, where Eleanor Holmes Norton replaced Walter Fauntroy, who had stepped down to run (unsuccessfully) for D.C. Mayor. From the moment she entered the race, Norton was the odds-on favorite to win, but her candidacy suffered a setback when it was learned that she had failed to file D.C. income taxes between 1982 and 1988. She eventually survived the flap and won comfortably in November. The victory in one sense was less than complete, however, as voters in the nation's capitol elect only a non-voting delegate to the U.S. Congress.

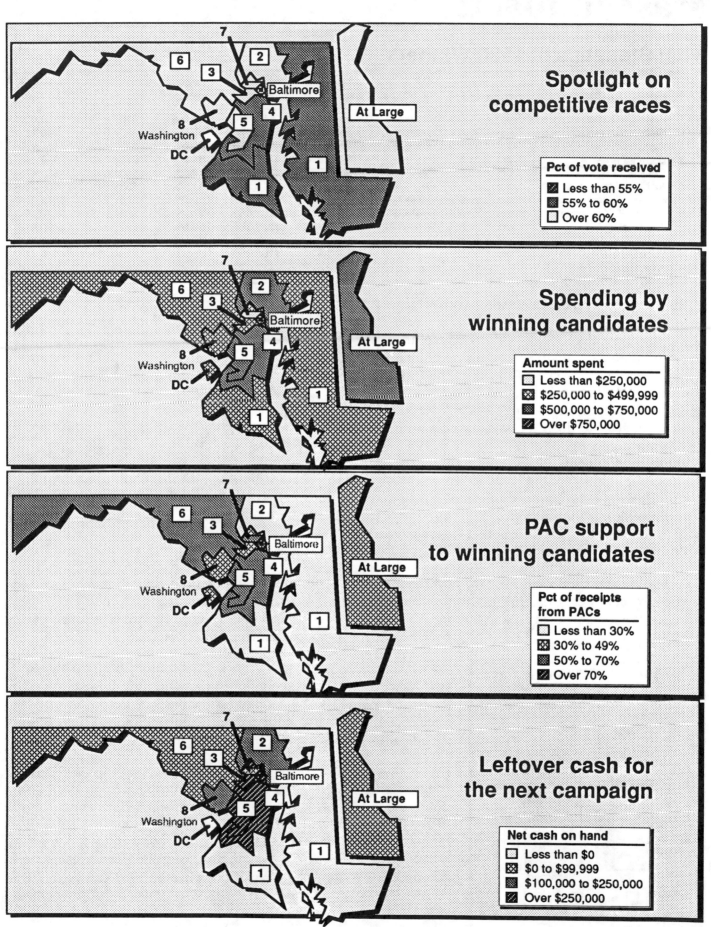

Spotlight on competitive races

Pct of vote received
- Less than 55%
- 55% to 60%
- Over 60%

Spending by winning candidates

Amount spent
- Less than $250,000
- $250,000 to $499,999
- $500,000 to $750,000
- Over $750,000

PAC support to winning candidates

Pct of receipts from PACs
- Less than 30%
- 30% to 49%
- 50% to 70%
- Over 70%

Leftover cash for the next campaign

Net cash on hand
- Less than $0
- $0 to $99,999
- $100,000 to $250,000
- Over $250,000

Massachusetts

Vital Statistics of 1990 Winners

Dist	Name	Party	Vote Pct	Race Type	Total Receipts	PAC Receipts	PAC Pct	Spent	Net cash on Hand
1	Silvio O. Conte	Rep	77.5%	Reelected	$146,537	$63,502	43.3%	$167,443	$258,037
2	Richard E. Neal	Dem	99.8%	Reelected	$462,672	$248,878	53.8%	$534,345	-$46,187
3	Joseph D. Early	Dem	99.4%	Reelected	$281,707	$86,348	30.6%	$282,012	$111,190
4	Barney Frank	Dem	65.5%	Reelected	$643,920	$220,517	34.2%	$718,160	$49,261
5	Chester G. Atkins	Dem	52.2%	Reelected	$843,893	$430	0.1%	$861,333	-$33,175
6	Nicholas Mavroules	Dem	65.0%	Reelected	$289,794	$119,249	41.1%	$333,912	$58,499
7	Edward J. Markey	Dem	99.9%	Reelected	$336,209	$0	0.0%	$207,273	$579,994
8	Joseph P. Kennedy II	Dem	72.2%	Reelected	$805,013	$103,550	12.9%	$832,815	$227,284
9	Joe Moakley	Dem	70.3%	Reelected	$512,858	$276,274	53.9%	$318,847	$489,816
10	Gerry E. Studds	Dem	53.4%	Reelected	$600,325	$221,581	36.9%	$620,387	$21,912
11	Brian Donnelly	Dem	99.7%	Reelected	$303,943	$168,850	55.5%	$104,221	$669,414
Sen	John Kerry	Dem	57.1%	Reelected	$8,042,413	$17,477	0.2%	$8,067,033	-$80,710

In a state where the Democratic Party has long been virtually the *only* party with any political power, the 1990 election was a trying one for the party and the voters alike. Soured by the humiliating defeat of Gov. Michael Dukakis in the 1988 presidential election, and angered by the subsequent economic plunge from the so-called "Massachusetts miracle" to deep recession, voters were ready for a change. They eventually got it — not in their congressional delegation, but in the governor's office, where the battle to replace the retiring Dukakis riveted voters' attention. A moderate Republican, William Weld, eventually captured the office, setting back the political ambitions of Boston University president John Silber, an outspokenly conservative Democrat.

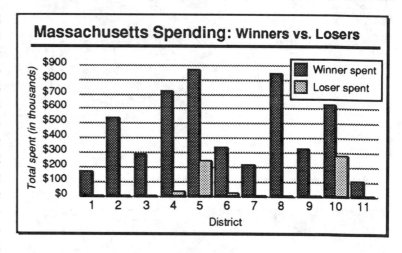

Massachusetts Spending: Winners vs. Losers

While attention was focused on the governor's race, the state's entire congressional delegation was reelected. Two House races were close, in the 6th and 10th districts. Those were also the only two districts where challengers managed to raise more than a token amount of money. But even in this volatile election year, the challengers were not able to topple Democratic incumbents Chet Atkins and Gerry Studds.

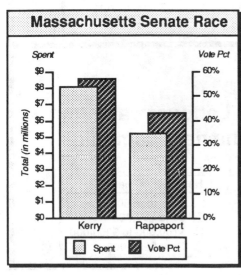

Massachusetts Senate Race

Democratic Sen. John Kerry also won reelection, though not without an expensive fight. His Republican opponent, developer-lawyer Jim Rappaport, poured $4.2 million of his own money into an overall $5.1 million campaign. Kerry more than matched the fundraising, however, spending just over $8 million before the campaign was over.

Though the 1990 elections did not alter the makeup of the state's congressional delegation, however, fate did. Liberal Republican Silvio Conte, the state's only Republican congressman, died in February 1991. In the special election to replace him the following June, the winner was Democrat John Olver. The state's 13-member congressional delegation is now entirely Democratic — though at least one of those Democrats is bound to lose their job in 1992. Following the 1990 census, the state is slated to lose one of its 11 seats in the U.S. House of Representatives.

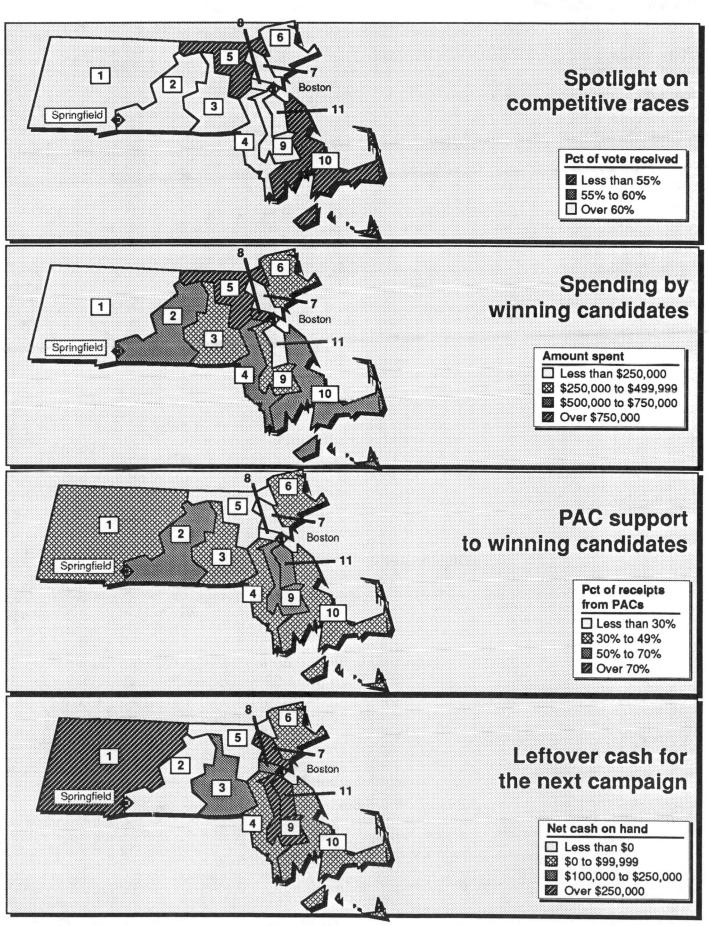

Spotlight on competitive races

Pct of vote received
- Less than 55%
- 55% to 60%
- Over 60%

Spending by winning candidates

Amount spent
- Less than $250,000
- $250,000 to $499,999
- $500,000 to $750,000
- Over $750,000

PAC support to winning candidates

Pct of receipts from PACs
- Less than 30%
- 30% to 49%
- 50% to 70%
- Over 70%

Leftover cash for the next campaign

Net cash on hand
- Less than $0
- $0 to $99,999
- $100,000 to $250,000
- Over $250,000

Michigan

Vital Statistics of 1990 Winners

Dist	Name	Party	Vote Pct	Race Type	Total Receipts	PAC Receipts	PAC Pct	Spent	Net cash on Hand
1	John Conyers Jr.	Dem	89.3%	Reelected	$288,877	$178,360	61.7%	$216,793	$5,925
2	Carl D. Pursell	Rep	64.1%	Reelected	$285,808	$96,415	33.7%	$135,801	$240,044
3	Howard Wolpe	Dem	57.9%	Reelected	$791,685	$414,976	52.4%	$815,244	$56,327
4	Fred Upton	Rep	57.8%	Reelected	$445,881	$152,154	34.1%	$503,164	$41,344
5	Paul B. Henry	Rep	75.4%	Reelected	$398,627	$92,880	23.3%	$241,151	$275,521
6	Bob Carr	Dem	99.8%	Reelected	$397,155	$207,450	52.2%	$223,595	$255,444
7	Dale E. Kildee	Dem	68.4%	Reelected	$259,480	$187,646	72.3%	$222,531	$39,580
8	Bob Traxler	Dem	68.6%	Reelected	$295,544	$186,685	63.2%	$176,479	$358,806
9	Guy Vander Jagt	Rep	54.8%	Reelected	$448,892	$267,971	59.7%	$452,960	$104,106
10	Dave Camp	Rep	65.0%	Open	$667,713	$173,525	26.0%	$657,229	-$106,670
11	Robert W. Davis	Rep	61.3%	Reelected	$340,079	$242,224	71.2%	$325,232	$114,637
12	David E. Bonior	Dem	64.7%	Reelected	$1,258,712	$732,737	58.2%	$1,218,178	$89,849
13	Barbara-Rose Collins	Dem	80.1%	Open	$335,736	$63,620	18.9%	$274,688	$8,520
14	Dennis M. Hertel	Dem	63.6%	Reelected	$306,850	$186,540	60.8%	$187,545	$281,310
15	William D. Ford	Dem	61.2%	Reelected	$384,737	$280,598	72.9%	$354,964	$186,613
16	John D. Dingell	Dem	66.6%	Reelected	$843,579	$621,927	73.7%	$602,952	$490,749
17	Sander M. Levin	Dem	69.7%	Reelected	$356,280	$241,525	67.8%	$271,072	$255,205
18	William S. Broomfield	Rep	66.4%	Reelected	$243,762	$56,200	23.1%	$78,205	$754,678
Sen	Carl Levin	Dem	57.5%	Reelected	$7,228,954	$1,405,557	19.4%	$7,082,164	$95,810

Whatever uneasiness Michigan voters may have felt about the state's economic doldrums, there was no popular move to replace their representatives in Congress in the 1990 elections. All 16 of the House incumbents who sought reelection were successful, as was Democratic Sen. Carl Levin. Not all the incumbents sailed to victory with huge majorities at the polls, but only one was held to less than 55 percent of the vote, and almost none faced opponents with the financial resources to mount a serious challenge.

The only changes in Michigan's congressional lineup came in the 10th and 13th districts, where the current office holders declined to run for new terms. The 10th district was vacated by Republican Bill Schuette, who ran for the Senate (and was defeated in November). The 13th, in Detroit, came open with the retirement of Democrat George Crockett. Both those seats stayed in the hands of the political party that had held them before.

Dave Camp was the winner in Schuette's old district, easily handling a little-known Democrat who tried to run a campaign with no money at all. (She didn't even file a spending report with the Federal Election Commission). Camp, meanwhile, spent $657,000 on his campaign and took nearly two-thirds of the vote on election day.

The contest in the 13th district was similarly one-sided — at least in November. The real contest for the downtown Detroit district was in the August Democratic primary. The winner then was Barbara-Rose Collins, a city councilwoman who topped the field of seven candidates. She won easily in November, polling 80 percent of the vote against a Republican who spent nothing to oppose her.

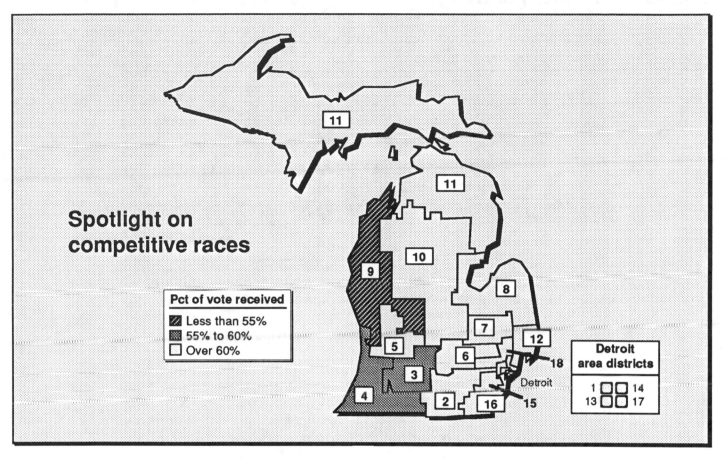

Spotlight on competitive races

Pct of vote received
- Less than 55%
- 55% to 60%
- Over 60%

Detroit area districts

| 1 | | | 14 |
| 13 | | | 17 |

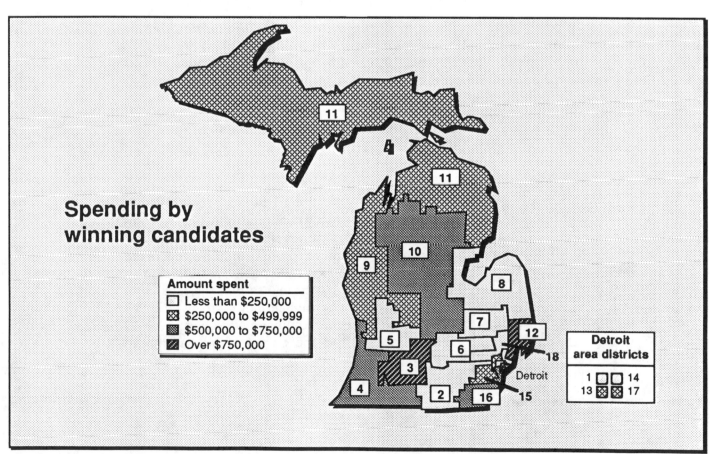

Spending by winning candidates

Amount spent
- Less than $250,000
- $250,000 to $499,999
- $500,000 to $750,000
- Over $750,000

Detroit area districts

| 1 | | | 14 |
| 13 | | | 17 |

Michigan *(cont'd)*

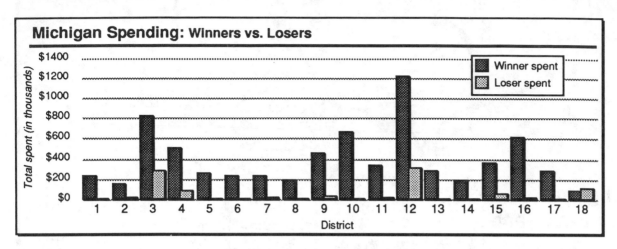

Michigan Spending: Winners vs. Losers

Total spent (in thousands)

Legend: Winner spent / Loser spent

District (x-axis): 1 2 3 4 5 6 7 8 9 10 11 12 13 14 15 16 17 18

The most expensive U.S. House race in Michigan during 1990 was northeast of Detroit in the 12th congressional district. Democrat David Bonior spent more than $1.2 million defending the seat he has held since 1976 against Republican Jim Dingeman. Dingeman spent nearly $300,000 in the campaign, but Bonior won handily in November, carrying nearly 65 percent of the vote.

The only other race with a reasonably well-financed challenger proved to be much closer. Howard Wolpe, a six-term Democrat from the 3rd district, has often had to face tough reelection battles. This time he had his hands full with Republican attorney Brad Haskins. Wolpe outspent his challenger three-to-one, and eventually carried the election with just under 58 percent of the vote.

The 1992 elections could be more difficult for Michigan incumbents. Like its neighboring industrial states in the Northeast and Midwest, Michigan will be losing ground in Congress to the fast-growing sunbelt states. While California, Florida and Texas will be gaining new seats in the U.S. House of Representatives after the 1990 census, Michigan will be losing two.

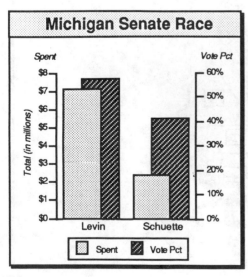

Michigan Senate Race

Spent / *Vote Pct*

Total (in millions)

x-axis: Levin / Schuette

Legend: Spent / Vote Pct

Carl Levin's reelection to a third term in the U.S. Senate came reasonably comfortably in 1990 — compared with the thin victories of his first two campaigns, where he never captured more than 52 percent of the vote. His 1990 opponent, Republican congressman Bill Schuette, was never able to pull the race close enough — or raise enough money — to give Levin a serious scare. Levin's campaign cost just over $7 million, nearly triple the output of his Republican challenger.

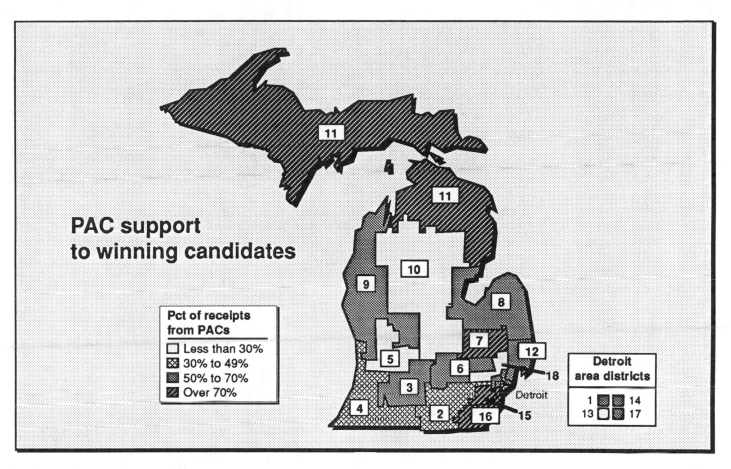

PAC support
to winning candidates

Pct of receipts
from PACs
Less than 30%
30% to 49%
50% to 70%
Over 70%

Detroit
area districts

1 14
13 17

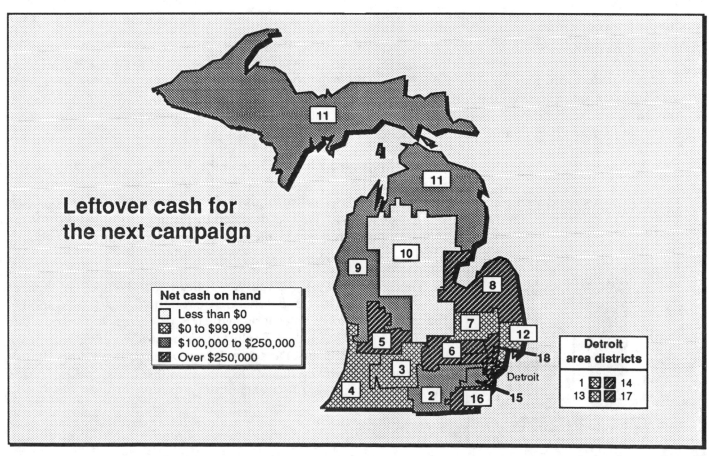

Leftover cash for
the next campaign

Net cash on hand
Less than $0
$0 to $99,999
$100,000 to $250,000
Over $250,000

Detroit
area districts

1 14
13 17

Minnesota

Vital Statistics of 1990 Winners

Dist	Name	Party	Vote Pct	Race Type	Total Receipts	PAC Receipts	PAC Pct	Spent	Net cash on Hand
1	Timothy J. Penny	Dem	78.1%	Reelected	$230,040	$113,050	49.1%	$197,442	$256,193
2	Vin Weber	Rep	61.8%	Reelected	$613,549	$240,653	39.2%	$670,684	$213,403
3	Jim Ramstad	Rep	66.9%	Open	$936,208	$237,745	25.4%	$935,454	-$121,827
4	Bruce F. Vento	Dem	64.7%	Reelected	$259,456	$187,095	72.1%	$265,699	$155,180
5	Martin Olav Sabo	Dem	72.9%	Reelected	$355,684	$226,950	63.8%	$321,644	$216,221
6	Gerry Sikorski	Dem	64.6%	Reelected	$443,201	$335,487	75.7%	$378,087	$306,294
7	Collin C. Peterson	Dem	53.5%	Beat Incumb	$270,273	$185,598	68.7%	$242,864	-$73,673
8	James L. Oberstar	Dem	72.9%	Reelected	$364,577	$248,780	68.2%	$229,262	$393,551
Sen	Paul Wellstone	Dem	50.4%	Beat Incumb	$1,403,208	$294,520	21.0%	$1,340,708	-$55,013

Minnesota was the scene of the biggest — in fact the *only* — upset in U.S. Senate races during 1990, as liberal activist and political science professor Paul Wellstone defeated two-term Repubican incumbent Rudy Boschwitz. It wasn't money that bought the victory though, since Wellstone spent only $1.3 million against a Boschwitz budget of nearly $8 million. Scandals and disarray in the Republicans' gubernatorial campaign didn't hurt either, nor did Boschwitz's last minute overreaction to what was finally seen as a serious threat to his reelection.

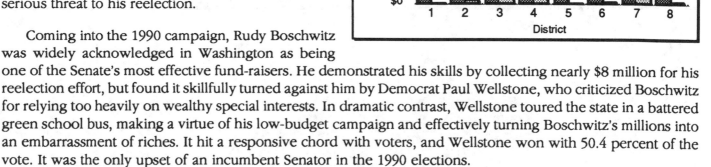

Coming into the 1990 campaign, Rudy Boschwitz was widely acknowledged in Washington as being one of the Senate's most effective fund-raisers. He demonstrated his skills by collecting nearly $8 million for his reelection effort, but found it skillfully turned against him by Democrat Paul Wellstone, who criticized Boschwitz for relying too heavily on wealthy special interests. In dramatic contrast, Wellstone toured the state in a battered green school bus, making a virtue of his low-budget campaign and effectively turning Boschwitz's millions into an embarrassment of riches. It hit a responsive chord with voters, and Wellstone won with 50.4 percent of the vote. It was the only upset of an incumbent Senator in the 1990 elections.

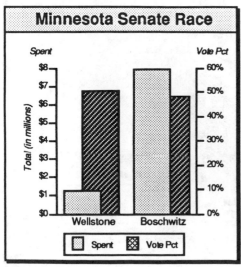

Scandal played a leading role in the 7th U.S. House district, where Republican Arlan Stangeland was unable to shirk off allegations that he had improperly used office funds to charge several hundred phone calls to a female lobbyist. He was defeated by Democrat Collin Peterson, an accountant and frequent challenger to Stangeland who came within a whisker of winning the seat four years earlier.

The retirement of veteran Republican Bill Frenzel in the 3rd congressional district, a traditional GOP stronghold, guaranteed another change in Minnesota's delegation in the U.S. Congress. Republican State Sen. Jim Ramstad had little difficulty taking the seat, winning nearly two-thirds of the vote against Democrat Lewis DeMars. The victory did not come cheaply however; Ramstad spent $935,000 in the contest, nearly triple the amount spent by DeMars.

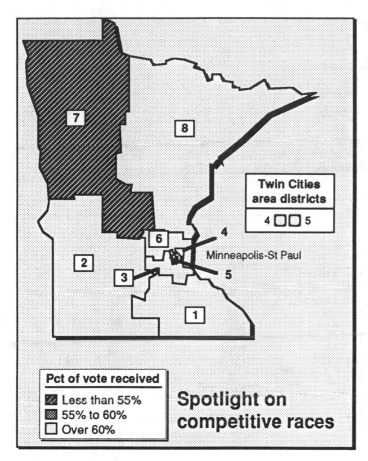

Pct of vote received
- ▨ Less than 55%
- ▦ 55% to 60%
- ☐ Over 60%

Spotlight on competitive races

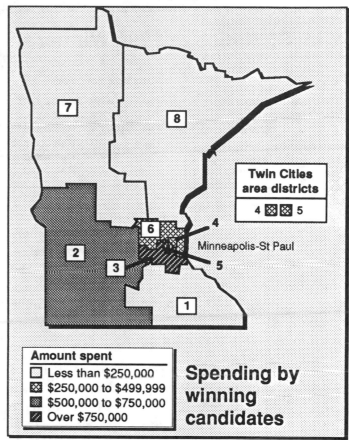

Amount spent
- ☐ Less than $250,000
- ▦ $250,000 to $499,999
- ▩ $500,000 to $750,000
- ▨ Over $750,000

Spending by winning candidates

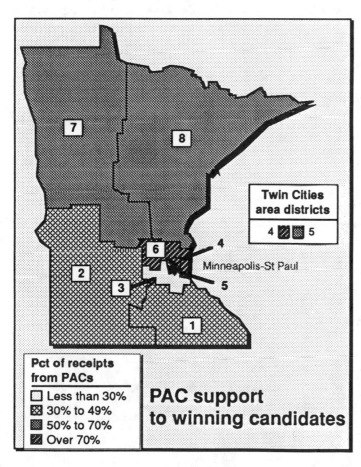

Pct of receipts from PACs
- ☐ Less than 30%
- ▦ 30% to 49%
- ▩ 50% to 70%
- ▨ Over 70%

PAC support to winning candidates

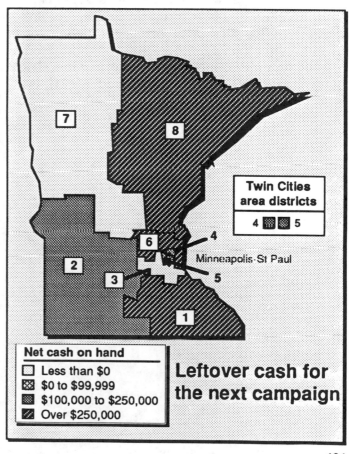

Net cash on hand
- ☐ Less than $0
- ▦ $0 to $99,999
- ▩ $100,000 to $250,000
- ▨ Over $250,000

Leftover cash for the next campaign

Mississippi

Vital Statistics of 1990 Winners

Dist	Name	Party	Vote Pct	Race Type	Total Receipts	PAC Receipts	PAC Pct	Spent	Net cash on Hand
1	Jamie L. Whitten	Dem	64.9%	Reelected	$183,612	$129,450	70.5%	$96,254	$435,724
2	Mike Espy	Dem	84.1%	Reelected	$448,212	$219,225	48.9%	$365,825	$57,666
3	G. V. "Sonny" Montgomery	Dem	100.0%	Reelected	$112,779	$55,250	49.0%	$71,181	$171,908
4	Mike Parker	Dem	80.6%	Reelected	$526,715	$285,973	54.3%	$479,951	$48,162
5	Gene Taylor*	Dem	81.4%	Reelected	$316,052	$143,426	45.4%	$322,048	-$39,180
Sen	Thad Cochran	Rep	100.0%	Reelected	$1,463,865	$553,386	37.8%	$693,907	$908,834

While members of Congress in many other states had to fend off a late surge of anti-incumbent sentiment among voters, lawmakers in Mississippi were skating to reelection with barely a ripple of opposition. The state's five congressmen enjoyed the highest average vote percentage — 82.2 percent — of any state in the union, and GOP Senate incumbent Thad Cochran didn't even face a challenger.

The only incumbent to face a financial challenge of any size at all was Democrat Gene Taylor in the 5th district. Taylor was running for his first full term in the House; he won the seat in an October 1989 special election, following the death in an air crash of fresh-man Republican Larkin Smith. Taylor's opponent in 1990 was Smith's widow Sheila, and she was able to raise a respectable $210,000 to try to win the seat. But after a strong campaign in 1989 and a year in office, Taylor proved unbeatable. He piled up 81 percent of the vote on election day.

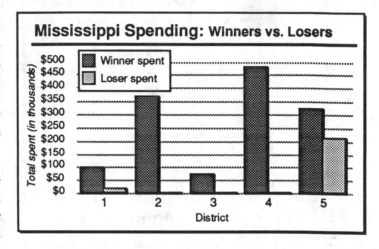

The only Mississippi congressman to win with less than two-thirds of the vote was 80-year-old Jamie Whitten of the 1st district. Whitten, first elected in 1941, is the longest-serving member of Congress currently in office.

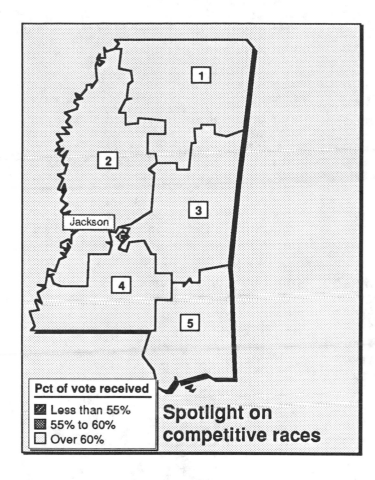

Pct of vote received
- Less than 55%
- 55% to 60%
- Over 60%

Spotlight on competitive races

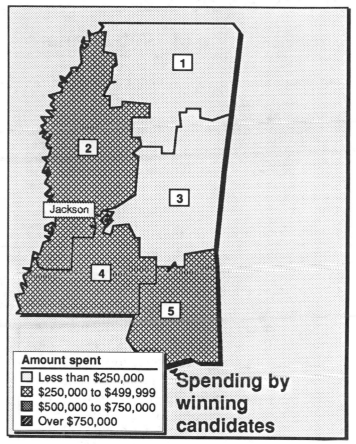

Amount spent
- Less than $250,000
- $250,000 to $499,999
- $500,000 to $750,000
- Over $750,000

Spending by winning candidates

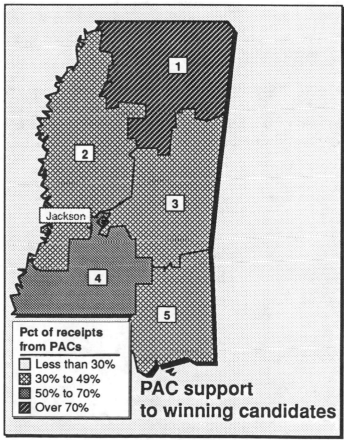

Pct of receipts from PACs
- Less than 30%
- 30% to 49%
- 50% to 70%
- Over 70%

PAC support to winning candidates

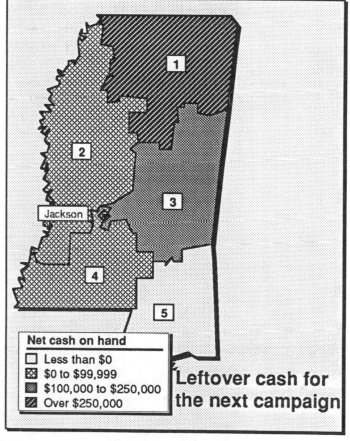

Net cash on hand
- Less than $0
- $0 to $99,999
- $100,000 to $250,000
- Over $250,000

Leftover cash for the next campaign

Missouri

Vital Statistics of 1990 Winners

Dist	Name	Party	Vote Pct	Race Type	Total Receipts	PAC Receipts	PAC Pct	Spent	Net cash on Hand
1	William L. Clay	Dem	60.9%	Reelected	$213,965	$182,550	85.3%	$186,909	$119,666
2	Joan Kelly Horn	Dem	50.0%	Beat Incumb	$356,066	$160,515	45.1%	$340,390	-$2,574
3	Richard A. Gephardt	Dem	56.8%	Reelected	$1,647,415	$761,537	46.2%	$1,455,794	$193,485
4	Ike Skelton	Dem	61.8%	Reelected	$390,115	$239,550	61.4%	$306,485	$311,648
5	Alan Wheat	Dem	62.1%	Reelected	$311,266	$224,435	72.1%	$245,132	$263,939
6	E. Thomas Coleman	Rep	51.9%	Reelected	$281,837	$184,870	65.6%	$315,922	$33,407
7	Mel Hancock	Rep	52.1%	Reelected	$280,787	$120,782	43.0%	$182,474	$129,033
8	Bill Emerson	Rep	57.3%	Reelected	$625,060	$326,541	52.2%	$704,447	$7,761
9	Harold L. Volkmer	Dem	57.5%	Reelected	$308,533	$218,715	70.9%	$238,679	$159,821

The 1990 elections proved to be more nerve-rattling than usual for incumbent congressmen in Missouri. Republican Jack Buechner in the 2nd district was turned out of office in the nation's closest race of the year, and five other incumbents won reelection with less than 60 percent of the vote. Even Dick Gephardt, the House majority leader who gained national prominence in his 1988 bid for the presidency, was held to a surprisingly close 57 percent on election day — despite spending more than $1.4 million on his campaign.

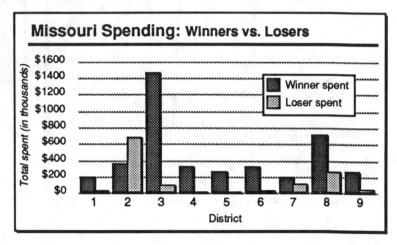

Buechner was ousted by Democrat Joan Kelly Horn, a political consultant whose margin of victory was just 54 votes out of nearly 190,000 cast. Though she spent $340,000 in her campaign, incumbent Buechner spent twice that amount.

Two other incumbents had uncomfortably close calls on election day. Republican E. Thomas Coleman, in the 6th district, carried just 52 percent of the vote against Bob McClure, a Democratic farmer who spent less than $17,000. To the south in the 7th district, Republican Bill Emerson won reelection by the same thin 52 percent margin, despite spending more than $700,000. Emerson's opponent was Russ Carnahan, the 32-year-old son of Missouri's Lt. Governor.

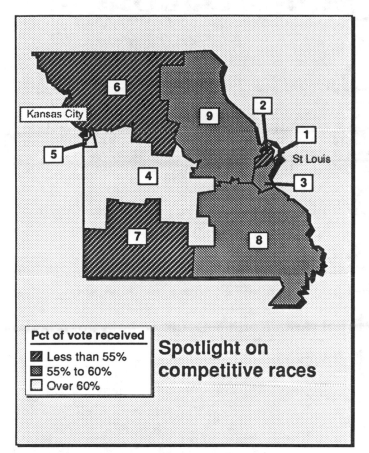

Pct of vote received
- ▨ Less than 55%
- ▦ 55% to 60%
- ☐ Over 60%

Spotlight on competitive races

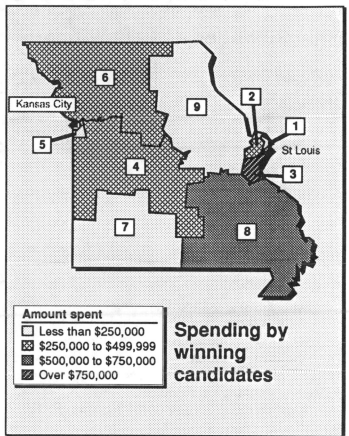

Amount spent
- ☐ Less than $250,000
- ▨ $250,000 to $499,999
- ▦ $500,000 to $750,000
- ▨ Over $750,000

Spending by winning candidates

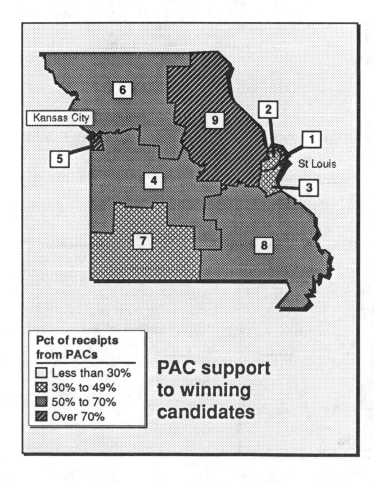

Pct of receipts from PACs
- ☐ Less than 30%
- ▨ 30% to 49%
- ▦ 50% to 70%
- ▨ Over 70%

PAC support to winning candidates

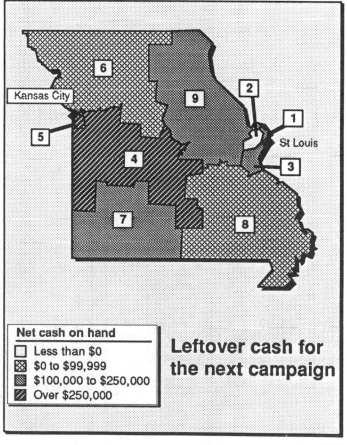

Net cash on hand
- ☐ Less than $0
- ▨ $0 to $99,999
- ▦ $100,000 to $250,000
- ▨ Over $250,000

Leftover cash for the next campaign

Nebraska/North & South Dakota

Vital Statistics of 1990 Winners

Dist	Name	Party	Vote Pct	Race Type	Total Receipts	PAC Receipts	PAC Pct	Spent	Net cash on Hand
Nebraska									
1	Doug Bereuter	Rep	64.7%	Reelected	$254,654	$147,250	57.8%	$223,898	$54,730
2	Peter Hoagland	Dem	57.9%	Reelected	$910,652	$614,287	67.5%	$929,247	-$138,820
3	Bill Barrett	Rep	51.1%	Open	$644,559	$193,583	30.0%	$624,575	-$50,018
Sen	Jim Exon	Dem	58.9%	Reelected	$2,636,125	$1,519,494	57.6%	$2,417,748	$270,574
North Dakota									
1	Byron L. Dorgan	Dem	65.2%	Reelected	$598,971	$449,050	75.0%	$504,800	$237,008
South Dakota									
1	Tim Johnson	Dem	67.6%	Reelected	$516,816	$251,800	48.7%	$463,625	$104,643
Sen	Larry Pressler	Rep	52.4%	Reelected	$2,368,218	$963,589	40.7%	$2,136,850	$556,585

Financially competitive U.S. House races — rare in most parts of the nation — were the rule rather than the exception in Nebraska and the Dakotas in 1990. Though all six of the area's incumbents were reelected, nearly all of them faced challengers with fairly substantial campaign budgets. None of the challengers were able to match the spending of the incumbents, however.

The one open-seat race was also competitive, both in dollars and votes. Republican Bill Barrett, speaker of Nebraska's unicameral legislature, was the eventual winner, polling a thin 51 percent majority against Democrat Sandra K. Scofield. The seat became vacant with the retirement of eight-term Republican Virginia Smith.

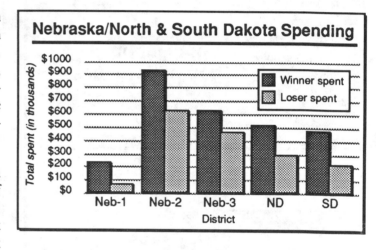

In Nebraska's 2nd congressional district, freshman Democrat Peter Hoagland spent nearly $930,000 ensuring his reelection to a seat he won two years earlier by one of the closest margins in the nation. Republican Ally Milder spent more than $625,000 in the 1990 contest, but Hoagland carried the district with nearly 58 percent of the vote.

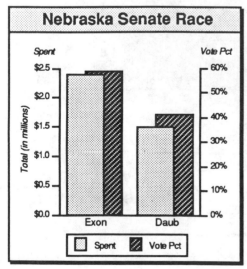

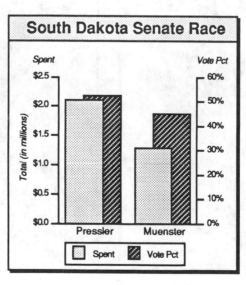

The Senate races in Nebraska and South Dakota were similar in spending and outcome, as both incumbents retained their seats. Democrat Jim Exon in Nebraska polled nearly 59 percent of the vote against former congressman Hal Daub, while Republican Larry Pressler of South Dakota won narrowly over Democratic challenger Ted Muenster.

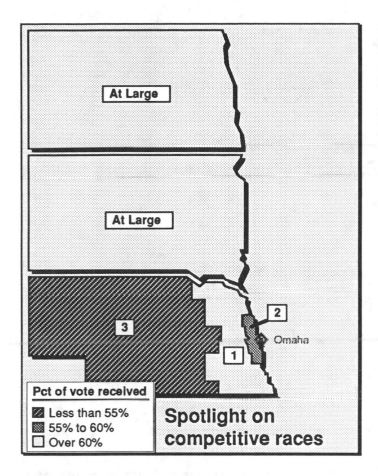

Pct of vote received
- ▨ Less than 55%
- ▨ 55% to 60%
- ☐ Over 60%

**Spotlight on
competitive races**

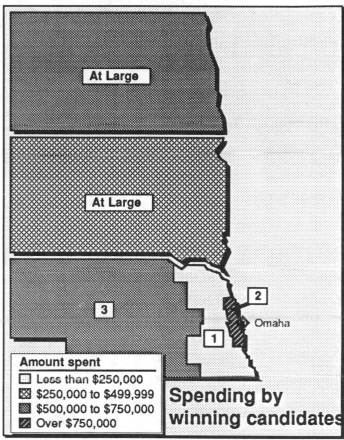

Amount spent
- ☐ Less than $250,000
- ▨ $250,000 to $499,999
- ▨ $500,000 to $750,000
- ▨ Over $750,000

**Spending by
winning candidates**

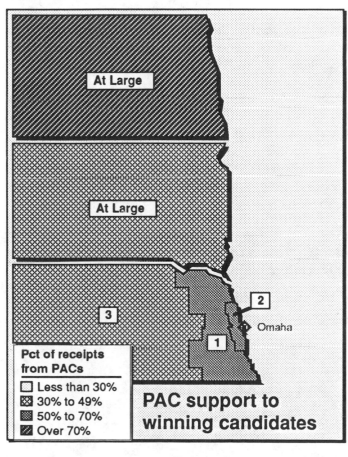

Pct of receipts
from PACs
- ☐ Less than 30%
- ▨ 30% to 49%
- ▨ 50% to 70%
- ▨ Over 70%

**PAC support to
winning candidates**

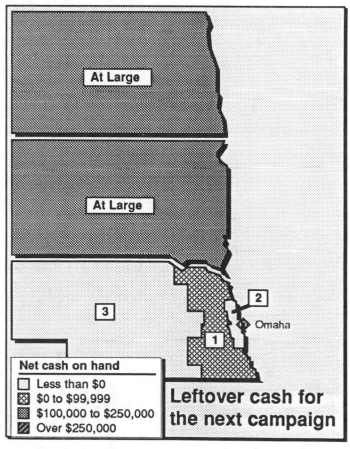

Net cash on hand
- ☐ Less than $0
- ▨ $0 to $99,999
- ▨ $100,000 to $250,000
- ▨ Over $250,000

**Leftover cash for
the next campaign**

Nevada/Utah

Vital Statistics of 1990 Winners

Dist	Name	Party	Vote Pct	Race Type	Total Receipts	PAC Receipts	PAC Pct	Spent	Net cash on Hand
Nevada									
1	James Bilbray	Dem	61.4%	Reelected	$686,010	$217,806	31.8%	$705,037	-$28,893
2	Barbara F. Vucanovich	Rep	59.1%	Reelected	$445,465	$165,675	37.2%	$441,075	-$9,295
Utah									
1	James V. Hansen	Rep	52.1%	Reelected	$271,159	$174,050	64.2%	$237,357	$41,944
2	Wayne Owens	Dem	57.6%	Reelected	$1,013,389	$540,732	53.4%	$1,083,427	-$7,098
3	Bill Orton	Dem	58.3%	Open	$86,601	$32,000	37.0%	$88,234	-$66,163

Though it is generally the most Republican-leaning state in the union in presidential elections, Utah now finds itself with a Democratic majority in its three-member U.S. House delegation — a fact that would have seemed improbable early in the 1990 election season.

Democratic incumbent Wayne Owens of Salt Lake City was considered vulnerable early in the race, but his odds improved dramatically when former congressman Dan Marriott was upset in the Republican primary by Genevieve Atwood, a former state legislator. Under Utah's open primary system, voters — whatever their party affiliation — may cast ballots for candidates of either party. In 1990, Democrats in large numbers crossed over to vote for Atwood, giving her the Republican nomination over the more potentially troublesome Marriott. In the general election, Democrat Owens poured over a million dollars into his reelection race and won with a relatively comfortable 57 percent of the vote.

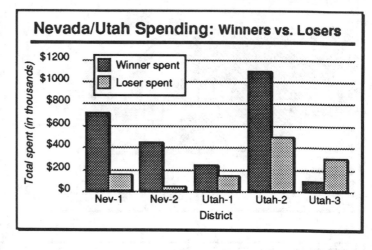

Nevada/Utah Spending: Winners vs. Losers

Meanwhile in Utah's rural 3rd congressional district, long considered a Republican stronghold, the retirement of incumbent Rep. Howard Nielson led to a scramble of candidates seeking the GOP nomination. While the Republicans were slugging it out, Democrat Bill Orton was busy staking out a conservative platform of his own. When the Republican nominee, Karl Snow, found himself unable to overcome lingering charges about questionable business dealings (charges originally brought to light during the Republican primary), Orton became the choice of the district's voters. The Democrat's victory was all the more unusual in that he spent only $88,000 on his election campaign — less than one-third the amount spent by Snow. It was the least expensive victory by a newly-elected candidate in the entire nation.

All in all, the 1990 elections were not entirely pleasant for the GOP in Utah. The one Republican incumbent who was reelected — James V. Hansen — carried only 52 percent of the vote.

Across the border in Nevada, both incumbents won by reasonably wide margins. Democrat James Bilbray and Republican Barbara Vucanovich substantially outspent their challengers.

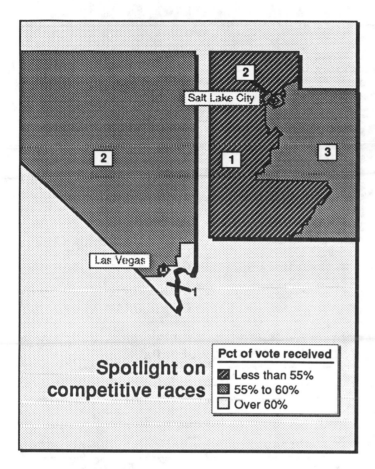

Spotlight on competitive races

Pct of vote received	
▨	Less than 55%
▨	55% to 60%
☐	Over 60%

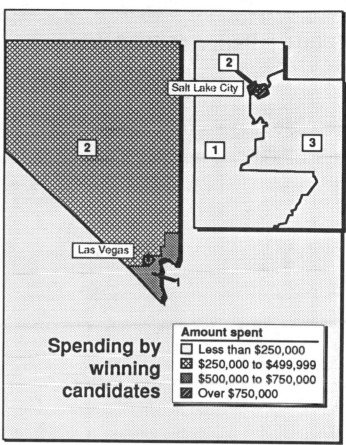

Spending by winning candidates

Amount spent	
☐	Less than $250,000
▨	$250,000 to $499,999
▨	$500,000 to $750,000
▨	Over $750,000

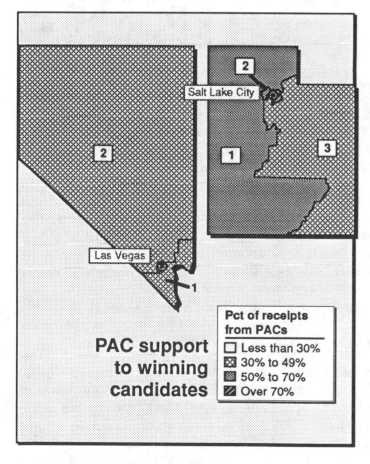

PAC support to winning candidates

Pct of receipts from PACs	
☐	Less than 30%
▨	30% to 49%
▨	50% to 70%
▨	Over 70%

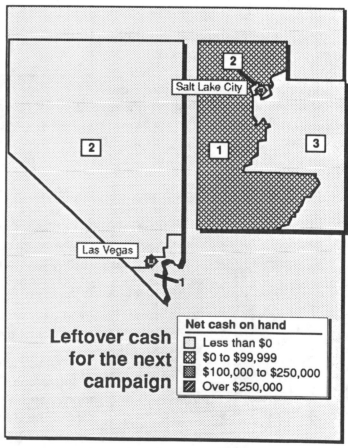

Leftover cash for the next campaign

Net cash on hand	
☐	Less than $0
▨	$0 to $99,999
▨	$100,000 to $250,000
▨	Over $250,000

New Jersey

Vital Statistics of 1990 Winners

Dist	Name	Party	Vote Pct	Race Type	Total Receipts	PAC Receipts	PAC Pct	Spent	Net cash on Hand
1	Robert E. Andrews	Dem	54.3%	Open	$542,535	$236,190	43.5%	$541,960	-$85,365
2	William J. Hughes	Dem	88.2%	Reelected	$282,731	$91,270	32.3%	$211,686	$208,172
3	Frank Pallone Jr.	Dem	49.1%	Reelected	$632,450	$394,314	62.4%	$634,109	-$53,610
4	Christopher H. Smith	Rep	62.9%	Reelected	$280,579	$113,116	40.3%	$292,826	$65,394
5	Marge Roukema	Rep	75.7%	Reelected	$446,589	$219,068	49.0%	$443,540	$96,290
6	Bernard J. Dwyer	Dem	50.5%	Reelected	$146,908	$125,747	85.6%	$147,925	$70,432
7	Matthew J. Rinaldo	Rep	74.6%	Reelected	$626,502	$240,920	38.5%	$405,355	$967,326
8	Robert A. Roe	Dem	76.9%	Reelected	$651,952	$328,910	50.5%	$558,625	$577,940
9	Robert G. Torricelli	Dem	57.0%	Reelected	$818,917	$236,389	28.9%	$495,219	$811,742
10	Donald M. Payne	Dem	81.5%	Reelected	$303,436	$185,642	61.2%	$168,522	$267,055
11	Dean A. Gallo	Rep	64.9%	Reelected	$652,386	$185,895	28.5%	$694,735	$71,891
12	Dick Zimmer	Rep	64.0%	Open	$1,228,793	$204,483	16.6%	$1,224,626	-$205,159
13	H. James Saxton	Rep	58.1%	Reelected	$628,142	$250,149	39.8%	$730,989	$48,861
14	Frank J. Guarini	Dem	66.1%	Reelected	$465,248	$303,133	65.2%	$316,782	$330,515
Sen	Bill Bradley	Dem	50.4%	Reelected	$12,874,229	$1,393,044	10.8%	$12,475,527	$692,770

New Jersey was the scene of two congressional races of particular note in 1990 — the open seat race in the state's 12th district was the most expensive in the nation, while the amazingly narrow reelection victory of Democratic Sen. Bill Bradley shocked both Bradley and political pundits nationwide.

Bradley's embarrassing close call — he captured just 50.4 percent of the vote against a political unknown — was attributed to the ferocity of New Jersey voters who were lashing out at Bradley for recent tax hikes by Democratic Gov. Jim Florio. Bradley, the highest-profile Democrat on the New Jersey ballot, spent $12.4 million in his reelection effort, against just $800,000 by Christine Todd Whitman, his Republican opponent. But in the end, the voters' anger was nearly enough to topple an incumbent widely assumed to be invulnerable both politically and financially.

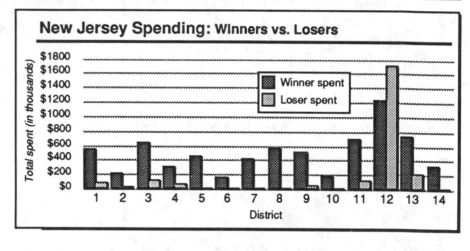

New Jersey Spending: Winners vs. Losers

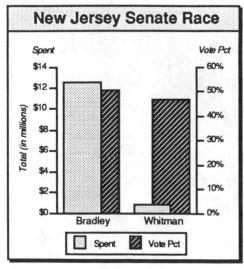

New Jersey Senate Race

Money seemed to be no object for either candidate in the open-seat race for New Jersey's 12th U.S. House district. The seat came open when Republican Jim Courter, the man who lost to Florio in the 1989 race for governor, decided not to seek another House term. Into the vacuum rushed Republican Dick Zimmer, former head of the New Jersey chapter of Common Cause, and Democrat Marguerite Chandler. Together, they spent $2.9 million fighting for the seat. Zimmer, though outspent, eventually prevailed. The loss was particularly costly for Chandler, since she put just over $1 million of her own money into the race.

Spending in the open seat race for New Jersey's 1st district was far more restrained. Democrat Robert Andrews spent the lion's share of money and captured 54 percent of the vote. The 12 incumbents in the rest of the state's House districts all won reelection, generally against candidates with extremely limited financial resources.

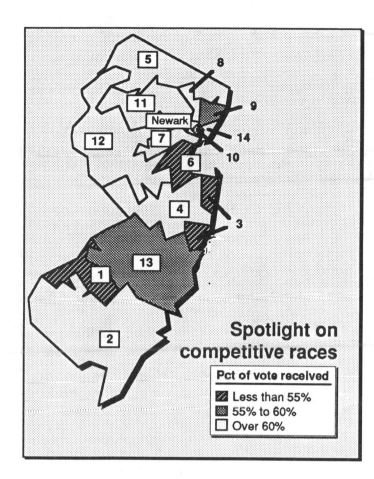

Spotlight on competitive races

Pct of vote received

- ▨ Less than 55%
- ▩ 55% to 60%
- ☐ Over 60%

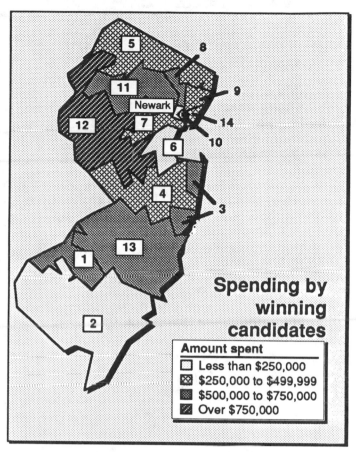

Spending by winning candidates

Amount spent

- ☐ Less than $250,000
- ▨ $250,000 to $499,999
- ▩ $500,000 to $750,000
- ▧ Over $750,000

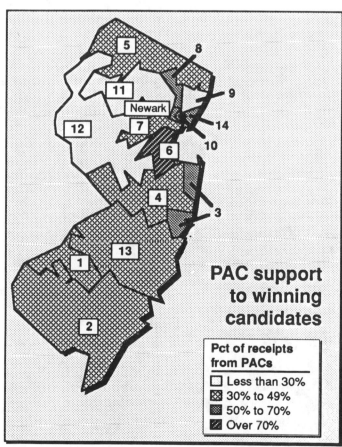

PAC support to winning candidates

Pct of receipts from PACs

- ☐ Less than 30%
- ▨ 30% to 49%
- ▩ 50% to 70%
- ▧ Over 70%

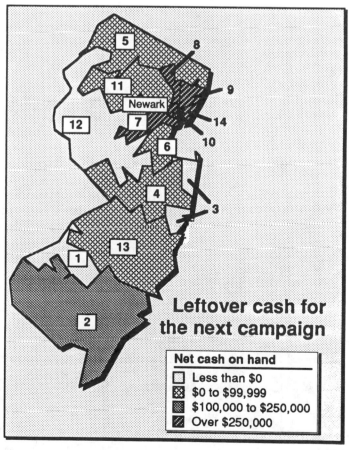

Leftover cash for the next campaign

Net cash on hand

- ☐ Less than $0
- ▨ $0 to $99,999
- ▩ $100,000 to $250,000
- ▧ Over $250,000

New Mexico

Vital Statistics of 1990 Winners

Dist	Name	Party	Vote Pct	Race Type	Total Receipts	PAC Receipts	PAC Pct	Spent	Net cash on Hand
1	Steven H. Schiff	Rep	70.2%	Reelected	$554,465	$222,203	40.1%	$538,273	$20,540
2	Joe Skeen	Rep	100.0%	Reelected	$197,830	$109,210	55.2%	$80,737	$195,431
3	Bill Richardson	Dem	74.5%	Reelected	$531,096	$346,707	65.3%	$420,907	$328,099
Sen	Pete V. Domenici	Rep	72.9%	Reelected	$2,434,289	$905,135	37.2%	$2,252,389	$218,513

Reelection was no problem for any of the incumbents in New Mexico during 1990. Only freshman congressman Steve Schiff, in the 1st district, faced an opponent with anything more than token financial resources. Schiff won easily, winning 70 percent of the vote and outspending Democratic state treasurer Rebecca Vigil-Giron by a margin of nearly five-to-one.

Bill Richardson, the Democratic incumbent in the 3rd district, took no chances in his reelection contest, pouring $420,000 into the race, versus the $21,000 spent by Republican challenger Phil Archuletta. Richardson captured three votes out of every four cast.

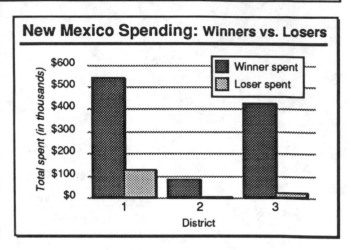

Republican Pete Domenici, meanwhile, coasted to his third term in the U.S. Senate with little difficulty. His opponent, State Sen. Tom Benavides, spent just $38,000 against Domenici's $2.2 million, and took only 27 percent of the vote.

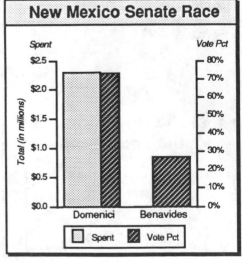

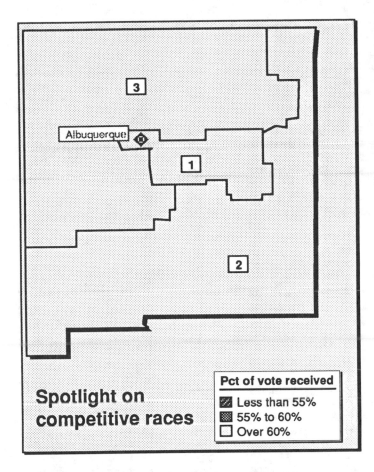

Spotlight on competitive races

Pct of vote received	
▨	Less than 55%
▨	55% to 60%
☐	Over 60%

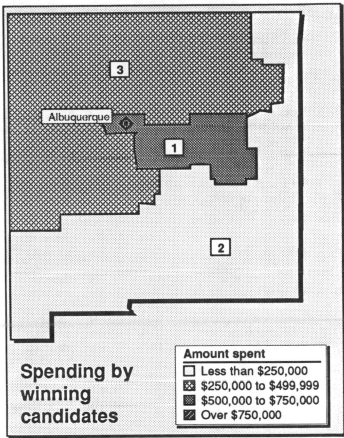

Spending by winning candidates

Amount spent	
☐	Less than $250,000
▨	$250,000 to $499,999
▨	$500,000 to $750,000
▨	Over $750,000

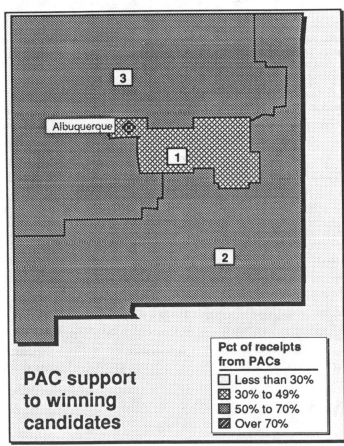

PAC support to winning candidates

Pct of receipts from PACs	
☐	Less than 30%
▨	30% to 49%
▨	50% to 70%
▨	Over 70%

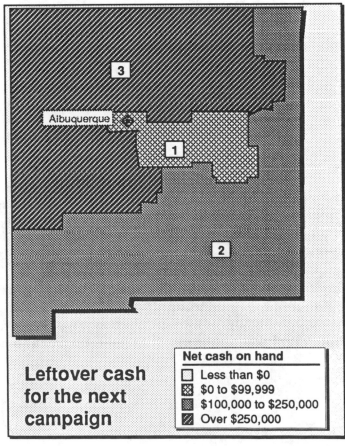

Leftover cash for the next campaign

Net cash on hand	
☐	Less than $0
▨	$0 to $99,999
▨	$100,000 to $250,000
▨	Over $250,000

New York

Vital Statistics of 1990 Winners

Dist	Name	Party	Vote Pct	Race Type	Total Receipts	PAC Receipts	PAC Pct	Spent	Net cash on Hand
1	George J. Hochbrueckner	Dem	56.3%	Reelected	$655,297	$394,362	60.2%	$638,635	$12,836
2	Thomas J. Downey	Dem	55.8%	Reelected	$612,878	$330,762	54.0%	$635,392	$486,556
3	Robert J. Mrazek	Dem	53.3%	Reelected	$602,613	$192,935	32.0%	$458,759	$351,185
4	Norman F. Lent	Rep	61.2%	Reelected	$596,305	$406,320	68.1%	$398,706	$687,015
5	Raymond J. McGrath	Rep	54.6%	Reelected	$537,366	$225,358	41.9%	$618,882	$244,622
6	Floyd H. Flake	Dem	73.1%	Reelected	$240,869	$122,440	50.8%	$205,031	$7,352
7	Gary L. Ackerman	Dem	100.0%	Reelected	$305,414	$186,537	61.1%	$272,549	$285,362
8	James H. Scheuer	Dem	72.3%	Reelected	$413,585	$95,040	23.0%	$400,349	-$293,151
9	Thomas J. Manton	Dem	64.4%	Reelected	$620,609	$452,323	72.9%	$316,301	$478,772
10	Charles E. Schumer	Dem	80.4%	Reelected	$841,900	$164,612	19.6%	$97,082	$1,580,475
11	Ed Towns	Dem	92.9%	Reelected	$335,807	$185,250	55.2%	$282,933	$151,035
12	Major R. Owens	Dem	94.9%	Reelected	$158,086	$111,525	70.5%	$172,498	-$18,410
13	Stephen J. Solarz	Dem	80.4%	Reelected	$1,218,914	$57,674	4.7%	$517,794	$1,859,603
14	Susan Molinari*	Rep	60.0%	Reelected	$157,229	$71,788	45.7%	$141,216	-$2,210
15	Bill Green	Rep	58.8%	Reelected	$705,383	$162,996	23.1%	$458,486	$73,107
16	Charles B. Rangel	Dem	97.2%	Reelected	$541,762	$351,150	64.8%	$601,550	$304,007
17	Ted Weiss	Dem	80.4%	Reelected	$144,408	$72,800	50.4%	$112,722	$80,492
18	José E. Serrano*	Dem	93.2%	Reelected	$111,390	$74,550	66.9%	$132,359	$11,391
19	Eliot L. Engel	Dem	61.2%	Reelected	$399,619	$324,173	81.1%	$389,698	-$35,119
20	Nita M. Lowey	Dem	62.8%	Reelected	$1,223,045	$448,797	36.7%	$911,766	-$65,515
21	Hamilton Fish Jr.	Rep	71.4%	Reelected	$348,209	$204,990	58.9%	$411,614	$134,830
22	Benjamin A. Gilman	Rep	68.6%	Reelected	$445,481	$195,968	44.0%	$497,635	$68,257
23	Michael R. Mcnulty	Dem	64.1%	Reelected	$240,736	$149,179	62.0%	$149,204	$100,394
24	Gerald B. H. Solomon	Rep	68.1%	Reelected	$255,758	$144,215	56.4%	$240,615	$111,840
25	Sherwood Boehlert	Rep	83.9%	Reelected	$303,746	$130,650	43.0%	$272,533	$189,652
26	David O'B Martin	Rep	100.0%	Reelected	$74,891	$52,050	69.5%	$59,112	$84,339
27	James T. Walsh	Rep	63.2%	Reelected	$365,536	$139,936	38.3%	$340,553	$38,110
28	Matthew F. McHugh	Dem	64.8%	Reelected	$227,716	$121,715	53.5%	$200,047	$137,521
29	Frank Horton	Rep	63.0%	Reelected	$207,092	$160,040	77.3%	$186,967	$162,845
30	Louise M. Slaughter	Dem	59.0%	Reelected	$446,664	$282,817	63.3%	$322,216	$117,797
31	Bill Paxon	Rep	56.6%	Reelected	$686,209	$230,219	33.5%	$506,343	$177,950
32	John J. LaFalce	Dem	55.0%	Reelected	$339,919	$195,675	57.6%	$145,079	$645,138
33	Henry J. Nowak	Dem	77.5%	Reelected	$150,832	$98,908	65.6%	$93,158	$238,450
34	Amo Houghton	Rep	69.6%	Reelected	$333,962	$102,000	30.5%	$178,401	$306,780

Every last incumbent in New York's 34 congressional districts was successfully reelected in 1990, but for three of them — at least — the term will be their last in the U.S. House of Representatives. No state in the union will be as negatively affected by reapportionment as New York, whose population growth has stagnated in the face of the nation's continuing southern and western migration. When the 103rd Congress convenes in January 1993, New York will be represented by only 31 members in the U.S. House — a loss of three seats from its current allocation. When the new districts are drawn, it seems inevitable that a number of incumbents will either have to retire, seek other office, or face the unhappy prospect of squaring off against a fellow incumbent in a district new to both of them.

Many members of the New York delegation may have been looking ahead at that difficult election when they ran in 1990, holding substantial sums in reserve. Twenty-one incumbents closed out 1990 with more than $100,000 in the bank, ready for the next election. Two Brooklyn lawmakers — Charles Schumer and Stephen Solarz — began 1991 with war chests of $1.5 million and $1.8 million respectively.

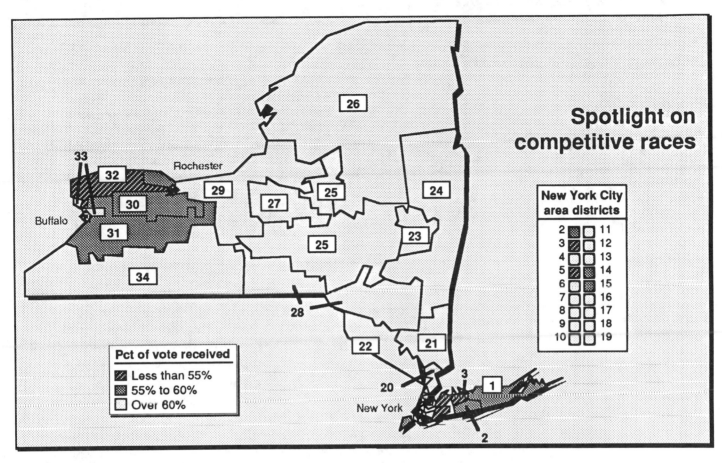

Spotlight on competitive races

New York City area districts

2	▦	11 □
3	▨	12 □
4		13 □
5		14 □
6		15 ▦
7	□	16 □
8	□	17 □
9	□	18 □
10	□	19 □

Pct of vote received
- ▨ Less than 55%
- ▦ 55% to 60%
- □ Over 60%

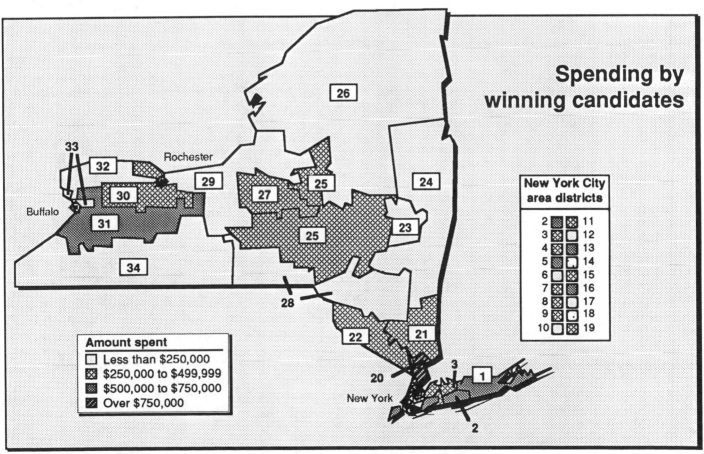

Spending by winning candidates

New York City area districts

2	▦	11 ▨
3	▨	12 □
4	▨	13 □
5		14 □
6	□	15 ▨
7	▨	16 ▨
8	▨	17 □
9	▨	18 □
10	□	19 ▨

Amount spent
- □ Less than $250,000
- ▨ $250,000 to $499,999
- ▦ $500,000 to $750,000
- ▨ Over $750,000

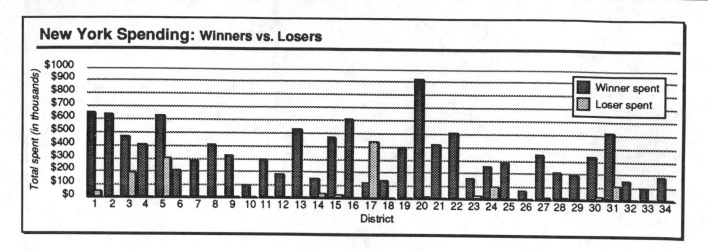

New York Spending: Winners vs. Losers

Total spent (in thousands) — District

Legend: ■ Winner spent / ▨ Loser spent

Not all New York congressman had the luxury of focusing on the election two years hence. Eight incumbents failed to draw at least 60 percent of the vote in 1990. Of those, the closest races were those of Long Island-based Robert Mrazek and Raymond McGrath, and John LaFalce of Buffalo. Mrazek, in the 3rd district, and McGrath, in the 5th, were two of a handful of incumbents whose opponents were able to muster more than a token amount of money. Mrazek's challenger, Republican Robert Previdi spent $184,000 in his upset bit. McGrath was challenged by Democrat Mark Epstein, who put more than $300,000 into the effort. Both Mrazek and McGrath still managed to outspend their challengers by more than two-to-one.

By contrast, LaFalce spent just $145,000 in his reelection effort. His opponent, Republican Michael Waring didn't report spending anything at all.

But money alone was no guarantee of victory. Democrat Ted Weiss, in the 17th district in New York City, was vastly outspent by Republican William Koeppel, who poured $431,000 into his campaign—more than half from his own pocket. But Weiss walked off with 80 percent of the vote on election day.

The most expensive campaign in the state was that of freshman congresswoman Nita Lowey in the 20th congressional district. Lowey first won the seat in 1988, in a top-dollar spending battle against incumbent Joseph DioGuardi. This time she polled nearly 63 percent of the vote, spending just over $900,000 against an opponent who spent $15,000.

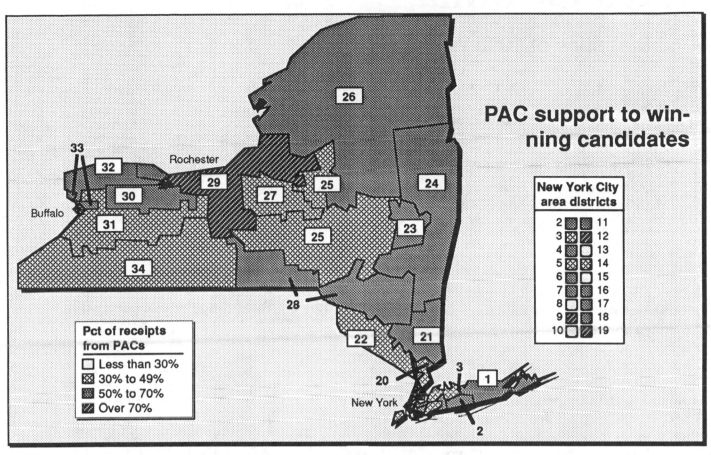

PAC support to win-
ning candidates

New York City area districts

2		11
3		12
4		13
5		14
6		15
7		16
8		17
9		18
10		19

Pct of receipts from PACs
- ☐ Less than 30%
- ▧ 30% to 49%
- ▦ 50% to 70%
- ▨ Over 70%

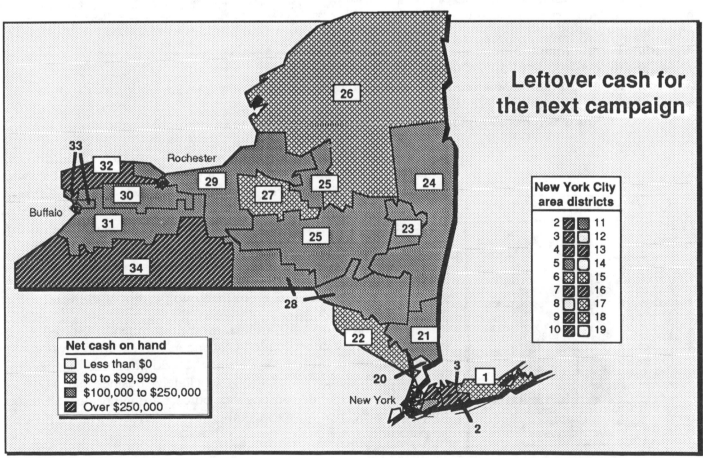

Leftover cash for
the next campaign

New York City area districts

2		11
3		12
4		13
5		14
6		15
7		16
8		17
9		18
10		19

Net cash on hand
- ☐ Less than $0
- ▧ $0 to $99,999
- ▦ $100,000 to $250,000
- ▨ Over $250,000

North Carolina

Vital Statistics of 1990 Winners

Dist	Name	Party	Vote Pct	Race Type	Total Receipts	PAC Receipts	PAC Pct	Spent	Net cash on Hand
1	Walter B. Jones	Dem	64.8%	Reelected	$127,710	$72,100	56.5%	$111,622	$328,428
2	Tim Valentine	Dem	74.7%	Reelected	$261,712	$159,202	60.8%	$286,351	$20,314
3	H. Martin Lancaster	Dem	59.3%	Reelected	$421,283	$203,700	48.4%	$499,436	$20,581
4	David E. Price	Dem	58.1%	Reelected	$771,624	$385,210	49.9%	$793,291	-$38,879
5	Stephen L. Neal	Dem	59.1%	Reelected	$671,884	$394,629	58.7%	$647,331	$25,591
6	Howard Coble	Rep	66.6%	Reelected	$572,043	$223,860	39.1%	$572,846	$15,846
7	Charlie Rose	Dem	65.6%	Reelected	$328,232	$193,404	58.9%	$153,315	$490,833
8	W. G. "Bill" Hefner	Dem	55.0%	Reelected	$660,311	$445,293	67.4%	$656,383	$100,710
9	Alex McMillan	Rep	62.0%	Reelected	$399,007	$275,435	69.0%	$385,183	$103,331
10	Cass Ballenger	Rep	61.8%	Reelected	$297,417	$183,749	61.8%	$302,006	$21,544
11	Charles H. Taylor	Rep	50.7%	Beat Incumb	$523,580	$111,689	21.3%	$523,867	-$433,924
Sen	Jesse Helms	Rep	52.6%	Reelected	$17,738,765	$994,336	5.6%	$17,761,579	-$901,962

Republican Sen. Jesse Helms, long a lightning rod for political activists (and fundraisers) of both left and right, spent more than $17.7 million defending his U.S. Senate seat in 1990. It was the most expensive Senate race ever run, breaking Helms' own record, set in 1984. After an acrimonious and expensive campaign that focused attention on North Carolina from contributors all over the nation, Helms defeated Democrat Harvey Gantt, former mayor of Charlotte. The prospect of the nation's best-known arch-conservative running against a progressive black prompted great national interest, and an outpouring of dollars to both

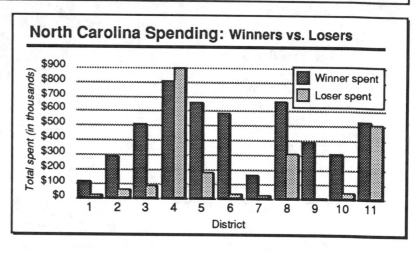

camps from all over the nation. Much of it came through direct-mail fundraising appeals — the style of fundraising that has long been Helms' favorite. The high cost of prospecting nationwide for small contributions through direct mail was one factor which has always made Helms' Senate campaigns the highest in the nation.

Though eclipsed in attention by the Helms-Gantt race, the U.S. House races in North Carolina were not without a drama of their own. The most contentious district of all, in the far-west 11th district, saw Republican Charles Taylor finally win the seat he lost narrowly two years earlier to James McClure Clarke, the incumbent Democrat. The district over the past eight years has proven to be the most topsy-turvy in the nation. Clarke first won the seat in 1982. He lost it again in 1984, won it again in 1986 and '88, then lost it in 1990. Not one of those elections was decided by a margin of more than two percent of the vote.

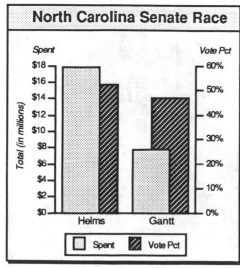

All other races in North Carolina saw the incumbents reelected, most commonly against under-funded challengers. An exception was in the 4th district, where incumbent Democrat David Price was outspent by Republican challenger John Carrington, a Raleigh businessman who had twice run unsuccessfully for statewide office. Carrington spent $890,000 trying to unseat Price, but the incumbent eventually won a new term with 58 percent of the vote.

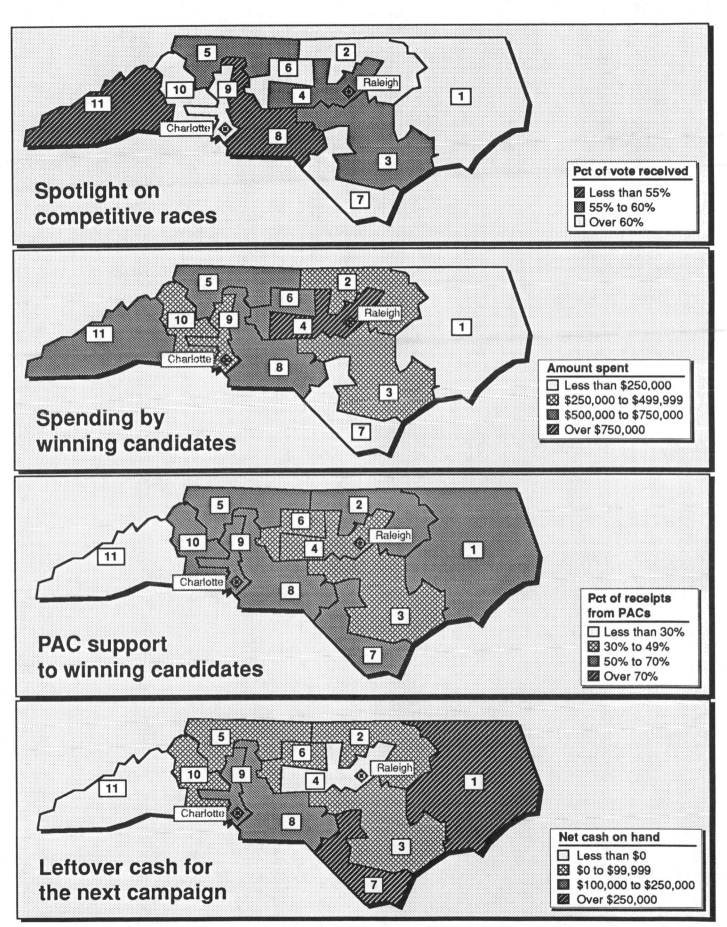

Spotlight on competitive races

Pct of vote received
- Less than 55%
- 55% to 60%
- Over 60%

Spending by winning candidates

Amount spent
- Less than $250,000
- $250,000 to $499,999
- $500,000 to $750,000
- Over $750,000

PAC support to winning candidates

Pct of receipts from PACs
- Less than 30%
- 30% to 49%
- 50% to 70%
- Over 70%

Leftover cash for the next campaign

Net cash on hand
- Less than $0
- $0 to $99,999
- $100,000 to $250,000
- Over $250,000

Ohio

Vital Statistics of 1990 Winners

Dist	Name	Party	Vote Pct	Race Type	Total Receipts	PAC Receipts	PAC Pct	Spent	Net cash on Hand
1	Charles Luken	Dem	51.1%	Open	$680,789	$369,725	54.3%	$651,544	$29,243
2	Bill Gradison	Rep	64.4%	Reelected	$202,259	$0	0.0%	$124,331	$442,751
3	Tony P. Hall	Dem	100.0%	Reelected	$173,805	$130,592	75.1%	$133,861	$312,635
4	Michael G. Oxley	Rep	61.7%	Reelected	$298,581	$200,233	67.1%	$330,272	$188,791
5	Paul E. Gillmor	Rep	68.5%	Reelected	$325,743	$230,425	70.7%	$254,688	$83,139
6	Bob McEwen	Rep	71.2%	Reelected	$292,650	$144,630	49.4%	$196,934	$118,666
7	David L. Hobson	Rep	62.1%	Open	$389,738	$202,177	51.9%	$389,136	-$13,406
8	John A. Boehner	Rep	61.1%	Beat Incumb	$737,441	$219,526	29.8%	$732,765	-$186,381
9	Marcy Kaptur	Dem	77.7%	Reelected	$227,820	$114,830	50.4%	$211,524	$58,129
10	Clarence E. Miller	Rep	63.2%	Reelected	$99,589	$69,250	69.5%	$75,367	$126,334
11	Dennis E. Eckart	Dem	65.7%	Reelected	$510,699	$370,536	72.5%	$453,883	$157,940
12	John R. Kasich	Rep	72.0%	Reelected	$328,624	$128,715	39.2%	$278,977	$93,542
13	Don J. Pease	Dem	56.7%	Reelected	$311,899	$184,728	59.2%	$348,032	$221,677
14	Thomas C. Sawyer	Dem	59.6%	Reelected	$262,812	$187,195	71.2%	$264,793	$47,519
15	Chalmers P. Wylie	Rep	59.1%	Reelected	$227,878	$167,153	73.3%	$242,592	$18,194
16	Ralph Regula	Rep	58.9%	Reelected	$110,331	$0	0.0%	$156,205	$52,654
17	James A. Traficant Jr.	Dem	77.7%	Reelected	$99,644	$54,930	55.1%	$79,064	$76,169
18	Douglas Applegate	Dem	74.3%	Reelected	$125,772	$78,205	62.2%	$94,754	$161,523
19	Edward F. Feighan	Dem	64.8%	Reelected	$323,072	$217,618	67.4%	$229,857	$287,445
20	Mary Rose Oakar	Dem	73.3%	Reelected	$337,442	$283,209	83.9%	$284,053	$54,525
21	Louis Stokes	Dem	80.0%	Reelected	$250,022	$137,575	55.0%	$198,984	$241,864

The first shuffling of the lineup in Ohio's congressional delegation came early in the election season, when Republican John A. Boehner ousted scandal-plagued incumbent Buzz Lukens in the May GOP primary. Lukens had become the bane of Ohio Republicans, refusing to step down from office after being convicted in a sex scandal involving a 16-year-old girl. Boehner won the general election as well, outspending Democrat Gregory Jolivette by more than six-to-one.

One of the closest races in the state, and the most expensive by far in total spending was in the 1st congressional district in Cincinnati. Incumbent Democrat Thomas Luken (no relation to Lukens in the 8th district) announced his retirement, setting up a contest between his son Charles, the mayor of Cincinnati, and Republican J. Kenneth Blackwell, a former city councilman who himself had served a one-year term as mayor. Blackwell and Luken each spent upwards of $650,000; on election day Luken was the winner, with just 51 percent of the vote.

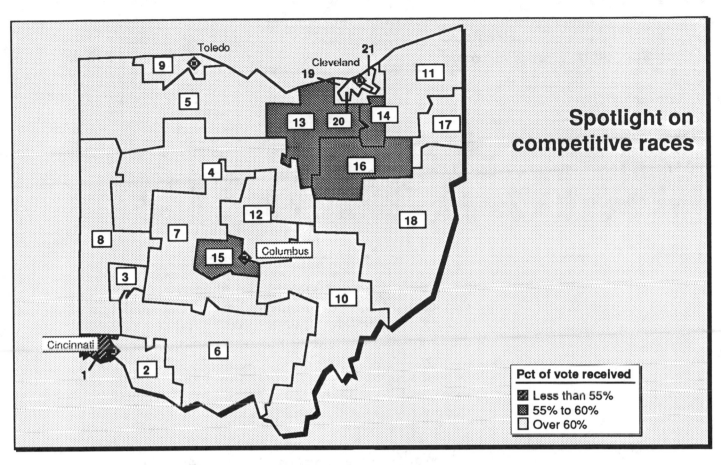

Spotlight on competitive races

Pct of vote received
- Less than 55%
- 55% to 60%
- Over 60%

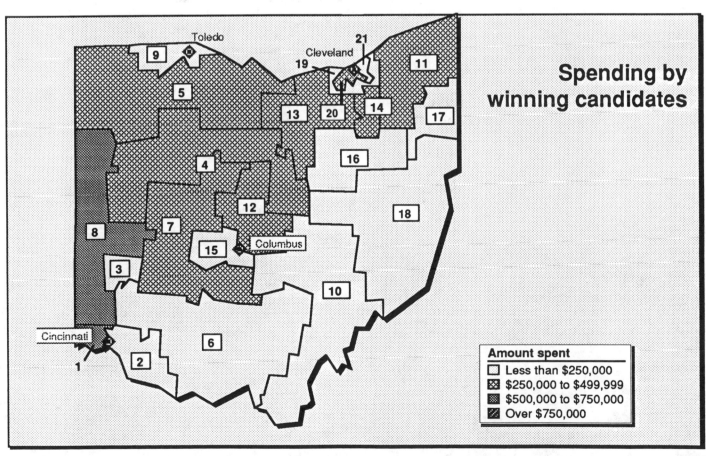

Spending by winning candidates

Amount spent
- Less than $250,000
- $250,000 to $499,999
- $500,000 to $750,000
- Over $750,000

Ohio *(cont'd)*

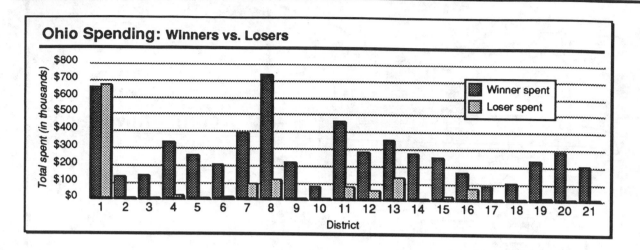

Ohio Spending: Winners vs. Losers

Total spent (in thousands) — Winner spent / Loser spent — *District*

Another open seat race, in the 7th district, was decided by a much wider margin — both in dollars and votes. Republican David Hobson, president pro tem of the Ohio state Senate, carried 62 percent of the vote, keeping the seat Republican after incumbent Mike DeWine stepped down to run for Lt. Governor. Hobson spent nearly $390,000 in the race, versus a Democratic challenger who spent less than $90,000.

Elsewhere in the state, all incumbents who sought reelection (with the exception of Buzz Lukens) were successful. Two of them, Republicans Bill Gradison of the 2nd district and Ralph Regula of the 16th, were among the handful of House members nationwide who financed their campaigns without the help of political action committees. On the opposite side of the spectrum was Cleveland Democrat Mary Rose Oakar, who relied on PACs for nearly 84 percent of her campaign cash.

Like several of its neighboring rust-belt states, Ohio lost ground to the faster-growing sunbelt states in the 1990 census. As a result, the state will lose two of its seats in the U.S. House of Representatives, beginning with the 1992 elections.

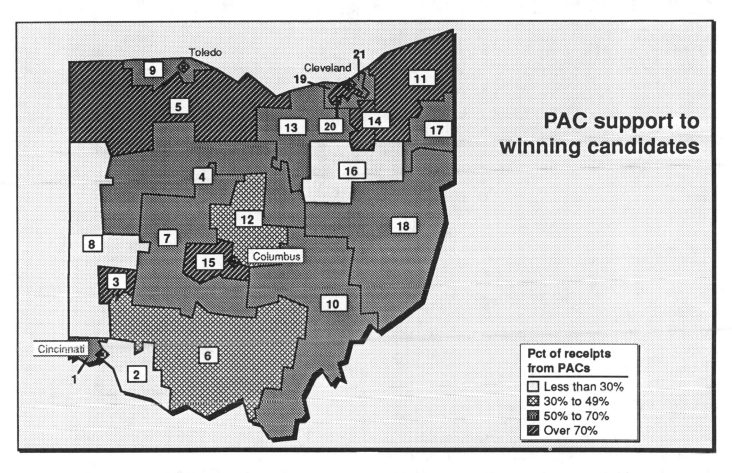

**PAC support to
winning candidates**

Pct of receipts
from PACs
- Less than 30%
- 30% to 49%
- 50% to 70%
- Over 70%

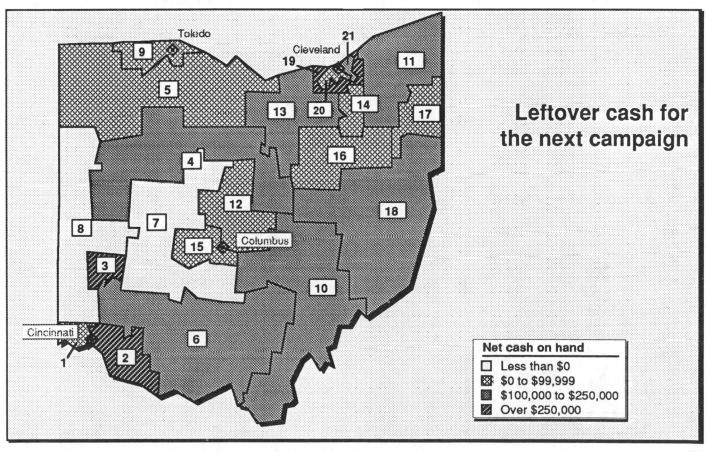

**Leftover cash for
the next campaign**

Net cash on hand
- Less than $0
- $0 to $99,999
- $100,000 to $250,000
- Over $250,000

Oklahoma

Vital Statistics of 1990 Winners

Dist	Name	Party	Vote Pct	Race Type	Total Receipts	PAC Receipts	PAC Pct	Spent	Net cash on Hand
1	James M. Inhofe	Rep	56.0%	Reelected	$609,786	$306,071	50.2%	$612,116	-$27,105
2	Mike Synar	Dem	61.3%	Reelected	$622,454	$2,038	0.3%	$631,839	$24,882
3	Bill Brewster	Dem	80.4%	Open	$448,824	$177,266	39.5%	$446,766	$2,055
4	Dave McCurdy	Dem	73.6%	Reelected	$342,376	$149,775	43.8%	$357,531	$81,622
5	Mickey Edwards	Rep	69.6%	Reelected	$326,283	$147,525	45.2%	$373,414	$13,371
6	Glenn English	Dem	80.0%	Reelected	$238,141	$145,150	61.0%	$157,414	$324,042
Sen	David L. Boren	Dem	83.2%	Reelected	$1,716,590	-$500	0.0%	$1,610,921	$158,133

Only one congressional race in Oklahoma was financially competitive in the 1990 elections, though even there the challenger did not prevail. Republican incumbent James Inhofe, in the 1st district, faced a rematch with the man who held him to less than 53 percent in 1988 — Democrat attorney Kurt Glassco. Glassco this time spent $406,000 on the race, while Inhofe increased his own spending to $612,000. On election day, Inhofe captured 56 percent of the vote.

That was the closest congressional race in Oklahoma in 1990. All other incumbents were reelected by comfortable margins. Even the one open seat race — in the 3rd district — was a runaway, as Democratic

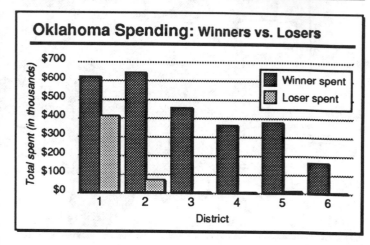

State Rep. Bill Brewster captured 80 percent of the vote and swamped a Republican rival who did not report spending any money at all on his campaign. The seat came open when incumbent Wes Watkins sought the Democratic nomination for governor instead of filing for reelection. Watkins later lost in the Democratic primary. The 3rd district has remained in Democratic hands ever since Oklahoma first became a state in 1907.

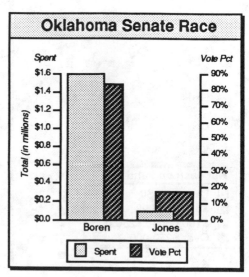

Democratic Sen. David Boren was never seriously challenged in his bid for a third U.S. Senate term. Boren's opponent, Stephen Jones, could only muster a campaign treasury of $140,000 — more than half of which came from his own pocket. Boren spent $1.6 million, a modest sum by Senate standards, but sufficient enough to bring the popular Oklahoman 83 percent of the vote on election day.

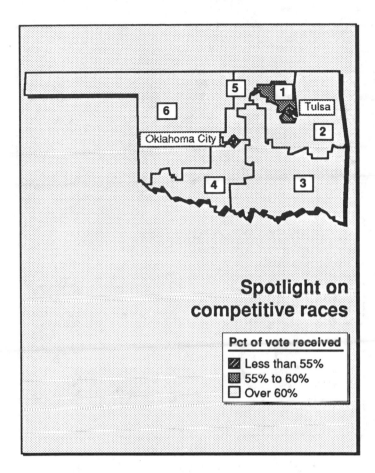

Spotlight on competitive races

Pct of vote received
- Less than 55%
- 55% to 60%
- Over 60%

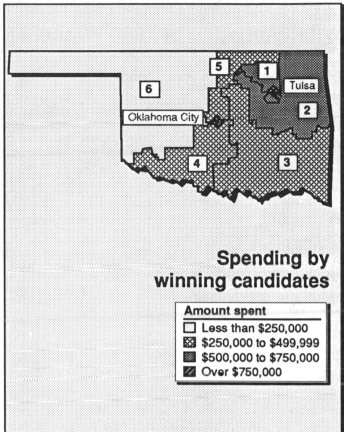

Spending by winning candidates

Amount spent
- Less than $250,000
- $250,000 to $499,999
- $500,000 to $750,000
- Over $750,000

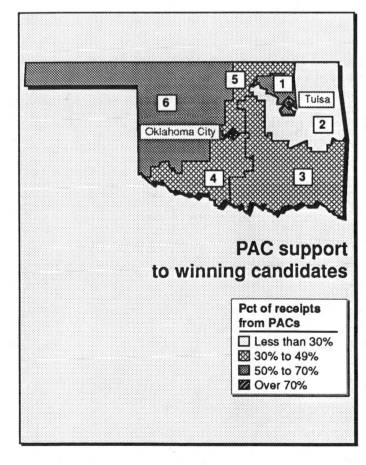

PAC support to winning candidates

Pct of receipts from PACs
- Less than 30%
- 30% to 49%
- 50% to 70%
- Over 70%

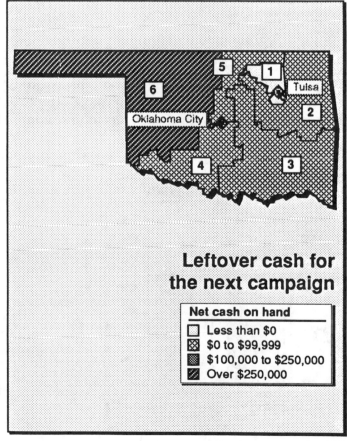

Leftover cash for the next campaign

Net cash on hand
- Less than $0
- $0 to $99,999
- $100,000 to $250,000
- Over $250,000

Oregon

Vital Statistics of 1990 Winners

Dist	Name	Party	Vote Pct	Race Type	Total Receipts	PAC Receipts	PAC Pct	Spent	Net cash on Hand
1	Les AuCoin	Dem	63.1%	Reelected	$599,295	$308,748	51.5%	$445,342	$361,578
2	Bob Smith	Rep	68.0%	Reelected	$374,114	$148,953	39.8%	$284,700	$179,736
3	Ron Wyden	Dem	80.8%	Reelected	$708,598	$340,642	48.1%	$693,855	$451,751
4	Peter A. DeFazio	Dem	85.8%	Reelected	$257,547	$172,635	67.0%	$217,527	$95,794
5	Mike Kopetski	Dem	55.0%	Beat Incumb	$850,229	$398,783	46.9%	$844,797	-$33,135
Sen	Mark O. Hatfield	Rep	53.7%	Reelected	$2,518,181	$1,049,085	41.7%	$2,749,232	-$20,891

In only two of Oregon's half-dozen congressional races in 1990 was the outcome ever in doubt: the cat-and-mouse contest between Mike Kopetski and incumbent Republican Denny Smith in the 5th U.S. House district, and the Senate race between Republican Mark Hatfield and millionaire businessman Harry Lonsdale.

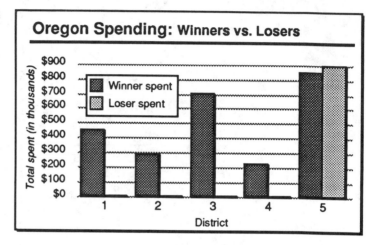

Borrowing a chapter from the successful tactics of Wisconsin entrepreneur Herb Kohl (who self-financed his 1988 Senate victory), Lonsdale attacked Hatfield's dependence on funding by political action committees and honoraria from special interests. At the same time, he dug deeper and deeper into his own pockets. By the time it was over, Lonsdale had put $743,000 of his own money into his $1.5 million campaign. It was enough to chip into the Republican's support, but not enough to derail him. On election day, Hatfield drew nearly 54 percent of the vote, winning election to his fifth term in the U.S. Senate.

Meanwhile, in the 5th congressional district south of Portland, Republican incumbent Denny Smith was facing a rematch of his 1988 contest with Democrat Mike Kopetski. Kopetski had nearly toppled Smith that year, losing by only 707 votes despite being heavily outspent. In 1990, both candidates stepped up their spending — Kopetski spent $844,000 while Smith spent $884,000. This time Kopetski prevailed, attracting 55 percent at the polls and becoming one of only 16 challengers to unseat incumbents in the U.S. House.

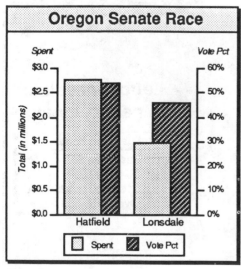

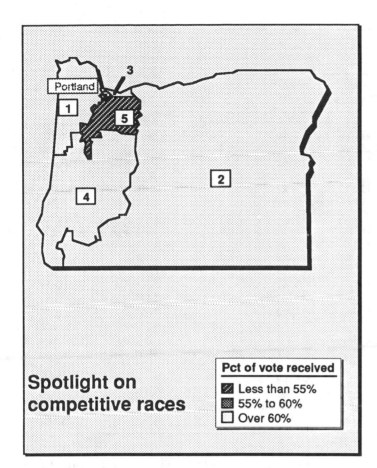

Spotlight on competitive races

Pct of vote received
- Less than 55%
- 55% to 60%
- Over 60%

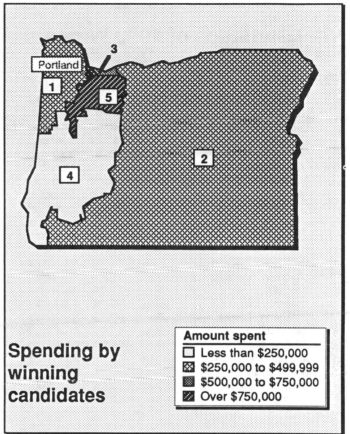

Spending by winning candidates

Amount spent
- Less than $250,000
- $250,000 to $499,999
- $500,000 to $750,000
- Over $750,000

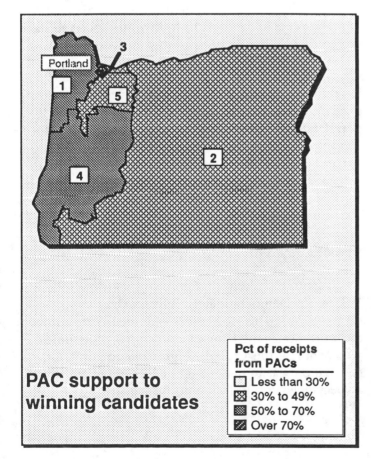

PAC support to winning candidates

Pct of receipts from PACs
- Less than 30%
- 30% to 49%
- 50% to 70%
- Over 70%

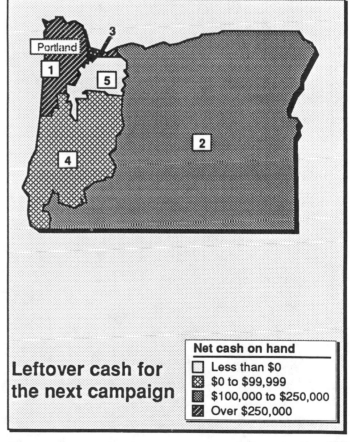

Leftover cash for the next campaign

Net cash on hand
- Less than $0
- $0 to $99,999
- $100,000 to $250,000
- Over $250,000

Pennsylvania

Vital Statistics of 1990 Winners

Dist	Name	Party	Vote Pct	Race Type	Total Receipts	PAC Receipts	PAC Pct	Spent	Net cash on Hand
1	Thomas M. Foglietta	Dem	79.4%	Reelected	$465,228	$226,918	48.8%	$234,057	$366,322
2	William H. Gray III	Dem	92.1%	Reelected	$725,717	$516,953	71.2%	$814,125	$54,497
3	Robert A. Borski	Dem	60.0%	Reelected	$325,222	$152,800	47.0%	$277,011	$155,234
4	Joe Kolter	Dem	55.9%	Reelected	$199,605	$162,520	81.4%	$132,920	$215,765
5	Richard T. Schulze	Rep	57.1%	Reelected	$578,161	$370,759	64.1%	$672,705	$182,353
6	Gus Yatron	Dem	57.0%	Reelected	$204,114	$127,955	62.7%	$191,152	$157,501
7	Curt Weldon	Rep	65.3%	Reelected	$504,744	$207,505	41.1%	$480,165	$135,094
8	Peter H. Kostmayer	Dem	56.6%	Reelected	$759,657	$295,528	38.9%	$826,742	-$36,288
9	Bud Shuster	Rep	100.0%	Reelected	$417,658	$181,469	43.5%	$429,942	$102,101
10	Joseph M. McDade	Rep	100.0%	Reelected	$383,030	$236,778	61.8%	$373,388	$335,857
11	Paul E. Kanjorski	Dem	100.0%	Reelected	$308,351	$223,935	72.6%	$405,637	$94,480
12	John P. Murtha	Dem	61.7%	Reelected	$878,887	$496,920	56.5%	$1,097,107	$33,122
13	Lawrence Coughlin	Rep	60.3%	Reelected	$373,205	$163,969	43.9%	$235,766	$356,517
14	William J. Coyne	Dem	71.8%	Reelected	$156,692	$141,600	90.4%	$130,904	$229,457
15	Don Ritter	Rep	60.6%	Reelected	$560,729	$273,606	48.8%	$577,790	$25,821
16	Robert S. Walker	Rep	66.1%	Reelected	$96,737	$43,810	45.3%	$98,284	$35,408
17	George W. Gekas	Rep	100.0%	Reelected	$128,438	$53,410	41.6%	$93,331	$141,544
18	Rick Santorum	Rep	51.4%	Beat Incumb	$257,786	$27,660	10.7%	$251,496	$6,289
19	Bill Goodling	Rep	100.0%	Reelected	$41,011	$0	0.0%	$40,698	$6,251
20	Joseph M. Gaydos	Dem	65.6%	Reelected	$191,541	$158,250	82.6%	$158,677	$123,222
21	Tom Ridge	Rep	100.0%	Reelected	$454,349	$246,265	54.2%	$361,712	$226,719
22	Austin J. Murphy	Dem	63.3%	Reelected	$199,802	$139,310	69.7%	$191,739	$111,254
23	William F. Clinger Jr.	Rep	59.4%	Reelected	$349,208	$190,302	54.5%	$338,431	$73,577

The 1990 election produced only one shift in the makeup of Pennsylvania's congressional delegation, though events in the months following shook the state more powerfully.

The April 1991 death of Republican Sen. John Heinz in a mid-air collision between a helicopter and the small plane in which he was riding removed a powerful and popular figure from Pennsylvania politics. The vacancy was filled a month later, when Democratic Gov. Robert P. Casey named fellow Democrat Harris Wofford to the Senate seat. A special election to fill the remainder of Heinz's unexpired term was scheduled for November 1991. Wofford's opponent in that race was former Attorney General (and former Pennsylvania Governor) Dick Thornburgh.

The other shakeup in Pennsylvania came June 26, 1991 when Democratic Rep. William Gray announced he would resign his House seat — as well as the number three position in the House leadership — to assume the presidency of the United Negro College Fund. Gray's resignation was to take effect in September 1991, with a special election to follow to fill the seat.

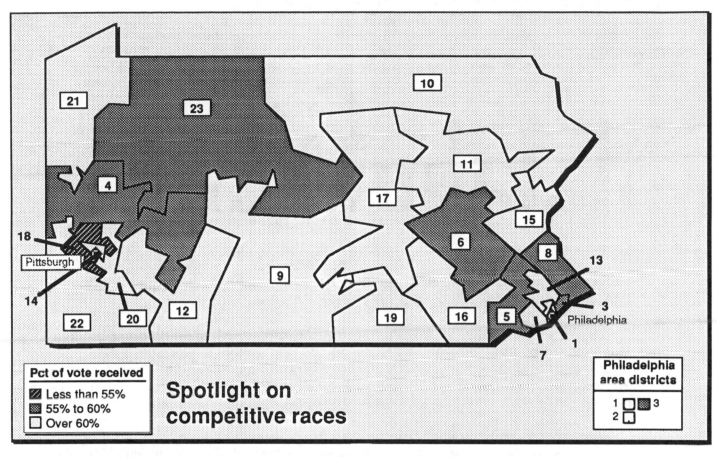

Pct of vote received

- Less than 55%
- 55% to 60%
- Over 60%

Spotlight on competitive races

Philadelphia area districts

1 □   3 ▦
2 □

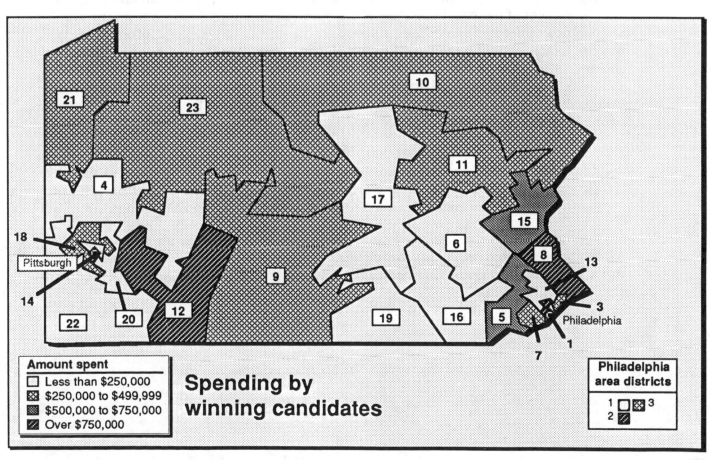

Amount spent

- Less than $250,000
- $250,000 to $499,999
- $500,000 to $750,000
- Over $750,000

Spending by winning candidates

Philadelphia area districts

1 □   3 ▦
2 ▨

129

Pennsylvania *(cont'd)*

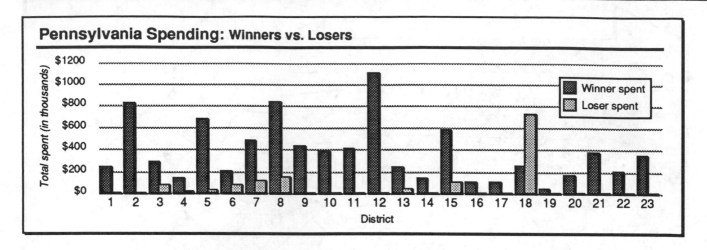

Pennsylvania Spending: Winners vs. Losers

Total spent (in thousands) — District

Legend: ■ Winner spent ▨ Loser spent

During the 1990 elections, Pennsylvania voters did remove one incumbent from office — and nearly dismissed a second in an unexpectedly close primary race.

Democrat Doug Walgren, a seven-term congressman from the 18th district near Pittsburgh, was defeated by Rick Santorum, a Republican attorney. Santorum overcame a formidable spending disadvantage, but played Walgren's extensive fund-raising from political action committees to his advantage. In all, the incumbent collected over $423,000 from PACs in a campaign that cost $717,000 in all. Santorum spent just $251,000.

The other incumbent who came within a hair's breadth of losing his seat was also embarrassed by his PAC riches. Veteran Democrat John P. Murtha, of the 12th district, carried only 51 percent of the vote in the May 15 Democratic primary — nearly losing his seat to a political newcomer who blasted the incumbent for becoming overly dependent on out-of-state defense contractors for his campaign funding. Murtha is chairman of the defense appropriations subcommittee, and was the top House recipient of defense industry PAC contributions in the 1990 elections. He took no chances after the unexpectedly close call in the primary, and eventually spent nearly $1.1 million on his reelection bid. He won the general election with over 61 percent of the vote.

Looking at the overall spending figures, it seems surprising that challengers did as well as they did. Few were able to attract anything near the level of money it takes to mount a competitive campaign. Rick Santorum was the only challenger to collect more than $200,000. Six Pennsylvania incumbents rode to reelection without even facing an opponent.

It is doubtful whether 1992 will be so kind to the incumbents. With reapportionment following the 1990 census, Pennsylvania is slated to lose two of its 23 U.S. House seats, ensuring that at least that many House incumbents will not be returning to Washington when the 103rd Congress convenes in 1993.

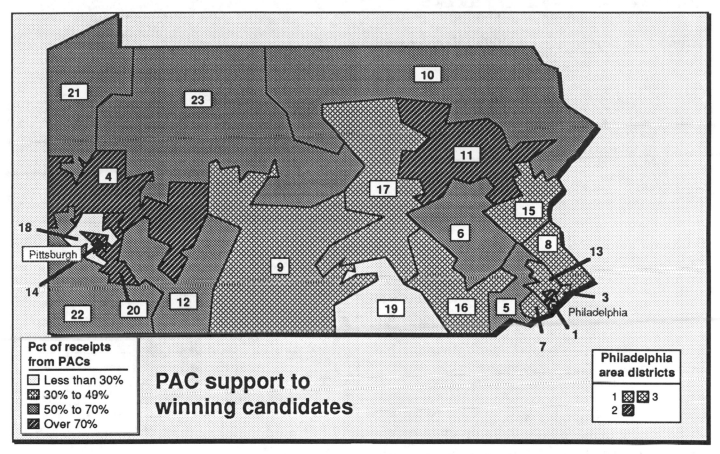

PAC support to winning candidates

Pct of receipts from PACs
- ☐ Less than 30%
- ▦ 30% to 49%
- ▨ 50% to 70%
- ▩ Over 70%

Philadelphia area districts
1 ▦ ▦ 3
2 ▨

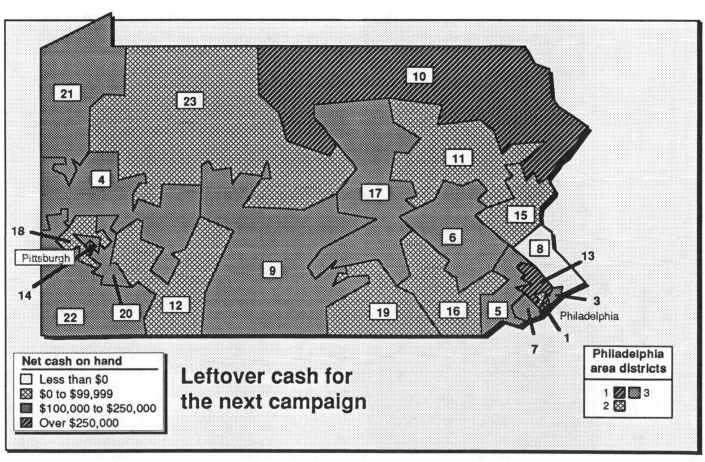

Leftover cash for the next campaign

Net cash on hand
- ☐ Less than $0
- ▦ $0 to $99,999
- ▪ $100,000 to $250,000
- ▨ Over $250,000

Philadelphia area districts
1 ▨ ▦ 3
2 ▦

South Carolina

Vital Statistics of 1990 Winners

Dist	Name	Party	Vote Pct	Race Type	Total Receipts	PAC Receipts	PAC Pct	Spent	Net cash on Hand
1	Arthur Ravenel Jr.	Rep	65.5%	Reelected	$221,611	$112,750	50.9%	$99,261	$284,458
2	Floyd D. Spence	Rep	88.7%	Reelected	$188,988	$106,533	56.4%	$130,173	$62.190
3	Butler Derrick	Dem	58.0%	Reelected	$848,063	$542,039	63.9%	$907,904	$106,192
4	Liz J. Patterson	Dem	61.4%	Reelected	$485,370	$303,154	62.5%	$485,095	-$64,485
5	John M. Spratt Jr.	Dem	99.9%	Reelected	$110,158	$84,950	77.1%	$173,157	$89,025
6	Robin Tallon	Dem	99.6%	Reelected	$231,293	$145,550	62.9%	$95,350	$347,441
Sen	Strom Thurmond	Rep	64.2%	Reelected	$2,207,157	$632,596	28.7%	$2,350,749	$221,092

The reelection of South Carolina's incumbents was a foregone conclusion in at least three of the state's six congressional districts in 1990, when no major party opponents even entered the race. The story was much the same in the U.S. Senate contest from the moment that 87-year-old Republican Strom Thurmond announced he would run for another term. Seventy-year-old Democrat Bob Cunningham filed against him, but spent only $6,232 on his campaign. On election day, Thurmond took nearly two-thirds of the vote.

The state's two other incumbents, Democrats Butler Derrick in the 3rd district and Liz Patterson in the 4th, far outmatched their Republican challengers in fundraising. Derrick waged a $900,000 campaign against real estate broker Ray Haskett, who mustered just $74,000 for his effort. Patterson's opponent, State Rep. Terry Haskins spent $144,000 in his bid to topple the incumbent, but Patterson outspent him six-to-one and won with a relatively comfortable 61 percent of the vote. Patterson was the only South Carolina incumbent to close the year with a deficit in her campaign account.

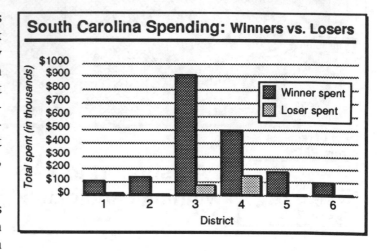

South Carolina Spending: Winners vs. Losers

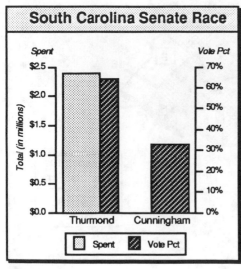

South Carolina Senate Race

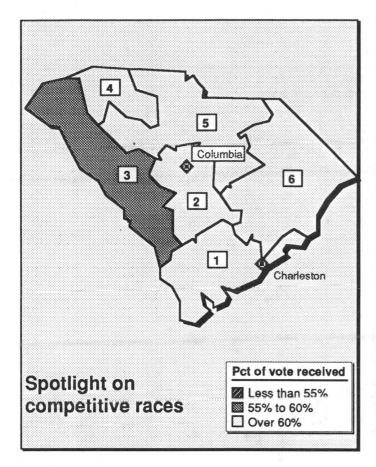

Spotlight on competitive races

Pct of vote received
- ▨ Less than 55%
- ▦ 55% to 60%
- ☐ Over 60%

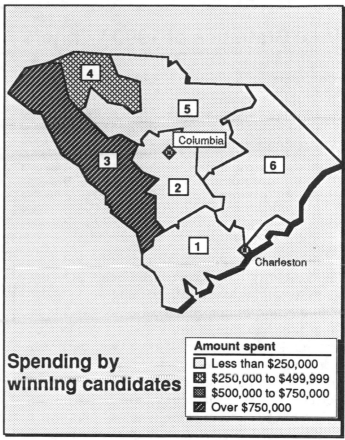

Spending by winning candidates

Amount spent
- ☐ Less than $250,000
- ▨ $250,000 to $499,999
- ▦ $500,000 to $750,000
- ▧ Over $750,000

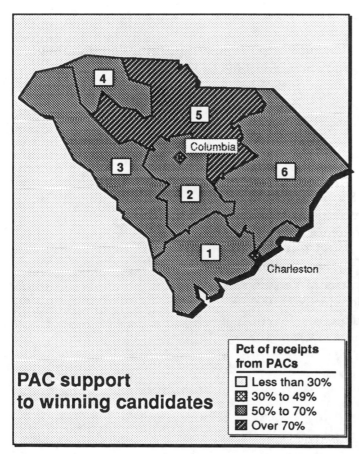

PAC support to winning candidates

Pct of receipts from PACs
- ☐ Less than 30%
- ▨ 30% to 49%
- ▦ 50% to 70%
- ▧ Over 70%

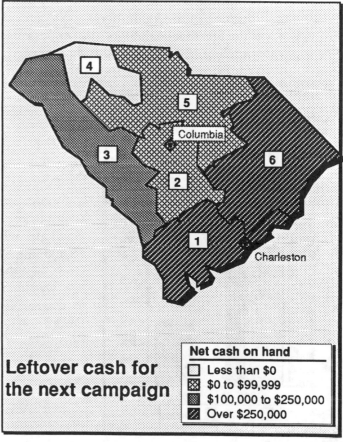

Leftover cash for the next campaign

Net cash on hand
- ☐ Less than $0
- ▨ $0 to $99,999
- ▦ $100,000 to $250,000
- ▧ Over $250,000

Tennessee

Vital Statistics of 1990 Winners

Dist	Name	Party	Vote Pct	Race Type	Total Receipts	PAC Receipts	PAC Pct	Spent	Net cash on Hand
1	James H. Quillen	Rep	99.9%	Reelected	$596,536	$360,350	60.4%	$263,291	$1,044,255
2	John J. "Jimmy" Duncan Jr.	Rep	80.6%	Reelected	$325,691	$165,501	50.8%	$200,935	$137,716
3	Marilyn Lloyd	Dem	53.0%	Reelected	$415,056	$233,750	56.3%	$234,107	$184,618
4	Jim Cooper	Dem	67.4%	Reelected	$183,494	$107,400	58.5%	$56,922	$205,616
5	Bob Clement	Dem	72.4%	Reelected	$424,581	$272,825	64.3%	$298,005	$163,739
6	Bart Gordon	Dem	66.7%	Reelected	$620,052	$355,275	57.3%	$367,090	$535,072
7	Don Sundquist	Rep	62.0%	Reelected	$648,472	$351,985	54.3%	$451,944	$471,904
8	John Tanner	Dem	100.0%	Reelected	$314,094	$134,800	42.9%	$153,941	$228,267
9	Harold E. Ford	Dem	58.1%	Reelected	$283,087	$169,925	60.0%	$284,282	-$22,124
Sen	Al Gore	Dem	67.7%	Reelected	$2,628,326	$1,153,761	43.9%	$1,918,372	$708,043

While a rising nationwide dissatisfaction with Congress may have given incumbents in many states something to fear in the closing weeks of the 1990 election campaigns, most office-holders in Tennessee had little to worry about. Even Democrat Harold Ford of Memphis, tarred with the brush of scandal in a fraud indictment (his 1990 trial ended with a hung jury), won reelection with 58 percent of the vote. Marilyn Lloyd in the 3rd district polled just 53 percent of the vote, but hers was a four-way race. Her closest challenger captured only 38 percent at the polls.

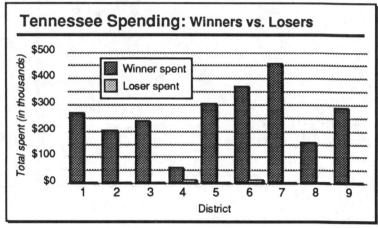

A telling measure of the incumbents' political insulation was the fact that challengers in Tennessee found it almost impossible to raise campaign contributions. The highest spending challenger in the state mustered a war chest of just over $12,000.

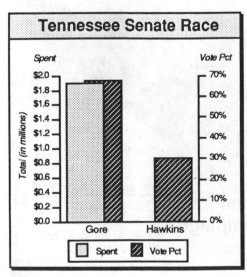

Democratic Sen. Al Gore was a shoo-in for reelection against Republican economist William Hawkins, who raised less than $8,400 in his bid to oppose him. Gore, like the voters of Tennessee, was likely looking past 1990 to a possible future run for the Democratic nomination for president.

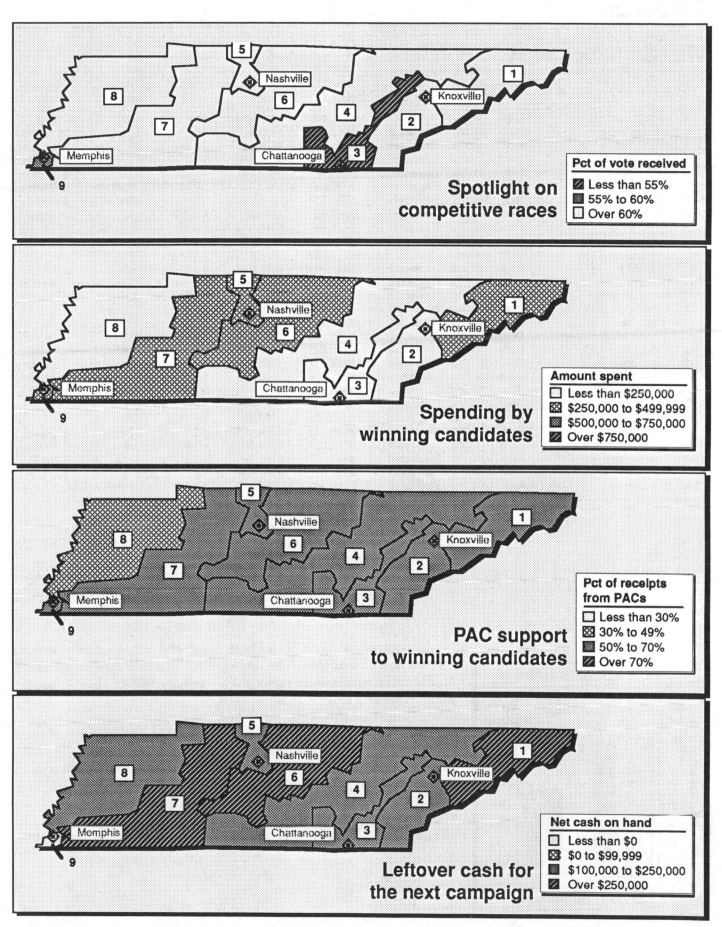

Spotlight on competitive races

Pct of vote received
- Less than 55%
- 55% to 60%
- Over 60%

Spending by winning candidates

Amount spent
- Less than $250,000
- $250,000 to $499,999
- $500,000 to $750,000
- Over $750,000

PAC support to winning candidates

Pct of receipts from PACs
- Less than 30%
- 30% to 49%
- 50% to 70%
- Over 70%

Leftover cash for the next campaign

Net cash on hand
- Less than $0
- $0 to $99,999
- $100,000 to $250,000
- Over $250,000

Texas

Vital Statistics of 1990 Winners

Dist	Name	Party	Vote Pct	Race Type	Total Receipts	PAC Receipts	PAC Pct	Spent	Net cash on Hand
1	Jim Chapman	Dem	61.0%	Reelected	$533,989	$296,589	55.5%	$463,377	$85,722
2	Charles Wilson	Dem	55.6%	Reelected	$663,504	$439,517	66.2%	$740,342	-$16,774
3	Steve Bartlett	Rep	99.6%	Reelected	$798,555	$278,249	34.8%	$837,944	$167,323
4	Ralph M. Hall	Dem	99.6%	Reelected	$261,431	$202,850	77.6%	$209,902	$213,621
5	John Bryant	Dem	59.6%	Reelected	$936,755	$453,721	48.4%	$588,019	$257,837
6	Joe L. Barton	Rep	66.5%	Reelected	$770,957	$253,403	32.9%	$458,346	$377,041
7	Bill Archer	Rep	100.0%	Reelected	$241,863	$0	0.0%	$200,871	$670,901
8	Jack Fields	Rep	100.0%	Reelected	$385,273	$269,275	69.9%	$420,288	$34,447
9	Jack Brooks	Dem	57.7%	Reelected	$775,167	$458,444	59.1%	$885,090	$330,424
10	J. J. "Jake" Pickle	Dem	64.9%	Reelected	$491,649	$247,200	50.3%	$562,967	$66,442
11	Chet Edwards	Dem	53.5%	Open	$672,399	$345,480	51.4%	$668,936	-$67,715
12	Pete Geren*	Dem	71.3%	Reelected	$497,798	$257,509	51.7%	$495,937	-$407,788
13	Bill Sarpalius	Dem	56.5%	Reelected	$684,754	$387,259	56.5%	$668,020	-$46,429
14	Greg Laughlin	Dem	54.3%	Reelected	$829,150	$431,314	52.0%	$851,294	-$133,705
15	E. "Kika" de la Garza	Dem	100.0%	Reelected	$86,524	$59,675	69.0%	$121,145	$137,477
16	Ronald D. Coleman	Dem	95.6%	Reelected	$279,452	$162,285	58.1%	$286,407	$9,538
17	Charles W. Stenholm	Dem	100.0%	Reelected	$254,175	$98,075	38.6%	$311,378	$89,736
18	Craig Washington*	Dem	99.6%	Reelected	$144,647	$87,250	60.3%	$157,053	-$9,269
19	Larry Combest	Rep	100.0%	Reelected	$197,121	$85,976	43.6%	$111,838	$129,221
20	Henry B. Gonzalez	Dem	100.0%	Reelected	$141,688	$80,800	57.0%	$112,901	$5,383
21	Lamar Smith	Rep	74.8%	Reelected	$608,876	$130,230	21.4%	$399,059	$363,182
22	Tom DeLay	Rep	71.2%	Reelected	$324,134	$168,475	52.0%	$297,153	$76,314
23	Albert G. Bustamante	Dem	63.5%	Reelected	$370,750	$192,375	51.9%	$236,046	$282,613
24	Martin Frost	Dem	100.0%	Reelected	$679,508	$409,905	60.3%	$597,310	$316,106
25	Michael A. Andrews	Dem	100.0%	Reelected	$539,864	$344,383	63.8%	$294,340	$811,150
26	Dick Armey	Rep	70.4%	Reelected	$441,625	$162,306	36.8%	$198,305	$362,311
27	Solomon P. Ortiz	Dem	100.0%	Reelected	$235,873	$100,790	42.7%	$140,756	$245,251
Sen	Phil Gramm	Rep	60.2%	Reelected	$16,268,341	$1,795,970	11.0%	$12,474,887	$4,147,378

It was not the races for Congress but the contest for the governor's mansion that riveted the attention of voters in Texas during 1990. The race to succeed retiring Gov. Bill Clements drew headlines both inside Texas and across the nation, as Democrat Ann Richards and Republican Clayton Williams squared off in freewheeling Texas style. Richards was the eventual winner.

By comparison, the 27 U.S. House races and one U.S. Senate contest offered little drama. All 26 incumbents who ran for new terms in the House were successfully reelected — exactly half of them faced no major-party challengers at all.

Republican Phil Gramm, who amassed a $16.2 million war chest to ensure his reelection, completely overpowered his Democratic opponent, State Sen. Hugh Parmer, outspending him more than seven-to-one. Gramm took 60 percent of the vote and closed out the year with more than $4 million in the bank. Under the terms of federal election laws, Gramm could transfer those funds to a new campaign committee if he decides to seek other office (such as running for President in 1996).

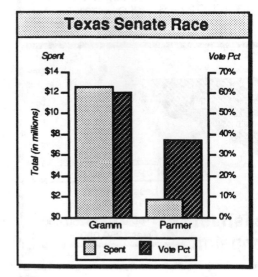

Texas Senate Race

136

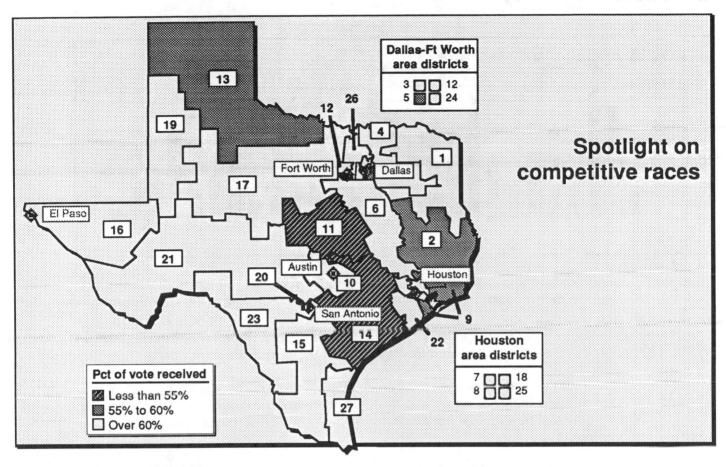

Spotlight on competitive races

Dallas-Ft Worth area districts

| 3 | | | 12 |
| 5 | | | 24 |

Houston area districts

| 7 | | | 18 |
| 8 | | | 25 |

Pct of vote received

- Less than 55%
- 55% to 60%
- Over 60%

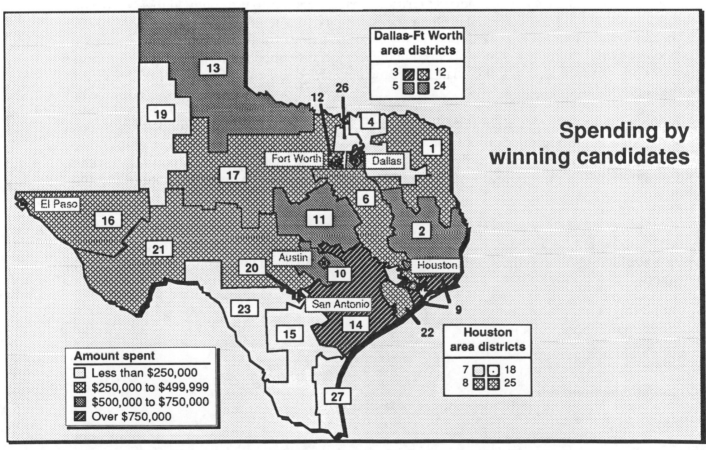

Spending by winning candidates

Dallas-Ft Worth area districts

| 3 | | | 12 |
| 5 | | | 24 |

Houston area districts

| 7 | | | 18 |
| 8 | | | 25 |

Amount spent

- Less than $250,000
- $250,000 to $499,999
- $500,000 to $750,000
- Over $750,000

Texas (cont'd)

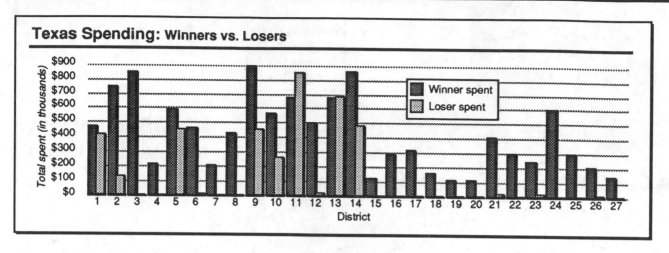

Texas Spending: Winners vs. Losers

Winner spent
Loser spent

Total spent (in thousands): $900, $800, $700, $600, $500, $400, $300, $200, $100, $0

District: 1 2 3 4 5 6 7 8 9 10 11 12 13 14 15 16 17 18 19 20 21 22 23 24 25 26 27

Unlike many other states, Texas did attract a number of high-spending challengers — even though none was successful in defeating the incumbents. The most expensive contest in the state overall was the open-seat race in the 11th district, made vacant by the retirement of Marvin Leath. Democrat Chet Edwards, a state senator, eventually outpolled Republican State Rep. Hugh Shine, though the Republican outspent Edwards by over $170,000. The combined spending by the two campaigns topped $1.5 million.

Up north in the Texas panhandle, freshman Democrat Bill Sarpalius had his hands full with a well-financed challenge by State Rep. Dick Waterfield. Waterfield matched the incumbent dollar for dollar, eventually outspending him by a narrow margin. But Sarpalius prevailed on election day, polling over 56 percent of the vote.

The state's closest race between incumbents and challengers was to the south, in the 14th district, where Greg Laughlin, another freshman Democrat, scrambled to defend his seat against cattle rancher and political newcomer Joe Dial. Dial spent nearly $480,000 trying to displace Laughlin in a district that has been known for turning out incumbents, but the Democrat stepped up his own spending to more than $850,000 and turned back the challenge. Laughlin carried just over 54 percent of the vote in November.

Newcomers to Congress were not the only ones having to deal with well-funded opponents, however. Veteran Democrat Jack Brooks, in the 9th district, fought off a challenge by former Beaumont Mayor Maury Meyers. Meyers put nearly $450,000 into the race, prompting Brooks to counter the attack with a campaign costing $885,000 — the most expensive House campaign in the state in the 1990 elections.

That figure will likely be topped in 1992, as reapportionment will give Texas three additional seats in the U.S. Congress, as well as a major redrawing of the state's existing 27 districts. Open seat races typically are high-spending affairs, as both candidates compete to boost their name recognition among the voters.

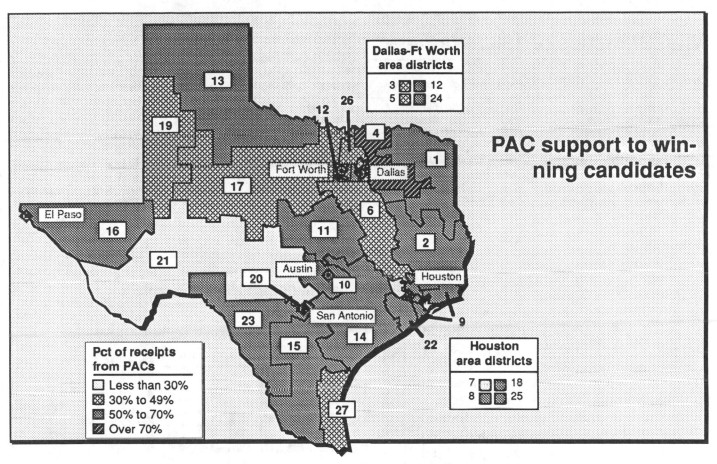

PAC support to win-
ning candidates

**Dallas-Ft Worth
area districts**

3 ▦ ▦ 12
5 ▦ ▦ 24

**Pct of receipts
from PACs**

☐ Less than 30%
▦ 30% to 49%
▦ 50% to 70%
▦ Over 70%

**Houston
area districts**

7 ☐ ▦ 18
8 ▦ ▦ 25

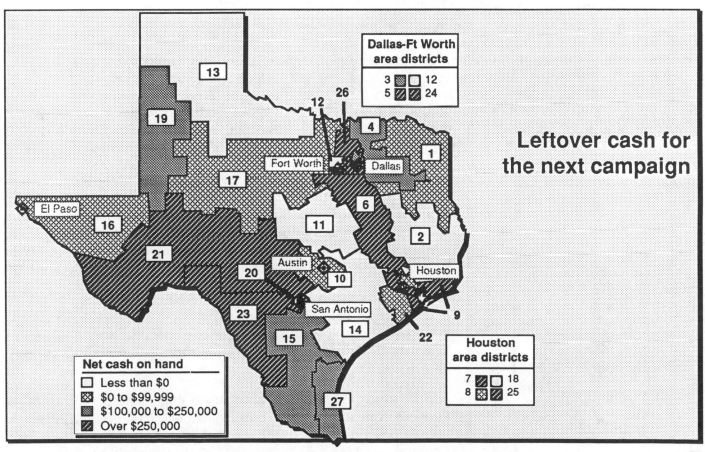

Leftover cash for
the next campaign

**Dallas-Ft Worth
area districts**

3 ▦ ☐ 12
5 ▦ ▦ 24

Net cash on hand

☐ Less than $0
▦ $0 to $99,999
▦ $100,000 to $250,000
▦ Over $250,000

**Houston
area districts**

7 ▦ ☐ 18
8 ▦ ▦ 25

Virginia

Vital Statistics of 1990 Winners

Dist	Name	Party	Vote Pct	Race Type	Total Receipts	PAC Receipts	PAC Pct	Spent	Net cash on Hand
1	Herbert H. Bateman	Rep	51.0%	Reelected	$526,099	$218,750	41.6%	$549,818	-$19,183
2	Owen B. Pickett	Dem	75.0%	Reelected	$240,133	$135,500	56.4%	$82,828	$185,854
3	Thomas J. Bliley Jr.	Rep	65.3%	Reelected	$632,395	$398,212	63.0%	$710,739	$30,293
4	Norman Sisisky	Dem	78.3%	Reelected	$240,553	$157,850	65.6%	$275,502	-$67,539
5	Lewis F. Payne Jr.	Dem	99.4%	Reelected	$317,828	$187,650	59.0%	$317,271	-$95,956
6	Jim Olin	Dem	82.7%	Reelected	$254,058	$153,200	60.3%	$199,904	$41,273
7	D. French Slaughter Jr.	Rep	58.1%	Reelected	$649,588	$152,865	23.5%	$826,942	-$72,143
8	James P. Moran Jr.	Dem	51.7%	Beat Incumb	$883,236	$257,821	29.2%	$883,216	-$82,667
9	Rick Boucher	Dem	97.1%	Reelected	$524,268	$366,584	69.9%	$252,685	$401,838
10	Frank R. Wolf	Rep	61.5%	Reelected	$514,240	$192,095	37.4%	$511,853	$59,412
Sen	John W. Warner	Rep	80.9%	Reelected	$1,514,081	$615,584	40.7%	$1,151,605	$222,138

Fast-growing northern Virginia, just across the Potomac from Washington, D.C., was the scene of the state's most contentious — and expensive — U.S. House race in 1990, as Alexandria Mayor Jim Moran successfully toppled incumbent Republican Stan Parris. Neither man is known for rhetorical restraint; the level of debate often reached so high a volume that the charges, counter-charges and expressions of mutual repugnance often spilled over the district to attract the attention of the rest of the state, and the nation's capital as well. Parris won the battle for dollars, spending nearly $1 million in his toughest reelection contest in years, but Moran's fundraising was nearly as fruitful. Between them, they spent more than $1.8 million on the race. On election day Moran was the victor, capturing just under 52 percent of the vote.

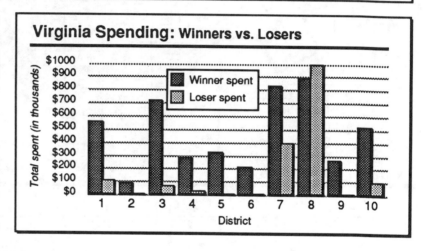

Virginia Spending: Winners vs. Losers

All other Virginia incumbents won reelection in 1990, but Republican Herbert Bateman in the 1st district avoided a near upset at the hands of TV reporter Andrew Fox. The challenger was only able to muster a $16,000 campaign — less than a fifth of Bateman's spending — but he held Bateman to just 51 percent at the polls.

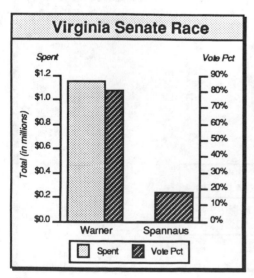

Virginia Senate Race

One other Virginia race featured a challenger with enough money to give the incumbent a serious challenge; that was in the 7th district where Democrat David Smith waged a $388,000 campaign against incumbent D. French Slaughter. Slaughter responded by punching his own fundraising into high gear, eventually outspending Smith better than two-to-one. Slaughter carried 58 percent of the vote on election day.

Republican Sen. John Warner had little difficulty winning a third term in the Senate in 1990. His only opponent on the ballot was independent candidate Nancy Spannaus, a supporter of political extremist Lyndon LaRouche. Spannaus spent no money on her campaign and drew only 18 percent of the vote.

The steady influx of new residents to Virginia during the 1980s — primarily in the suburbs south of Washington, D.C. — boosted the state's population enough to give it one additional seat in the next U.S. Congress.

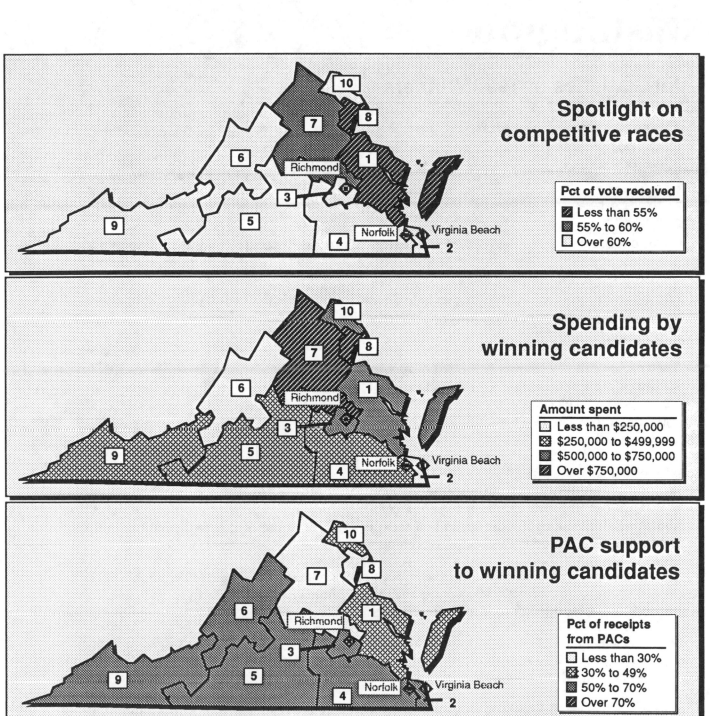

Spotlight on competitive races

Pct of vote received
- ▨ Less than 55%
- ▦ 55% to 60%
- ☐ Over 60%

Spending by winning candidates

Amount spent
- ☐ Less than $250,000
- ▧ $250,000 to $499,999
- ▦ $500,000 to $750,000
- ▨ Over $750,000

PAC support to winning candidates

Pct of receipts from PACs
- ☐ Less than 30%
- ▨ 30% to 49%
- ▦ 50% to 70%
- ▩ Over 70%

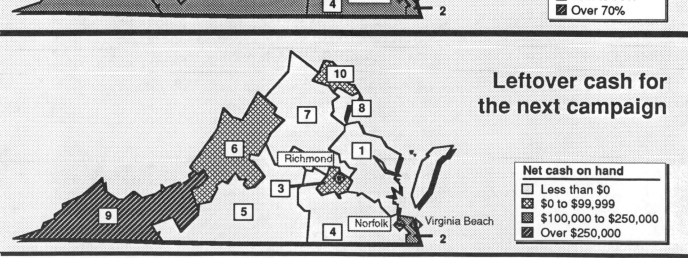

Leftover cash for the next campaign

Net cash on hand
- ☐ Less than $0
- ▨ $0 to $99,999
- ▦ $100,000 to $250,000
- ▧ Over $250,000

Washington

Vital Statistics of 1990 Winners

Dist	Name	Party	Vote Pct	Race Type	Total Receipts	PAC Receipts	PAC Pct	Spent	Net cash on Hand
1	John Miller	Rep	52.0%	Reelected	$913,407	$265,457	29.1%	$912,969	-$42,804
2	Al Swift	Dem	50.5%	Reelected	$503,123	$272,542	54.2%	$465,249	$168,462
3	Jolene Unsoeld	Dem	53.8%	Reelected	$1,302,285	$624,248	47.9%	$1,279,382	$1,623
4	Sid Morrison	Rep	70.7%	Reelected	$111,371	$42,200	37.9%	$49,935	$218,433
5	Thomas S. Foley	Dem	68.8%	Reelected	$467,084	$326,337	69.9%	$457,754	$596,708
6	Norm Dicks	Dem	61.4%	Reelected	$392,043	$240,055	61.2%	$565,257	$107,649
7	Jim McDermott	Dem	72.3%	Reelected	$232,919	$197,674	84.9%	$211,961	$39,680
8	Rod Chandler	Rep	56.2%	Reelected	$472,433	$300,515	63.6%	$451,296	$127,364

Four Washington incumbents were held to less than 60 percent of the vote in 1990, but all held on to their seats, as the state's entire congressional delegation won reelection.

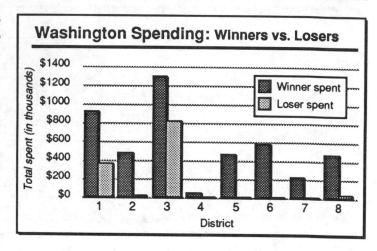

Washington Spending: Winners vs. Losers

The costliest race by far was in the 3rd district, in the southwest corner of the state. Freshman Democrat Jolene Unsoeld won election to the seat in 1988 in the closest race in the nation. This time she spared no expense in holding onto it against Bob Williams, an unusually well-funded Republican challenger. Williams, a former state lawmaker, poured $817,000 into the race, but he could not match the nearly $1.3 million spent by Unsoeld. The two candidates spent a combined $2.1 million, making this the second-most expensive U.S. House contest in the nation. Unsoeld eventually carried the district in November with just under 54 percent of the vote.

The closest race in the state this year was in Seattle, where Republican John Miller, in the 1st district, spent more than $900,000 against challenger Cynthia Sullivan. Sullivan spent just over $350,000, but held Miller to just 52 percent at the polls.

Veteran Democrat Al Swift had a lower vote percentage in November — just 50.5 percent — but his was a three-way race. Swift's closest competitor, Republican Doug Smith, drew 41 percent of the vote.

One other statistic of note in Washington was the low-budget campaign of Sid Morrison, a five-term Republican from the 4th district in the center of the state. Morrison was one of only four House incumbents nationwide to spend less than $50,000 while winning reelection.

Based on the results of the 1990 census, Washington state will gain one additional U.S. House seat in the next Congress.

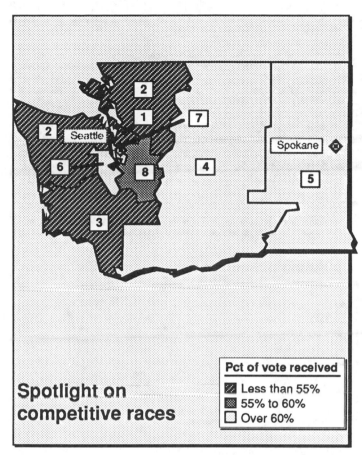

Spotlight on competitive races

Pct of vote received	
	Less than 55%
	55% to 60%
	Over 60%

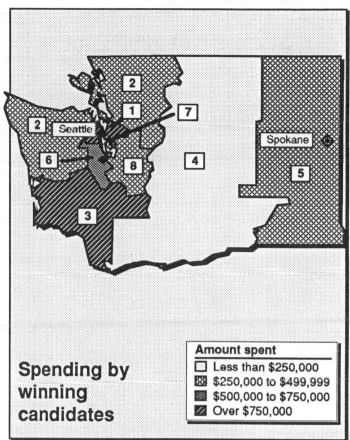

Spending by winning candidates

Amount spent	
	Less than $250,000
	$250,000 to $499,999
	$500,000 to $750,000
	Over $750,000

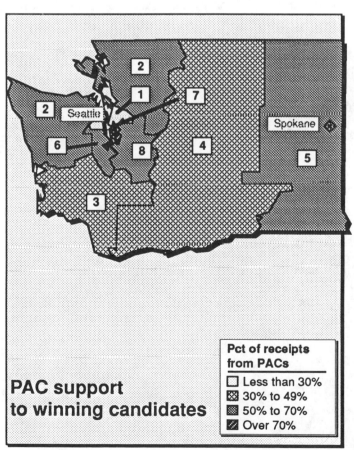

PAC support to winning candidates

Pct of receipts from PACs	
	Less than 30%
	30% to 49%
	50% to 70%
	Over 70%

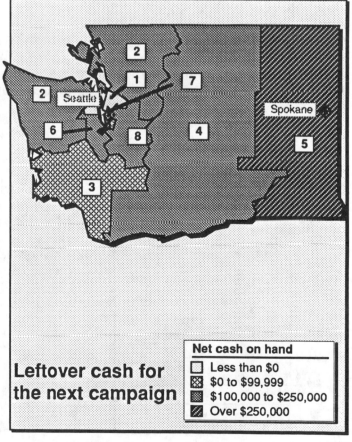

Leftover cash for the next campaign

Net cash on hand	
	Less than $0
	$0 to $99,999
	$100,000 to $250,000
	Over $250,000

143

West Virginia

Vital Statistics of 1990 Winners

Dist	Name	Party	Vote Pct	Race Type	Total Receipts	PAC Receipts	PAC Pct	Spent	Net cash on Hand
1	Alan B. Mollohan	Dem	67.1%	Reelected	$197,997	$131,498	66.4%	$206,688	$136,457
2	Harley O. Staggers Jr.	Dem	55.5%	Reelected	$419,859	$301,800	71.9%	$500,133	-$40,651
3	Bob Wise	Dem	100.0%	Reelected	$182,913	$126,118	69.0%	$53,137	$179,230
4	Nick J. Rahall II	Dem	52.0%	Reelected	$536,855	$285,750	53.2%	$566,348	$353,763
Sen	John D. Rockefeller IV	Dem	68.3%	Reelected	$3,597,376	$1,470,406	40.9%	$2,731,687	$902,198

West Virginia's full slate of Democrats all won reelection in 1990, though the going is not likely to be as easy in 1992, when the state loses one of its four congressional districts due to reapportionment.

Even the past election was a difficult one for Nick Rahall, the state's senior House Democrat, who won reelection with only 52 percent of the vote after a particularly strong primary challenge from former congressman Ken Hechler. Rahall's general election opponent, Marianne Brewster, spent just $61,000, against the incumbent's total spending of $566,000.

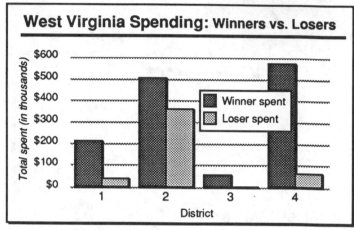

The one well-financed challenger in West Virginia during 1990 was Oliver Luck, a Republican attorney and former college football star who spent $356,000 against Harley Staggers in the 2nd district. Staggers spent half a million dollars defending his seat, and eventually drew more than 55 percent of the vote.

But though he won the race, the tough competition did cost Staggers a potentially important asset. He closed the election year with a $40,000 deficit, while the rest of his Democratic colleagues finished up with large surpluses — money that could come in handy as the state's four congressional districts get squeezed into three and two incumbents face the unhappy prospect of running against each other in 1992.

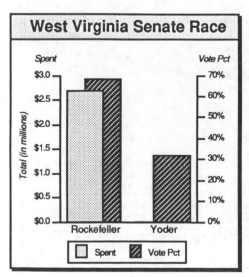

First-term Democratic Sen. Jay Rockefeller had little difficulty winning another six-year Senate term in 1990. His opponent, Republican attorney John Yoder, spent less than $23,000 against Rockefeller's $2.7 million. It may have been fiscal overkill, but it was positively low-budget compared with the 1984 campaign, when Rockefeller spent $12 million and eked out a narrow victory against a political unknown.

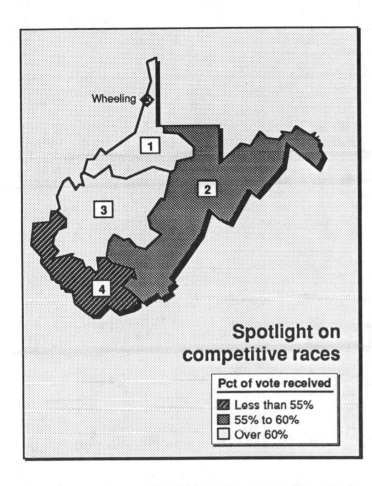

Spotlight on competitive races

Pct of vote received	
▨	Less than 55%
▦	55% to 60%
☐	Over 60%

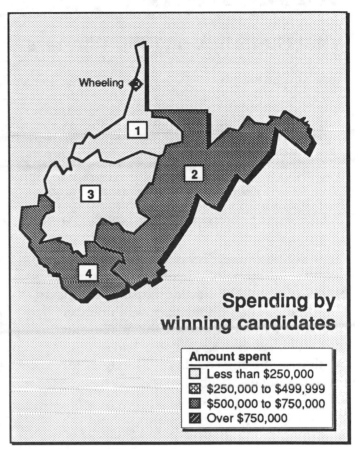

Spending by winning candidates

Amount spent	
☐	Less than $250,000
▨	$250,000 to $499,999
■	$500,000 to $750,000
▧	Over $750,000

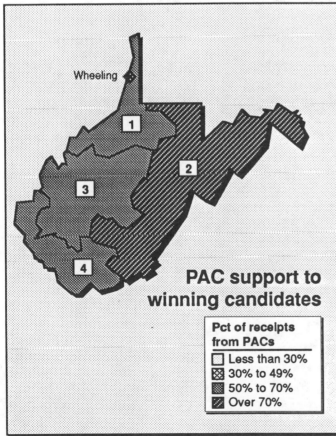

PAC support to winning candidates

Pct of receipts from PACs	
☐	Less than 30%
▨	30% to 49%
■	50% to 70%
▧	Over 70%

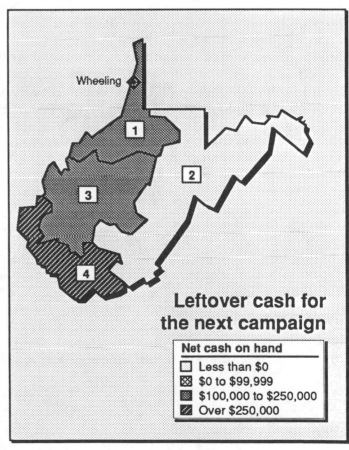

Leftover cash for the next campaign

Net cash on hand	
☐	Less than $0
▨	$0 to $99,999
■	$100,000 to $250,000
▧	Over $250,000

Wisconsin

Vital Statistics of 1990 Winners

Dist	Name	Party	Vote Pct	Race Type	Total Receipts	PAC Receipts	PAC Pct	Spent	Net cash on Hand
1	Les Aspin	Dem	99.4%	Reelected	$892,153	$322,900	36.2%	$795,806	$162,669
2	Scott L. Klug	Rep	53.2%	Beat Incumb	$183,789	$32,550	17.7%	$178,129	-$770
3	Steve Gunderson	Rep	61.0%	Reelected	$388,310	$194,195	50.0%	$341,458	$98,169
4	Gerald D. Kleczka	Dem	69.2%	Reelected	$304,440	$186,048	61.1%	$393,562	$86,327
5	Jim Moody	Dem	68.0%	Reelected	$735,212	$450,204	61.2%	$515,159	$237,639
6	Thomas E. Petri	Rep	99.5%	Reelected	$240,501	$98,455	40.9%	$131,156	$397,666
7	David R. Obey	Dem	62.1%	Reelected	$620,219	$311,550	50.2%	$467,346	$334,565
8	Toby Roth	Rep	53.5%	Reelected	$390,432	$203,083	52.0%	$499,968	$84,068
9	F. James Sensenbrenner Jr.	Rep	99.7%	Reelected	$266,285	$98,635	37.0%	$98,609	$312,478

Wisconsin's 2nd district, in and around Madison, was the scene of one of the most surprising upsets of the 1990 election season, as veteran Democrat Robert Kastenmeier was upended by Scott Klug, a former TV newscaster making his first run for public office. Kastenmeier had represented the district in Congress almost as long as the 37-year-old Klug had been alive (he was first elected in 1958), but the Republican challenger prevailed on election day, winning 53 percent of the vote. Klug's campaign budget of $178,000 was the lowest in the nation among challengers who defeated incumbents.

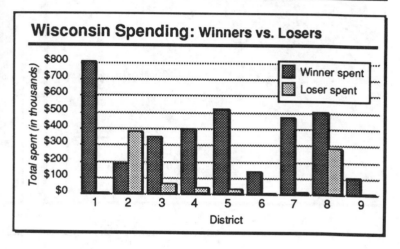

In the northeast corner of the state, Republican incumbent Toby Roth had his hands full with a relatively well-financed challenge from Democratic State Sen. Jerome Van Sistine. The challenger spent nearly $275,000 against Roth's half-million and took 46 percent of the vote — the most anyone has polled against Roth since he was first elected in 1978.

No other challengers in Wisconsin were able to muster enough cash to wage financially competitive campaigns.

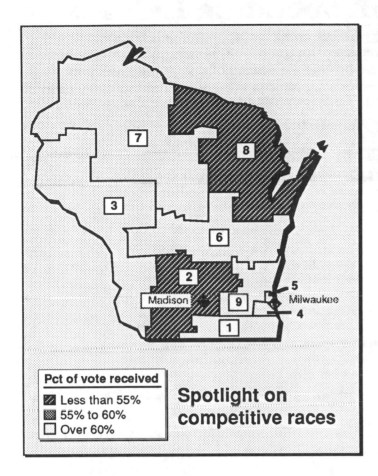

Pct of vote received
- ▨ Less than 55%
- ▦ 55% to 60%
- ☐ Over 60%

Spotlight on competitive races

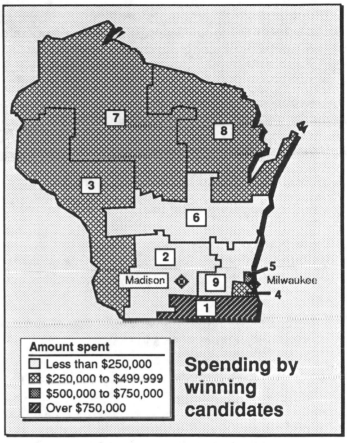

Amount spent
- ☐ Less than $250,000
- ▨ $250,000 to $499,999
- ▦ $500,000 to $750,000
- ▨ Over $750,000

Spending by winning candidates

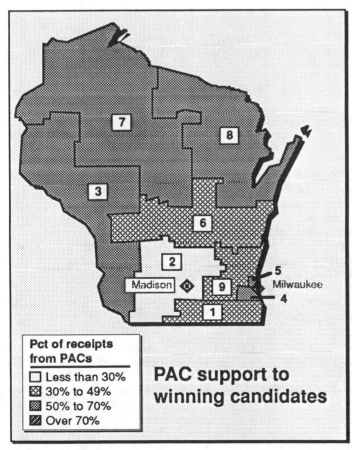

Pct of receipts from PACs
- ☐ Less than 30%
- ▨ 30% to 49%
- ▦ 50% to 70%
- ▨ Over 70%

PAC support to winning candidates

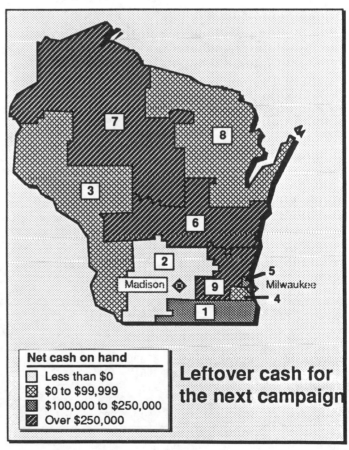

Net cash on hand
- ☐ Less than $0
- ▨ $0 to $99,999
- ▦ $100,000 to $250,000
- ▨ Over $250,000

Leftover cash for the next campaign

Appendix: Campaign Spending Indexes

The indexes on the following pages provide a quick reference tool for comparing the campaign spending statistics of each member of Congress elected in 1990. Instead of showing the actual dollar amounts (which are listed elsewhere in this book), this list presents an *index* of the amount. An index value of 100 represents the national average for that category, while 200 would be double the average, 50 would be half the average, and so on. Negative index numbers in the "Cash on Hand" category indicate an end-of-the-year deficit in the winner's campaign account. The scale is identical, but the values are all negative. Figures for Senate incumbents are based on their fundraising and spending activities over the full six-year cycle in which they have held office. Figures for House members are based on the regular two-year cycle which ran from Jan. 1, 1989 to Dec. 31, 1990.

The categories indexed include:

Amount spent. This is the total amount spent by the candidate in their campaign. It includes only spending that was charged directly to the campaign. Transfers to other campaign committees, such as contributions to other candidates, or to political party organizations, are not included.

Senate average:	$3,870,621
House average:	$407,556

Opponent spent. The basis for this rating is the same one used in the "spent" category — namely, the average spent by *winning* candidates. This category is included to provide a quick and informative comparison between the winner's spending versus that of his or her opponent.

Senate and House averages: *Same as above*

PAC receipts. This is the total amount received from political action committees, as reported to the FEC by the candidate. Any refunds of PAC contributions have been deducted from the total.

Senate average:	$978,329
House average:	$209,581

Cash on hand. This is the net cash on hand remaining in the campaign's treasury at the end of 1990, as reported by the congressman or senator's campaign. It includes all cash on hand *minus all outstanding debts*. A negative dollar sign indicates an end-of-the-year deficit.

Senate average:	$465,153
House average:	$156,821

1990 Senate Winners

Name	Spent	Opp Spent	PAC Rcpts	Cash on hand	Name	Spent	Opp Spent	PAC Rcpts	Cash on hand
Akaka, Daniel K.	45	62	87	-20	Johnston, J. Bennett	150	68	148	203
Baucus, Max	67	19	170	109	Kassebaum, Nancy Landon	14	0	18	47
Biden Jr., Joseph R.	67	6	73	30	Kerry, John	208	134	2	-17
Boren, David L.	42	4	-0	34	Levin, Carl	183	62	144	21
Bradley, Bill	322	21	142	149	McConnell, Mitch	140	76	135	41
Brown, Hank	96	50	142	95	Nunn, Sam	32	0	64	333
Coats, Daniel R.	96	28	113	78	Pell, Claiborne	62	54	90	46
Cochran, Thad	18	0	57	195	Pressler, Larry	55	34	98	120
Cohen, William S.	42	42	57	4	Pryor, David	17	0	60	216
Craig, Larry E.	43	14	82	20	Rockefeller IV, John D.	71	1	150	194
Domenici, Pete V.	58	1	93	47	Simon, Paul	226	127	172	181
Exon, Jim	62	38	155	58	Simpson, Alan K.	37	0	82	91
Gore, Al	50	0	118	152	Smith, Robert C.	37	8	68	19
Gramm, Phil	322	43	184	892	Stevens, Ted	42	0	89	51
Harkin, Tom	146	131	185	2	Thurmond, Strom	61	0	65	48
Hatfield, Mark O.	71	38	107	-4	Warner, John W.	34	0	66	48
Heflin, Howell	89	48	154	223	Wellstone, Paul	35	161	30	-12
Helms, Jesse	459	202	102	-194					

Senate Index values: Spent/Opponent spent: 100 = $3,870,621   PAC Receipts: 100 = $978,329   Cash on hand: 100 = $460,635

1990 House Winners

Name	Spent	Opp Spent	PAC Rcpts	Cash on hand
Abercrombie, Neil (D-Hawaii)	108	66	69	4
Ackerman, Gary L. (D-NY)	67	0	89	182
Alexander, Bill (D-Ark)	193	9	193	-69
Allard, Wayne (R-Colo)	88	118	83	-4
Anderson, Glenn M. (D-Calif)	113	2	123	20
Andrews, Michael (D-Texas)	72	0	164	517
Andrews, Robert (D-NJ)	133	20	113	-54
Andrews, Thomas (D-Maine)	170	114	116	-59
Annunzio, Frank (D-Ill)	210	100	226	23
Anthony, Beryl Jr. (D-Ark)	118	0	179	233
Applegate, Douglas (D-Ohio)	23	0	37	103
Archer, Bill (R-Texas)	49	0	0	428
Armey, Dick (R-Texas)	49	4	77	231
Aspin, Les (D-Wis)	195	0	154	104
Atkins, Chester G. (D-Mass)	211	58	0	-21
AuCoin, Les (D-Ore)	109	0	147	231
Bacchus, Jim (D-Fla)	215	90	196	-10
Baker, Richard H. (R-La)	82	0	73	43
Ballenger, Cass (R-NC)	74	9	88	14
Barnard, Doug Jr. (D-Ga)	230	39	125	173
Barrett, Bill (R-Nebr)	153	112	92	-32
Bartlett, Steve (R-Texas)	206	0	133	107
Barton, Joe L. (R-Texas)	112	2	121	240
Bateman, Herbert H. (R-Va)	135	25	104	-12
Beilenson, Anthony C. (D-Calif)	49	89	0	29
Bennett, Charles E. (D-Fla)	27	3	14	177
Bentley, Helen Delich (R-Md)	179	0	102	81
Bereuter, Doug (R-Nebr)	55	16	70	35
Berman, Howard L. (D-Calif)	111	20	87	128
Bevill, Tom (D-Ala)	41	0	50	361
Bilbray, James (D-Nev)	173	37	104	-18
Bilirakis, Michael (R-Fla)	200	22	112	-2
Bliley, Thomas J. Jr. (R-Va)	174	14	190	19
Boehlert, Sherwood (R-NY)	67	3	62	121
Boehner, John A. (R-Ohio)	180	28	105	-119
Bonior, David E. (D-Mich)	299	72	350	57
Borski, Robert A. (D-Pa)	68	18	73	99
Boucher, Rick (D-Va)	62	0	175	256
Boxer, Barbara (D-Calif)	161	8	160	318
Brewster, Bill (D-Okla)	110	0	85	1
Brooks, Jack (D-Texas)	217	110	219	211
Broomfield, William S. (R-Mich)	19	24	27	481
Browder, Glen (D-Ala)	43	6	91	76
Brown, George E. Jr. (D-Calif)	202	132	216	-34
Bruce, Terry L. (D-Ill)	63	1	146	366
Bryant, John (D-Texas)	144	111	216	164
Bunning, Jim (R-Ky)	138	19	108	62
Burton, Dan (R-Ind)	76	10	97	256
Bustamante, Albert G. (D-Texas)	58	6	92	180
Byron, Beverly B. (D-Md)	80	1	78	22
Callahan, Sonny (R-Ala)	45	0	81	151
Camp, Dave (R-Mich)	161	0	83	-68
Campbell, Ben Nighthorse (D-Colo)	82	7	100	9
Campbell, Tom (R-Calif)	161	25	119	404
Cardin, Benjamin L. (D-Md)	89	1	96	160
Carper, Thomas R. (D-Del)	128	12	97	34
Carr, Bob (D-Mich)	55	0	99	163
Chandler, Rod (R-Wash)	111	8	143	81
Chapman, Jim (D-Texas)	114	100	142	55
Clay, William L. (D-Mo)	46	3	87	76
Clement, Bob (D-Tenn)	73	0	130	104
Clinger, William F. Jr. (R-Pa)	83	2	91	47
Coble, Howard (R-NC)	141	8	107	10
Coleman, E. Thomas (R-Mo)	78	6	88	21
Coleman, Ronald D. (D-Texas)	70	0	77	6
Collins, Barbara-Rose (D-Mich)	67	0	30	5
Collins, Cardiss (D-Ill)	98	0	110	57
Combest, Larry (R-Texas)	27	0	41	82
Condit, Gary (D-Calif)	52	13	36	12
Conte, Silvio O. (R-Mass)	41	0	30	165
Conyers, John Jr. (D-Mich)	53	0	85	4
Cooper, Jim (D-Tenn)	14	3	51	131
Costello, Jerry F. (D-Ill)	97	6	110	175
Coughlin, Lawrence (R-Pa)	58	10	78	227
Cox, C. Christopher (R-Calif)	167	9	85	-36
Cox, John W (D-Ill)	91	121	91	-4
Coyne, William J. (D-Pa)	32	0	68	146
Cramer, Bud (D-Ala)	157	45	118	-42
Crane, Philip M. (R-Ill)	40	0	0	74
Cunningham, Randy "Duke" (R-Calif)	131	183	102	-16
Dannemeyer, William E. (R-Calif)	154	0	62	62
Darden, George "Buddy" (D-Ga)	99	5	95	64
Davis, Robert W. (R-Mich)	80	1	116	73
de la Garza, E. "Kika" (D-Texas)	30	0	28	88
DeFazio, Peter A. (D-Ore)	53	1	82	61
DeLauro, Rosa (D-Conn)	235	75	192	-54
DeLay, Tom (R-Texas)	73	0	80	49
Dellums, Ronald V. (D-Calif)	206	0	34	24
Derrick, Butler (D-SC)	223	18	259	68
Dickinson, Bill (R-Ala)	146	40	104	160
Dicks, Norm (D-Wash)	139	2	115	69
Dingell, John D. (D-Mich)	148	1	297	313
Dixon, Julian C. (D-Calif)	28	1	59	87
Donnelly, Brian (D-Mass)	26	0	81	427
Dooley, Calvin (D-Calif)	132	153	82	-34
Doolittle, John T. (R-Calif)	127	54	112	1
Dorgan, Byron L. (D-ND)	124	70	214	151
Dornan, Robert K. (R-Calif)	355	0	17	107
Downey, Thomas J. (D-NY)	156	0	158	310
Dreier, David (R-Calif)	42	7	48	1065
Duncan, John J. "Jimmy" Jr. (R-Tenn)	49	0	79	88
Durbin, Richard J. (D-Ill)	51	11	98	196
Dwyer, Bernard J. (D-NJ)	36	2	60	45
Dymally, Mervyn M. (D-Calif)	103	0	80	16
Early, Joseph D. (D-Mass)	69	0	41	71
Eckart, Dennis E. (D-Ohio)	111	18	177	101
Edwards, Chet (D-Texas)	164	207	165	-43
Edwards, Don (D-Calif)	51	1	82	35
Edwards, Mickey (R-Okla)	92	2	70	9
Emerson, Bill (R-Mo)	173	61	156	5
Engel, Eliot L. (D-NY)	96	0	155	-22
English, Glenn (D-Okla)	39	0	69	207
Erdreich, Ben (D-Ala)	28	0	82	232
Espy, Mike (D-Miss)	90	0	105	37
Evans, Lane (D-Ill)	96	28	109	20
Fascell, Dante B. (D-Fla)	123	39	78	349

Index values: Spent/Opponent spent: 100 = $407,556   PAC Receipts: 100 = $209,581   Cash on hand: 100 = $156,821

Name	Spent	Opp Spent	PAC Rcpts	Cash on hand	Name	Spent	Opp Spent	PAC Rcpts	Cash on hand
Fawell, Harris W. (R-Ill)	67	0	57	66	Hubbard, Carroll Jr. (D-Ky)	59	0	129	214
Fazio, Vic (D-Calif)	253	10	215	124	Huckaby, Jerry (D-La)	59	2	51	174
Feighan, Edward F. (D-Ohio)	56	2	104	183	Hughes, William J. (D-NJ)	52	7	44	133
Fields, Jack (R-Texas)	103	0	128	22	Hunter, Duncan (R-Calif)	92	0	53	4
Fish, Hamilton Jr. (R-NY)	101	0	98	86	Hutto, Earl (D-Fla)	39	45	45	70
Flake, Floyd H. (D-NY)	50	0	58	5	Hyde, Henry J. (R-Ill)	66	0	62	120
Foglietta, Thomas M. (D-Pa)	57	2	108	234	Inhofe, James M. (R-Okla)	150	100	146	-17
Foley, Thomas S. (D-Wash)	112	1	156	380	Ireland, Andy (R-Fla)	94	0	81	63
Ford, Harold E. (D-Tenn)	70	0	81	-14	Jacobs, Andrew Jr. (D-Ind)	4	3	0	21
Ford, William D. (D-Mich)	87	11	134	119	James, Craig T. (R-Fla)	156	262	101	-91
Frank, Barney (D-Mass)	176	8	105	31	Jefferson, William J. (D-La)	110	104	50	-101
Franks, Gary (R-Conn)	143	215	85	-44	Jenkins, Ed (D-Ga)	78	33	88	286
Frost, Martin (D-Texas)	147	0	196	202	Johnson, Nancy L. (R-Conn)	137	5	121	75
Gallegly, Elton (R-Calif)	110	3	75	134	Johnson, Tim (D-SD)	114	52	120	67
Gallo, Dean A. (R-NJ)	170	26	89	46	Johnston, Harry A. (D-Fla)	115	52	121	27
Gaydos, Joseph M. (D-Pa)	39	0	76	79	Jones, Ben (D-Ga)	174	171	199	-19
Gejdenson, Sam (D-Conn)	114	28	89	-20	Jones, Walter B. (D-NC)	27	5	34	209
Gekas, George W. (R-Pa)	23	0	25	90	Jontz, Jim (D-Ind)	160	192	193	-26
Gephardt, Richard A. (D-Mo)	357	20	363	123	Kanjorski, Paul E. (D-Pa)	100	0	107	60
Geren, Pete (D-Texas)	122	6	123	-260	Kaptur, Marcy (D-Ohio)	52	0	55	37
Gibbons, Sam M. (D-Fla)	203	0	151	178	Kasich, John R. (R-Ohio)	68	12	61	60
Gilchrest, Wayne T. (R-Md)	65	189	29	-2	Kennedy, Joseph P. II (D-Mass)	204	0	49	145
Gillmor, Paul E. (R-Ohio)	62	0	110	53	Kennelly, Barbara B. (D-Conn)	100	0	141	113
Gilman, Benjamin A. (R-NY)	122	1	94	44	Kildee, Dale E. (D-Mich)	55	2	90	25
Gingrich, Newt (R-Ga)	378	82	207	-69	Kleczka, Gerald D. (D-Wis)	97	8	89	55
Glickman, Dan (D-Kan)	87	1	140	123	Klug, Scott L. (R-Wis)	44	91	16	-0
Gonzalez, Henry B. (D-Texas)	28	0	39	3	Kolbe, Jim (R-Ariz)	62	0	64	52
Goodling, Bill (R-Pa)	10	0	0	4	Kolter, Joe (D-Pa)	33	2	78	138
Gordon, Bart (D-Tenn)	90	2	170	341	Kopetski, Mike (D-Ore)	207	217	190	-21
Goss, Porter J. (R-Fla)	60	0	58	41	Kostmayer, Peter H. (D-Pa)	203	35	141	-23
Gradison, Bill (R-Ohio)	31	1	0	282	Kyl, Jon (R-Ariz)	109	10	81	210
Grandy, Fred (R-Iowa)	79	11	120	-10	LaFalce, John J. (D-NY)	36	0	93	411
Gray, William H. III (D-Pa)	200	0	247	35	Lagomarsino, Robert J. (R-Calif)	162	59	69	-12
Green, Bill (R-NY)	112	5	78	47	Lancaster, H. Martin (D-NC)	123	21	97	13
Guarini, Frank J. (D-NJ)	78	0	145	211	Lantos, Tom (D-Calif)	152	24	58	407
Gunderson, Steve (R-Wis)	84	14	93	63	LaRocco, Larry (D-Idaho)	110	118	114	-45
Hall, Ralph M. (D-Texas)	52	0	97	136	Laughlin, Greg (D-Texas)	209	118	206	-85
Hall, Tony P. (D-Ohio)	33	0	62	199	Leach, Jim (R-Iowa)	21	0	0	30
Hamilton, Lee H. (D-Ind)	96	0	90	37	Lehman, Richard H. (D-Calif)	74	0	96	61
Hammerschmidt, John Paul (R-Ark)	26	4	79	319	Lehman, William (D-Fla)	91	9	103	176
Hancock, Mel (R-Mo)	45	25	58	82	Lent, Norman F. (R-NY)	98	0	194	438
Hansen, James V. (R-Utah)	58	33	83	27	Levin, Sander M. (D-Mich)	67	0	115	163
Harris, Claude (D-Ala)	59	14	72	50	Levine, Mel (D-Calif)	144	36	114	1093
Hastert, Dennis (R-Ill)	77	0	86	122	Lewis, Jerry (R-Calif)	52	1	139	216
Hatcher, Charles (D-Ga)	73	0	101	13	Lewis, John (D-Ga)	27	2	84	166
Hayes, Charles A. (D-Ill)	31	11	41	12	Lewis, Tom (R-Fla)	99	0	38	77
Hayes, Jimmy (D-La)	76	39	79	-47	Lightfoot, Jim Ross (R-Iowa)	103	16	70	90
Hefley, Joel (R-Colo)	27	4	55	54	Lipinski, William O. (D-Ill)	42	10	66	12
Hefner, W. G. "Bill" (D-NC)	161	74	212	64	Livingston, Bob (R-La)	27	0	67	180
Henry, Paul B. (R-Mich)	59	0	44	176	Lloyd, Marilyn (D-Tenn)	57	0	112	118
Herger, Wally (R-Calif)	126	2	102	73	Long, Jill (D-Ind)	185	141	214	-7
Hertel, Dennis M. (D-Mich)	46	0	89	179	Lowery, Bill (R-Calif)	141	18	98	10
Hoagland, Peter (D-Nebr)	228	154	293	-89	Lowey, Nita M. (D-NY)	224	4	214	-42
Hobson, David L. (R-Ohio)	95	22	96	-9	Luken, Charles (D-Ohio)	160	165	176	19
Hochbrueckner, George J. (D-NY)	157	11	188	8	Machtley, Ronald K. (R-RI)	216	91	159	1
Holloway, Clyde C. (R-La)	95	27	69	40	Madigan, Edward (R-Ill)	68	0	129	346
Hopkins, Larry J. (R-Ky)	30	0	44	441	Manton, Thomas J. (D-NY)	78	0	216	305
Horn, Joan Kelly (D-Mo)	84	165	77	-2	Markey, Edward J. (D-Mass)	51	0	0	370
Horton, Frank (R-NY)	46	0	76	104	Marlenee, Ron (R-Mont)	76	8	67	49
Houghton, Amo (R-NY)	44	2	49	196	Martin, David O'B. (R-NY)	14	0	25	54
Hoyer, Steny H. (D-Md)	176	2	199	205	Martinez, Matthew G. (D-Calif)	46	18	45	28

Index values: Spent/Opponent spent: 100 = $407,556   PAC Receipts: 100 = $209,581   Cash on hand: 100 = $156,821

Name	Spent	Opp Spent	PAC Rcpts	Cash on hand	Name	Spent	Opp Spent	PAC Rcpts	Cash on hand
Matsui, Robert T. (D-Calif)	180	1	275	720	Pease, Don J. (D-Ohio)	85	31	88	141
Mavroules, Nicholas (D-Mass)	82	5	57	37	Pelosi, Nancy (D-Calif)	108	38	122	62
Mazzoli, Romano L. (D-Ky)	82	81	0	-24	Penny, Timothy J. (D-Minn)	48	0	54	163
McCandless, Al (R-Calif)	148	153	86	-9	Perkins, Carl C. (D-Ky)	85	42	128	-25
McCloskey, Frank (D-Ind)	109	36	154	15	Peterson, Collin C. (D-Minn)	60	120	89	-47
McCollum, Bill (R-Fla)	139	6	71	65	Peterson, Pete (D-Fla)	75	206	63	-39
McCrery, Jim (R-La)	118	75	91	23	Petri, Thomas E. (R-Wis)	32	0	47	254
McCurdy, Dave (D-Okla)	88	0	71	52	Pickett, Owen B. (D-Va)	20	0	65	119
McDade, Joseph M. (R-Pa)	92	0	113	214	Pickle, J. J. "Jake" (D-Texas)	138	64	118	42
McDermott, Jim (D-Wash)	52	0	94	25	Porter, John (R-Ill)	77	0	52	46
McEwen, Bob (R-Ohio)	48	3	69	76	Poshard, Glenn (D-Ill)	25	4	2	1
McGrath, Raymond J. (R-NY)	152	72	108	156	Price, David E. (D-NC)	195	219	184	-25
McHugh, Matthew F. (D-NY)	49	4	58	88	Pursell, Carl D. (R-Mich)	33	2	46	153
McMillan, Alex (R-NC)	95	0	131	66	Quillen, James H. (R-Tenn)	65	0	172	666
McMillen, Tom (D-Md)	138	10	201	209	Rahall II, Nick J. (D-WVa)	139	15	136	226
McNulty, Michael R. (D-NY)	37	6	71	64	Ramstad, Jim (R-Minn)	230	83	113	-78
Meyers, Jan (R-Kan)	52	19	53	1	Rangel, Charles B. (D-NY)	148	0	168	194
Mfume, Kweisi (D-Md)	50	0	61	54	Ravenel, Arthur Jr. (R-SC)	24	3	54	181
Michel, Robert H. (R-Ill)	142	0	237	154	Ray, Richard (D-Ga)	93	17	74	96
Miller, Clarence E. (R-Ohio)	18	0	33	81	Reed, John F. (D-RI)	220	140	144	-136
Miller, George (D-Calif)	110	12	125	279	Regula, Ralph (R-Ohio)	38	17	0	34
Miller, John (R-Wash)	224	86	127	-27	Rhodes, John J. III (R-Ariz)	79	0	81	6
Mineta, Norman Y. (D-Calif)	158	0	172	219	Richardson, Bill (D-NM)	103	5	165	209
Mink, Patsy T. (D-Hawaii)	157	50	71	-122	Ridge, Tom (R-Pa)	89	0	118	145
Moakley, Joe (D-Mass)	78	0	132	312	Riggs, Frank (R-Calif)	62	101	4	-90
Molinari, Susan (R-NY)	35	9	34	-1	Rinaldo, Matthew J. (R-NJ)	99	0	115	617
Mollohan, Alan B. (D-WVa)	51	8	63	87	Ritter, Don (R-Pa)	142	25	131	16
Montgomery, G. V. "Sonny" (D-Miss)	17	0	26	110	Roberts, Pat (R-Kan)	38	4	64	255
Moody, Jim (D-Wis)	126	5	215	152	Roe, Robert A. (D-NJ)	137	0	157	369
Moorhead, Carlos J. (R-Calif)	98	10	110	425	Roemer, Tim (D-Ind)	116	183	128	20
Moran, James P. Jr. (D-Va)	217	242	123	-53	Rogers, Harold (R-Ky)	27	0	34	170
Morella, Constance A. (R-Md)	87	0	114	128	Rohrabacher, Dana (R-Calif)	98	7	57	31
Morrison, Sid (R-Wash)	12	0	20	139	Ros-Lehtinen, Ileana (R-Fla)	138	59	81	9
Mrazek, Robert J. (D-NY)	113	45	92	224	Rose, Charlie (D-NC)	38	5	92	313
Murphy, Austin J. (D-Pa)	47	1	66	71	Rostenkowski, Dan (D-Ill)	73	0	94	710
Murtha, John P. (D-Pa)	269	1	237	21	Roth, Toby (R-Wis)	123	67	97	54
Myers, John T. (R-Ind)	55	0	47	66	Roukema, Marge (R-NJ)	109	0	105	61
Nagle, Dave (D-Iowa)	85	2	125	13	Rowland, J. Roy (D-Ga)	90	26	109	134
Natcher, William H. (D-Ky)	2	35	0	0	Roybal, Edward R. (D-Calif)	47	0	38	126
Neal, Richard E. (D-Mass)	131	0	119	-29	Russo, Marty (D-Ill)	133	0	182	4
Neal, Stephen L. (D-NC)	159	43	188	16	Sabo, Martin Olav (D-Minn)	79	2	108	138
Nichols, Dick (R-Kan)	139	17	48	-196	Sanders, Bernard (O-Vt)	140	168	34	-14
Nowak, Henry J. (D-NY)	23	0	47	152	Sangmeister, George E. (D-Ill)	116	158	170	11
Nussle, Jim (R-Iowa)	114	140	70	-18	Santorum, Rick (R-Pa)	62	176	13	4
Oakar, Mary Rose (D-Ohio)	70	0	135	35	Sarpalius, Bill (D-Texas)	164	167	185	-30
Oberstar, James L. (D-Minn)	56	4	119	251	Savage, Gus (D-Ill)	47	0	28	-35
Obey, David R. (D-Wis)	115	3	149	213	Sawyer, Thomas C. (D-Ohio)	65	1	89	30
Olin, Jim (D-Va)	49	0	73	26	Saxton, H. James (R-NJ)	179	52	119	31
Ortiz, Solomon P. (D-Texas)	35	0	48	156	Schaefer, Dan (R-Colo)	69	1	109	78
Orton, Bill (D-Utah)	22	71	15	-42	Scheuer, James H. (D-NY)	98	0	45	-187
Owens, Major R. (D-NY)	42	0	53	-12	Schiff, Steven H. (R-NM)	132	30	106	13
Owens, Wayne (D-Utah)	266	120	258	-5	Schroeder, Patricia (D-Colo)	128	40	54	116
Oxley, Michael G. (R-Ohio)	81	5	96	120	Schulze, Richard T. (R-Pa)	165	6	177	116
Packard, Ron (R-Calif)	36	0	48	111	Schumer, Charles E. (D-NY)	24	0	79	1008
Pallone, Frank Jr. (D-NJ)	156	29	188	-34	Sensenbrenner, F. James Jr. (R-Wis)	24	0	47	199
Panetta, Leon E. (D-Calif)	67	6	62	130	Serrano, Jose E. (D-NY)	32	0	36	7
Parker, Mike (D-Miss)	118	0	136	31	Sharp, Philip R. (D-Ind)	190	147	236	19
Patterson, Liz J. (D-SC)	119	35	145	-41	Shaw, E. Clay Jr. (R-Fla)	30	0	116	195
Paxon, Bill (R-NY)	124	25	110	113	Shays, Christopher (R-Conn)	97	22	26	48
Payne, Donald M. (D-NJ)	41	0	89	170	Shuster, Bud (R-Pa)	105	0	87	65
Payne, Lewis Jr. (D-Va)	78	0	90	-61	Sikorski, Gerry (D-Minn)	93	4	160	195

Index values: Spent/Opponent spent: 100 = $407,556   PAC Receipts: 100 = $209,581   Cash on hand: 100 = $156,821

Name	Spent	Opp Spent	PAC Rcpts	Cash on hand	Name	Spent	Opp Spent	PAC Rcpts	Cash on hand
Sisisky, Norman (D-Va)	68	5	75	-43	Torres, Esteban E. (D-Calif)	53	18	42	95
Skaggs, David E. (D-Colo)	97	12	116	14	Torricelli, Robert G. (D-NJ)	122	8	113	518
Skeen, Joe (R-NM)	20	0	52	125	Towns, Ed (D-NY)	69	0	88	96
Skelton, Ike (D-Mo)	75	2	114	199	Traficant, James A. Jr. (D-Ohio)	19	0	26	49
Slattery, Jim (D-Kan)	124	21	156	34	Traxler, Bob (D-Mich)	43	0	89	229
Slaughter, D. French Jr. (R-Va)	203	95	73	-46	Udall, Morris K. (D-Ariz)	28	0	65	47
Slaughter, Louise M. (D-NY)	79	6	135	75	Unsoeld, Jolene (D-Wash)	314	201	298	1
Smith, Bob (R-Ore)	70	0	71	115	Upton, Fred (R-Mich)	123	19	73	26
Smith, Christopher H. (R-NJ)	72	14	54	42	Valentine, Tim (D-NC)	70	14	76	13
Smith, Lamar (R-Texas)	98	4	62	232	Vander Jagt, Guy (R-Mich)	111	5	128	66
Smith, Lawrence J. (D-Fla)	68	0	118	264	Vento, Bruce F. (D-Minn)	65	14	89	99
Smith, Neal (D-Iowa)	14	0	56	240	Visclosky, Peter J. (D-Ind)	73	5	80	28
Snowe, Olympia J. (R-Maine)	75	56	47	-1	Volkmer, Harold L. (D-Mo)	59	9	104	102
Solarz, Stephen J. (D-NY)	127	0	28	1186	Vucanovich, Barbara F. (R-Nev)	108	10	79	-6
Solomon, Gerald B. H. (R-NY)	59	23	69	71	Walker, Robert S. (R-Pa)	24	0	21	23
Spence, Floyd D. (R-SC)	32	0	51	40	Walsh, James T. (R-NY)	84	3	67	24
Spratt, John M. Jr. (D-SC)	42	0	41	57	Washington, Craig (D-Texas)	39	0	42	-6
Staggers, Harley O. Jr. (D-WVa)	123	87	144	-26	Waters, Maxine (D-Calif)	186	0	101	18
Stallings, Richard (D-Idaho)	100	35	127	-10	Waxman, Henry A. (D-Calif)	71	0	150	299
Stark, Pete (D-Calif)	74	52	129	231	Weber, Vin (R-Minn)	165	4	115	136
Stearns, Cliff (R-Fla)	114	7	96	-7	Weiss, Ted (D-NY)	28	106	35	51
Stenholm, Charles W. (D-Texas)	76	0	47	57	Weldon, Curt (R-Pa)	118	27	99	86
Stokes, Louis (D-Ohio)	49	0	66	154	Wheat, Alan (D-Mo)	60	0	107	168
Studds, Gerry E. (D-Mass)	152	67	106	14	Whitten, Jamie L. (D-Miss)	24	4	62	278
Stump, Bob (R-Ariz)	55	2	63	72	Williams, Pat (D-Mont)	85	22	142	137
Sundquist, Don (R-Tenn)	111	0	168	301	Wilson, Charles (D-Texas)	182	31	210	-11
Swett, Dick (D-NH)	114	133	89	-3	Wise, Bob (D-WVa)	13	0	60	114
Swift, Al (D-Wash)	114	3	130	107	Wolf, Frank R. (R-Va)	126	23	92	38
Synar, Mike (D-Okla)	155	15	1	16	Wolpe, Howard (D-Mich)	200	67	198	36
Tallon, Robin (D-SC)	23	0	69	222	Wyden, Ron (D-Ore)	170	1	163	288
Tanner, John (D-Tenn)	38	0	64	146	Wylie, Chalmers P. (R-Ohio)	60	4	80	12
Tauzin, W. J. "Billy" (D-La)	116	0	116	31	Yates, Sidney R. (D-Ill)	206	4	128	34
Taylor, Charles H. (R-NC)	129	123	53	-277	Yatron, Gus (D-Pa)	47	18	61	100
Taylor, Gene (D-Miss)	79	52	68	-25	Young, C. W. Bill (R-Fla)	49	0	62	218
Thomas, Bill (R-Calif)	122	0	112	100	Young, Don (R-Alaska)	139	40	133	-60
Thomas, Craig (R-Wyo)	107	59	84	-10	Zeliff, Bill (R-NH)	227	93	63	-239
Thomas, Lindsay (D-Ga)	98	5	80	43	Zimmer, Dick (R-NJ)	300	419	98	-131
Thornton, Ray (D-Ark)	166	106	116	-15					

Index values: Spent/Opponent spent: 100 = $407,556   PAC Receipts: 100 = $209,581   Cash on hand: 100 = $156,821

Index